# Under the Cherry Trees
## The Autobiography of a Gloucestershire Lad

Dumbleton church and fountain

# UNDER THE CHERRY TREES

## The Autobiography of a Gloucestershire Lad

Ivor M. Cave

The Book Guild Ltd.
Sussex, England

The Book Guild Ltd.
25 High Street,
Lewes, Sussex.

First published 1992
© Ivor M. Cave 1992
Set in Baskerville
Typesetting by APS,
Salisbury, Wiltshire.
Printed in Great Britain by
Antony Rowe Ltd.,
Chippenham, Wiltshire.

A catalogue record for this book is
available from the British Library.

ISBN 0 86332 685 4

# CONTENTS

# LIST OF ILLUSTRATIONS

*I have very few regrets about my past except perhaps the length of it. Given the opportunity to live my life over again I should probably make the same mistakes but with a great deal more enthusiasm.*

Author

# PREFACE

Most of us have a story to tell, but few bother to commit it to paper. We are apt to think of our lives as being mundane and ordinary, but this is not always so. Departing from the world, we hope that we have left it a little better than when we came into it, some having made their mark whilst others pass by unnoticed.

Our childhood days are our happiest, but are soon forgotten, the memory of them being overtaken by the task of growing up and all its attendant difficulties. Then, sometimes years later, the old places and old faces will bring the experience flooding back. Throughout our lives we are at work weaving a pattern which, ragged as it may be at the edges, invariably stands the test of time, until at last the finished article is taken with us to our graves unseen.

This is the story of two people, of no account in the larger frame of history, but who in the hearts and minds of those who knew them will always be remembered. I shared their childhood and was privileged to be with them in the autumn of their lives.

It was then, during one of my many visits, that the idea came to me. September was upon us and the evenings had begun to draw in, a time for cosy log fires and soft lamplight. Sitting together after tea we talked of the old days and of all the things that had happened to us since; of childhood friends, and of how, carefree and young, we had played our games and whilst doing so had grown up. It began to dawn on me that theirs was a story worth telling and so, discussing it with them, I took up the challenge. With the help of Reg's many diaries which he had kept all his life, and after many hours of patient note-taking, the project began to take shape: it is here written more or less as told to me.

Kathy would sometimes join us and, sitting beside Reg, would put an arm round his shoulder and listen intently as incidents and events were recalled. I felt honoured to be

9

admitted to that part of their lives which up to then had been unknown to me. No doubt similar stories might be told of others, but having shared a great part of their experience, it became in a way very special. Now they have both gone and I feel free to set to work on the final manuscript.

So, as all story tellers must, I will begin at the beginning.

# 1

*Carefree days when I renew my acquaintance*
*with my friend the frog, get my first*
*pair of boots, meet Kathy, and commence school.*

The train steamed slowly into the station and with a last protesting screech, jolted to a halt. Flurries of snow drifted this way and that before settling briefly on the oil lamps which swung from their ornate fixings above the platform. In the clouds of warm steam that came hissing up from under the now stationary carriages, the solitary porter, coat collar pulled well nigh up to his ears, walked up and down swinging his lamp and calling out the name of the station. Pausing now and then he exchanged words with one or other of the descending passengers who, with heads bowed against the wind, were making their way towards the exit, there to fumble with gloved hands for the tickets to hand to the collector who received them in silence.

The soldier stood for a moment on the now deserted platform, the collar of his khaki greatcoat drawn close about his face. Then, swinging his kit bag on to his shoulder he made his way into the street, pausing only to drop the expired portion of his ticket into the waste-bin, the collector having long since forsaken his post to return to the waiting room and its cheerful coal fire.

The road from Beckford to Dumbleton is a long lonely one, and the snow, now thickening, swirled about him, driven by a wind that moaned its way round the tip of Bredon Hill. Each step, a fight against the elements, bent him forward as he made his way towards the lights of the village, now faintly visible across the meadows. Rounding the corner by the Lodge gates he paused for a moment to shift the kit bag to a more comfortable position before making his way towards the cluster of houses from whose windows warm shafts of light escaping from curtain chinks, reached out in welcome.

It was on this bitter night in the year 1916 that I was born and the soldier was my father returning to be present at my birth. I came into a world ravaged by war, a war which very few understood and which had already taken its toll in human misery. It was the year of the terrible slaughter on the battlefields of the Somme where the lives of thousands of young men, both friend and foe, had been sacrificed for a few yards of shell-pocked ground. The nation, weary and uncomprehending, watched as the casualty lists grew longer and longer.

Fortunately my father was still in England, being stationed on the East Coast from where my mother and elder brother had returned to launch me on an unsuspecting world.

At birth I was a puny child and not expected to live, at least according to the doctor. Little did he know how determined I was to prove him wrong. I was christened Reginald James Chamberlain, my father walking the six miles each way to Winchcombe to register the fact. Then, when only six months old, I contracted bronchitis and became gravely ill; indeed I would have died had it not been for the dedicated nursing of my Aunty Dora who wrapped me in brown paper liberally smeared with goose grease and sat with me during the long crisis hours. Dear Aunty Dora, long since gone to her rest, she holds a very special place in my affections. She was a commanding figure, capable and honest, and she and Mumford, my grandmother, assumed responsibility for me in the absence of my mother – who by then had returned to the East Coast, taking my brother with her.

Except for a few brief episodes I remember very little of those early days. The war ended and men returned to pick up the threads of life. They came back to a changed world where memories of loved ones, never to return, were still fresh. Father, now demobbed, settled in Hereford with my mother and brother, leaving me with Mumford. The young grew up to fill the sorrowing gaps and slowly life returned to normal.

Our village hall, which during the war had served as a military hospital, reverted to its community role; occasionally a stranger calling at the cottages would be asked inside to renew old friendships made during those days. However, as the years passed their visits became less and less frequent until at last all that remained were the sepia photographs standing on mantelpieces, showing stiff starched nurses grouped around wounded Tommies in their hospital blues.

Of happenings in the world outside the village we knew very little and slowly life reverted to its slow leisurely pattern. On Armistice Days we gathered round the war memorial which had been erected at the top end of the village near to the church, where, with caps in hand and heads bowed we stood to remember the fallen whose freshly carved names filled the spaces below the stone cross. Widows clasped the hands of small children who understood little of their adult misery other than that father or brother would never return to their young lives. We stood bare headed in silence while the autumn wind searched the scanty clothing we wore and blew icy fingers through the trees which, stripped of their leaves were bare as a monks habit. All that now remained were names, a record of those who had not returned and who lay buried in the fields of Flanders, on the beaches of Gallipoli, and in other places where death had reached out to them. Recorded for posterity they would all too soon be joined by others from a war, which, mercifully as yet, we had no knowledge.

My early life now starts in a small cottage standing tight to the main street of the village, and next door to the estate office of which my grandmother was the sole custodian, being responsible for the cleaning of it and the lighting of fires in the winter. She was a widow, Grandfather having died the year before I was born and the cottage had been given to her in recognition of his service to the estate. It had a kitchen, parlour, and two bedrooms, all on one floor. In years gone by it had apparently been the village school where, due to the generosity of the then lord of the manor poor children had been educated at a cost to them of one penny per week. At the rear was a fair-sized garden which Mumford cultivated with flowers and vegetables, while at the far end, forming a boundary with Grinnel's orchard, stood the old pig-sty, now converted into a hen house, where lived an assorted collection of hens and pullets. Toilet arrangements were primitive, consisting as they did of an earth privy adjacent to the hen house. It was a double seater affair upon which at times Mumford and I would sit side by side. Access for emptying was provided by a large hinged flap which gave entrance from the orchard: on the days when

Charlie Bennet came to empty the trays it was as well to be as far away as possible. On dark winter nights, with night shirt flapping around my ankles, feet encased in unlaced boots, and guided by lantern light, I made many a perilous journey down the garden path propelled by the call of nature, the hole over which I sat holding endless terrors. Relieved in more ways than one, on my return my childish imagination lent wings to my feet as I scampered back to the safety of the cottage and my warm bed – which incidentally I shared with Mumford.

Often on summer mornings with the bedroom window open wide, I would lie and watch the shadows made by the early sun as it filtered through the arbour of pink roses, dance on the walls. As the breeze lifted the leaves the pattern created would shift this way and that, only to be stilled for a brief moment when the wind calmed. Occasionally an inquisitive bird would flutter near the window peering in as if to say 'Be up and about'. The shadow of its tiny wings seemed to dance with all the others on the wall until at last, tired of its play, it fled away to perch itself on the topmost branch of the pear tree at the bottom of the garden where, in song, it would declare itself ready to begin its day.

Facing the bed end there was a large built in bookcase, unglazed but having its door secured with a fine wire grill. The books it contained had a smell of their own, a dank musty smell; some of their titles stay with me now, *King Solomons Mines* by Rider Haggard was one, and *The Sorrows of Satan*. This last one was one of Mumford's favourites, which she had read and re-read until I swear she must have known its contents by heart. In the years to come, when able to read, I was to get to know their secrets and through their magic be transported to far away places.

Mumford would rise long before me to rekindle the fire in the parlour and get the kettle into its best singing mood on the hob. Lying in my warm bed I would hear her as she hammered the large lumps of coal in the coal house with which to fill the scuttles for the estate office fires. Reluctantly I made my way kitchenwards, loitering for a while in front of the fire, where, with nightshirt tucked up around my middle, I stood to watch the steam from the now protesting kettle hiss and dance its way up the smoke blackened chimney. As I stood there my eyes rested, as they often did, on the mantelpiece above on which were arranged a multitude of small ornaments, mementoes of visits Mumford had made to various seaside resorts in the past. But there, in pride of place as ever, was the photograph of Mumford and Grandad in its silver frame. How proud they looked, she sitting demurely on a straight backed chair, he standing behind her, one hand resting lightly on her shoulder, the other clasping a bowler hat. How fine he looked in his dark suit and stiff white collar, his moustache neatly trimmed and waxed! I often saw Mumford, when she thought no one was looking, take the picture down and carefully dust it, then stand for a while remembering.

My washing was soon done, in the large white enamel bowl placed in the stone sink and filled with rainwater from the butt outside.

Even more hastily I dressed, with the speed which only small boys are capable of when in a hurry, and took my place before the scrubbed table top. There, waiting for my plate of porridge, I passed away the time by spooning brown sugar crystals from bowl to plate and back again, a practice which, when discovered, brought recriminations.

Oh, that lovely plate of porridge, what poetry could be written on such a subject! To watch the milk being poured into a place cleared in the centre of it, then carefully to eat around the edge, seeing how much liquid could be contained until the very last minute, was pure joy. To me it was a lagoon on some remote island upon which sailed pirate ships from the Spanish Main. Many a fierce battle did I fight in secret in that milky sea with matchsticks deftly propelled and controlled by my spoon handle. What lovely and silly things youth can indulge in before the formality and niceties of later years sweep them away!

The kitchen, though small in size and dimly lit, served us well. Under the window stood the square stone sink which was built up to working height on bricks. Above it a single tap stretched its neck from a steel pipe, from which came the spring water brought down from the hills above the village. Washing, I ought to have said, was always fraught with danger for me, as due to the height of the sink I had to stand on a stool to reach both bowl and tap.

To one side stood the lead-lined copper, maid of all work. Heated by a coal fire beneath, it provided the hot water for

15

bathing, washing and the accomplishment of a multitude of other chores. Each year a week or so before Christmas our plum puddings in white basins neatly topped with tied cloths, would be plunged into its boiling recess for their long steaming.

The range, which was nearby, was never used for the purpose for which it had been intended, as the down draughts from its short chimney invariably sent smoke billowing into the room, and should the door have been left open into the parlour, a frantic scene would then ensue. Mumford would rush about throwing doors and windows wide and all the time flapping her apron in an attempt to disperse the black cloud, which left sooty smuts hanging from the cobwebs in the rafters of the high ceiling.

Our cooking arrangements were conducted on a large Valor oil stove, to me a fascinating piece of equipment. It had two burners, each with their separate chimneys, above which when necessary was placed a large tin oven. Thus it was that on dull wet days with nothing much else to do, I would sit and watch the blue flames tinged with yellow, dancing behind the crazed and flaky mica screens. The stove, which in later years I christened Old Faithful, could at times, however, be very temperamental, when it too would fill the kitchen with acrid blue smoke.

It was a hungry beast, consuming immense quantities of paraffin from the village store, which I would fetch in a bright metal can whose handle reached half way up my chest. These journeys from store to stove took the form of a series of short staggers and long rests. Fortunately, time was not of the essence, as inevitably the proceedings would be interrupted by my floating matchsticks down the gutter, or sitting to watch some helpless insect endeavouring to climb the steep stone curb to escape the swirling waters below. Arriving back at the cottage I would, as often as not, be smartly turned about to search for the small change which I had somehow managed to lose on the way. Most likely it had been deposited down the drain outside the stores, as by some inexplicable urge, I could never pass it without dropping the coins through the grating to hear them plop into the water below.

On the highest shelves of the kitchen stood an assortment of the home-made wines which Mumford seemed to produce in vast quantities, each bottle being neatly labelled to show its contents. Sometimes at night, in the agony of their fermentation, corks would be blown, causing Mumford to rise from her bed and proceed, candle in hand, to the kitchen to administer to their needs. Occasionally, a bottle would burst, scattering its contents all over the place, and it was a mystery to me why they always seemed to choose the dead of night for their activities.

On Saturday mornings we observed the ritual knife cleaning, when out would come the well-worn piece of board and tin of Monkey Brand cleaner. Setting to with a will, we polished away until all the cutlery, shining in steely splendour, was ready to be replaced in the table drawer. Strange to relate, on the rare occasions when thunder threatened, Mumford would cover up all the knives and mirrors, a superstition which was not explained, but which no doubt had been handed down through the generations. How I hated those storms! To me there was something frightening and awesome about them, and sitting in the dark passage between parlour and bedrooms, a finger stuffed tightly in each ear, I would count the seconds between the flashes of lightning and the accompanying thunder, so as to judge, as it was claimed, how far away the storm was.

Our domestic life in those early days was well ordered, and each week saw its familiar sequence of events. One of these was bath time, when the old high-backed hip bath was placed on the floor in the middle of the kitchen and filled with hot water from the copper. The act of bathing presented very little difficulty for me, but for Mumford it necessitated a time-honoured and well practised procedure. Seeing that only one part of the body could be accommodated at any one time, the bathing had to be carried out in two stages. First came the upper part and then, in a standing position, the rest could be attended to: but it was essential at such times that a partner be present to assist in the scrubbing of the back and the getting in and out, especially where older people were concerned. In the absence of any other help I took great delight in officiating at these weekly ablutions, carrying out the task with a zeal which more often than not resulted in there being more water on the kitchen floor than was left in the bath. I remember Mumford once telling me how Mrs Halling, a widow living in the village, had spent the best part of the day unable to get out of her hip bath. There she remained until a passing neighbour happening to peer in through the window, realized her predicament and hurried to her assistance.

Hair cutting days I avoided if at all possible. Fred Walker who performed this service had probably learnt the art in his days at sheep shearing; however, in spite of this he managed fairly well in those far off days when fashion had not yet dictated to young boys, and when all that was required was that the finished job should be serviceable and as long lasting as possible. Fred was a familiar figure in the village, to be seen summer and winter propelling his old three-wheeled tricycle along the roads, wearing an ancient Panama hat which, bleached by the sun, had a greenish look about it, almost as if it had started to grow moss.

Seated on a stool in the yard behind the cottage, with a large white sheet enveloping me, well tucked in around the neck, I awaited the onslaught. Fred, by then usually fortified with several glasses of Mumford's home-made wine, took up his stance behind me and commenced operations, pausing now and then to snort noisily into a large red handkerchief, or to blow vigorously down my neck to remove any loose hairs. What with the blowing, the smell of his breath and the pulling of the scissors, which always seemed non too sharp, I was mightily glad when the job was done and, shorn and chilly round the neck, I was allowed to scamper out into the street to regain some sort of dignity. Having partaken of a further glass of wine, Fred would pedal off to his next assignment. I often wondered what sort of state he would be in after three or more haircuts, assuming that the hospitality received at Mumford's was repeated – particularly if a pig killing, which was another concern of his – happened to come between his appointments.

My first duty each morning was to fetch the milk from the dairy. Off up the lane I would go, swinging the milk can gaily. Fortunately, this had a tight fitting lid or on the return journey there would have been trouble, as invariably it was subjected to the same treatment. On the way there were, of course, numerous distractions, the first and best being the estate timber yard. Here the trees brought down from the woods were trimmed and sawn into planks. Great stacks of them stood about, to be seasoned before being used. Pride of place in my affections, however, was taken by the stationary steam engine which drove the large circular saw. I watched intently as the broad drive belt stretched between saw and engine and crossed in the middle, tightened and slackened as the load was applied. One moment the old engine would be running quietly and smoothly, and the next, as the blade met the resistance of the load, it would strain and puff over its task, with steam hissing from valve and cylinder. Its work done, as if in relief, it would relax once more into its steady beat. Now and then the boiler mouth would be opened for shovel loads of coal to be heaped into its demanding belly, the glow of the fire lighting up the face of the toiling labourer. It got so with me that, lying half asleep in the bed in the early morning, I could tell to a second when the large tree trunks were being presented to the hungry saw. First would come the altered beat of the engine, followed by the keen sound as steel ripped into timber. Then, its task complete, it would take up its normal quiet running as before.

Resuming my journey towards the dairy, I braced myself for the inevitable verbal battle with George Nurden, the head man: he seemed to delight in tormenting me. Short and plump, he could show a deceptive turn of speed, as I sometimes found out to my cost when daring to play in the rickyard across the paddock. However, as I halted at the entrance to the preparing room, there was no sign of him this morning – only Charlie, one of his sons, was busy with the butter churn which stood inside. Butter-making was a long and arduous operation, but it was fun to watch, especially when the top of the churn was at last opened and the yellow butter came out, to be patted into blocks on the cool slab alongside.

From the milking sheds out in the yard came the sound of the steady splash of milk into bucket and the occasional low moo of protest from some doe-eyed Jersey cow. Somewhere out of sight, the milker was at work, hunched on his stool, head pressed firmly into the animal's flank. He knew each of his charges by name, and the particular temperament of each, for they were all different and, like children, they could have their off days when no amount of coaxing would induce them to give of their best.

For me, however, the dairy's most provocative and interesting inhabitant was the large ginger tom cat who sat crouched on the yard fence, fixing me with a rigid, malevolent stare. I never did get to know its name, if indeed it had one, but its fierce look, made more daunting by one partially closed eye – a casualty no doubt of some feline battle – ensured that I treated it with extreme caution. The old tom was said to be the best mouser in the district, besides having fathered half the cat population of the village. There it would sit on the top rail, defying all my insults and efforts to dislodge it, the only indication that it was aware of my presence coming from its tail which it switched now and then. How I would love to have owned that cat – what tricks I could have taught it! But it was not to be; having been a law unto itself for so long, it was beyond taming.

And so I entered the separating room where Charlie filled my can with skimmed milk. With the lid firmly secured and my penny piece deposited on the table, it was time to set off homewards.

My next stop was outside the village hall, where there was a shallow well. Raising the wooden cover, I renewed my daily acquaintance with a large frog who each morning awaited my visit, sitting patiently on a protruding brick just above the water level. With a short piece of stick I gently nudged him towards, and then over the edge into the water, he dropped with a faint plop and immediately climbed back on to the brick. As soon as he was comfortably settled I repeated the procedure, carrying on with the game until one or other of us got tired. Over the years he had become accustomed to our morning ritual, no doubt to pass it on to his descendants, one of whom, even now, may be sitting on that protruding brick waiting for some other small boy to lift the cover and start the game all over again.

There were however other highlights in my young life, which, although perhaps forgotten as time passed, were at the time of their happening very important. In order that I might take my rightful place amongst the other older foot scuffing, can-kicking boys, suitable footwear had to be found: this necessitated a trip to Evesham.

At eight o'clock we gathered outside the village stores to board Bill Woods's carrier cart, a simple open dray on which were placed wooden forms. Only in extremely inclement weather would a tarpaulin be provided to protect the passengers from the elements, and many a journey I was forced to make sitting under an umbrella held by Mumford, from the edges of which the rain would drip down between collar and skin. Mr Wood's old horse, Rafnally, stood patiently waiting in the shafts, head hung down, seemingly contemplating one small patch of ground in front of him. As the bustle of activity taking place behind diminished, and the command 'Walk On' was given, he would raise his head and gaze mournfully towards the driveway leading to his stables where no doubt he would rather be. Eventually, after much coaxing and threatening, he shambled off up the village making it quite plain that he was getting very little pleasure from his enforced labours.

Along the way stops were made at cottages and farms to collect written orders for goods to be purchased by Bill and delivered on the return journey. Empty paraffin cans were stacked on the floor of the dray and punnets of fruit in their seasons would also be accommodated. One landmark which I remember clearly on those journeys was a stately pair of old elms which stood one each side of the road just beyond Little Cheltenham; chained together for support, they were said to mark the boundary between Gloucestershire and Worcestershire. Sadly, they are no longer there, having succumbed to old age, or possibly the ravages of Dutch elm disease.

Arriving at Evesham we made our way over the river bridge and up Bridge Street, our heads dodging from side to side to catch the first glimpse of the contents of the shop windows as we passed. Journey's end was in the High Street where, once alighted, the passengers went their separate ways, shopping bags in hand, leaving Bill to throw a blanket over Rafnally's back and hitch on the nose bag.

Our first port of call was inevitably the 'Bon Marché', a large store in the centre of the town, where one could be fitted out from head to foot without ever leaving the premises. Here were boots of all sizes, standing unboxed in long silent rows, each with a pair of leather laces attached, with steel tips to both toe and heel and fully studded between. To me they represented the ultimate in my progress into the grown-up world. Tantalizingly, they stood on the shelves, inviting some small boy to take them and introduce them to the streets and lanes outside, and I could hardly wait for the assistant to pick out a pair for me to try on.

At last Mumford seemed satisfied. As for myself, I felt enormously important. Never would I have admitted the effort needed to lift my feet off the ground. The feel of them was so grand, the sheer joy of clomping along the boarded floor! Indeed, I would have walked straight out of the shop in them had I been allowed to do so, in order that the whole of Evesham might admire my new footwear. But, instead, carefully wrapped they were placed in Mumford's shopping bag, never to be out of my sight, for in truth I feared that some mishap might befall them.

So the long day wore on, until our shopping done, we retired to a small tea shop where the other villagers were already to be found, fortifying themselves with cups of strong tea. With a large sugared bun in one hand, I sat with elbows propped, listening to the conversation which drifted backwards and forwards across the room until the time came to seek out Rafnally and Bill Wood's carrier cart for the return journey.

Balanced precariously on the wooden seat, I snuggled up to Mumford, who put her arm around me to stop me falling off, and soon Evesham was left far behind. Along the way stops were made to deliver purchased goods. Gossip was exchanged and often Bill would be fortified with a mug of cider or a glass of home-made wine. Consequently, long before Nutmeadow was reached, he had dropped off into sleepy silence, leaving the horse to negotiate the last mile on its own.

At the unloading stop villagers were waiting to collect their daily newspapers. The news was already old by then, but no matter: life went on much the same. Then, half asleep, I staggered the last few steps to the cottage where, once inside and with oil lamp lit and purchases safely stowed away, I lay full length on the hearth rug in front of the fire to enjoy the antics of Rupert the Bear in the newspaper. There is an unforgettable smell to a brand new newspaper, a fresh printy smell which invites you to open its pages and discover the delights within. However, being then only at the picture stage and not having any knowledge of reading, much of the enjoyment was lost to me: nevertheless, through all those years of literary ignorance, Rupert the Bear created a world of fantasy and I followed his adventures with avid interest.

Early next morning, donning my splendid boots, I ventured out into the street. Walking up and down, I kicked at anything that would move and some things that wouldn't, all the time marvelling at the sparks which were made when the steel tips struck against the granite curbstones. At length, tiring of this activity, I carefully removed any marks made on the toe caps with my handkerchief which soon began to show signs of wear and tear. Much later I was to learn the correct procedure: this involved standing on one leg while the boot on the other was rubbed vigorously on the back of one's stocking. There was no doubt that this gave them a good shine, and the fact that the backs of the stockings became liberally coated with Cherry Blossom boot polish seemed at the time of little consequence. This ritual, together with that of wiping one's nose on the sleeve of one's jersey in the absence of a handkerchief clean enough to carry out the operation, seemed common to all small boys. Other items of equipment necessary for survival consisted, apparently, of a pen knife, a piece of string, and one sticky toffee usually to be found adhering to the lining of the trouser pocket. There were, besides, a number of skills which it was as well to be adept in. These included being able to emit a shrill whistle through the front teeth, and the playing of a mouth organ – not both at once I hasten to add. These arts Mumford taught me together with the finer points of whip and top spinning, which I practised on the tarmac road outside.

Mumford was an accomplished entertainer in her own right, and I remember well her renderings of *My Old Man Said Follow The Van* which she was apt to perform on the stage at the village hall, accompanied by Mrs Davis from the power house. Her repertoire of songs also included *Smiling Through, Daisy Daisy, Come Into The Garden Maud* and many others of the old time music hall favourites. This was an age that produced its own amusements and entertainment: when with oil lamps lit, families gathered around the piano to render demure songs of the day, assisted by others whose vocal limitations debarred them from Going Into The Garden With Maud. The star of such occasions would invariably be a large middle-aged lady whose heaving bosoms seemed a necessary part of the performance, her chest being inflated to immense proportions each time a high note was delivered. On the rare occasion when allowed to attend these gatherings I would sit enthralled – not by the song, but by the bosoms which would fight madly to escape from their corsage prisons.

In those early days we pursued our lives within the confines of the village, except of course for the occasional visit to

Cheltenham or Evesham. Nestled under its wooded hills, Dumbleton had a charm of its own, bounded as it was by the Cotswolds to the south, while close by to the west the sharp rise beyond Ashton Under Hill showed where Bredon Hill formed a boundary between us and the flat Vale of Evesham. Everything was estate-orientated, the village depending on Lord Monsell, up at the Hall, for its livelihood, while he in turn relied on the villagers for the estate's smooth running. Dairy, power house, school and stores, together with stables and smithy, were all to be found here, making a community that was almost self-sufficient, where generations of the same families had been born, married and buried. There was a women's institute in which Lady Monsell took a keen interest, whilst to become a playing member of the cricket club, one had to be employed by the estate or at least be resident in the village. All this tended to weave a pattern of strength, wielding us into a tightly knit family dependent on each other and quick to help in times of trouble. I was enriched by it more than I knew, never ceasing to marvel at the changing seasons, and getting to know the beauty and variety of the wild life around. And it was this feeling of warmth and security that supported me during my early days, preparing me for the next important milestone along the way – school and the beginning of my education proper.

She came skipping along the road, resplendent in her white cotton frock hemmed with lace, her ribboned pigtails bobbing with each movement. Shifting from one booted foot to the other I watched as she approached, uncertain what to do or say. Finally, pulling my cap lower over my eyes, I tried to give the impression that as yet I had not noticed her; but Kathy, for that was her name, had no intention of being ignored. She halted in front of me and, with steady gaze, looked me up and down, all the while swinging her school satchel like an athlete preparing to execute a hammer throw. There is something very disturbing about a young female swinging a school satchel, particularly when you meet her for the first time, so, deciding for the moment that discretion might well be the better part of valour, I hastily dragged up my stockings – which always

She came skipping along the road, resplendent in her white cotton frock hemmed with lace, her ribboned pigtails bobbing with each movement.

seemed to be resting over my boot tops – and fled down the path into school. Little did I realize the role she was to play in my life in the years to come.

However these were early days and I was far too busy enjoying my childhood to give any thoughts to the future. Squatting in my favourite corner of the playground, I awaited the arrival of the rest of the gang, and was soon joined by Ernie Lane, Ted Pulley, Lofty and Titch Harris, Bumper Davis and Badger Robinson. We were an ill-assorted lot, always in trouble and a continual challenge to our teachers, particularly to our headmaster, Mr Prior, who rejoiced in the nickname of Old Thunder. Hunched in friendly silence, we passed away the time flicking small pebbles at a fly sunning itself in the dust of the playground until stirred into action by the clanging of the school bell, wielded in the capable hands of Miss Ermison. Slowly we filed into the large hall which, with the aid of a curtain, was divided into two classrooms, and made our way to our respective desks where, with much shuffling of feet and whispered conversation, we awaited the arrival of the head-master.

Prompt as ever, Mr Prior emerged from the school house, striding down the short garden path in a half crouch, hands in trouser pockets, eyes fixed firmly on the ground in front of him. The suit he wore, I swear, was the only one he possessed for it appeared to give service at weddings, funerals, church Sundays, and even the annual flower show in the summer; the jacket was patched with leather at the elbows, and the knees of his thick worsted trousers were baggy and creased.

His one pride and joy was his old motor cycle combination which he kept in a shed at the bottom of the school garden. In this fearsome contraption Mrs Prior, much to her obvious discomfort, and clutching the sides of the sidecar, would be transported round the countryside at a furious pace, her large brimmed hat kept firmly in place with a scarf tied under her chin. Old Thunder was my original conception of Biggles, when, with helmet and goggles on, and his motor cycling coat flapping about him, he passed us in the lanes, the wind tightening his face to a look of grim determination. A ride to Evesham with Mr Prior was something to which very few of the villagers would avail themselves, preferring the more sedate journey by Bill Wood's carrier cart. That was certainly much

26

slower, but at least it ensured that they would arrive with nervous systems more or less intact.

Mounting the dais, Old Thunder settled himself in his chair and pushed the gold-rimmed spectacles he wore more firmly on the bridge of his nose. Clearing his throat, he viewed the assembly below, then opened the register and began to call the names. For a while after that, all that would be heard was a 'Present, sir', or when some absentee was unable to answer to his or her name, a dead silence. On such occasions he would raise his head and gaze round the room to make sure that the offender was indeed missing and that it was not just a case of some dozy pupil who, half asleep, had failed to hear his name called. The daily check completed, he slammed the book shut with a bang that brought the dozy ones back to life and caused the more timid to grip the edge of their desks until their knuckles showed white. Then followed the singing of the morning hymn which he led in a thundering baritone voice, much to the consternation of those of us sitting in the front row who were apt to receive the full blast of his offering. With all formalities duly attended to we sat in silence, awaiting the pre-lesson pep talk he invariably gave before disappearing back to the school house where his breakfast would be waiting. Blowing furiously into a large handkerchief with a noise like both barrels of Charlie Done's shotgun going off at once, he commenced: 'As you are by now no doubt aware, we have a new addition to our dubious collection of scholastic geniuses, a Miss Kathy Lockwood. To demonstrate that my faith in human nature has not been entirely ruined, I intend that she should sit next to our Master Chamberlain – not, I fear, in the hope that she will learn much from him, but rather that she might be a sobering influence!' Here he paused for a while, fixing his gaze on me. To have to sit next to a girl was bad enough, but her being a newcomer only made matters worse. However, Old Thunder knew this and the arrangement had been deliberate on his part.

Resigning myself glumly to the situation, I rose to my feet, and Ernie Lane, who usually sat beside me, gathered up his belongings and moved to the back of the class. In his new position he would find it almost impossible to effect any sort of communication with me, owing to the proximity of the large coke burning stove against which, on cold winter mornings,

Old Thunder was wont to warm his backside.

The next morning she was beside me, busily arranging her books. As she did so, she slyly bent her head and whispered: 'Serves you jolly well right.' That remark caused me to endeavour to deliver a crafty kick to her ankle; however, I only succeeded in barking my shin on the side of the desk, much to the amusement of Dorothy Clark, sitting behind. (Dear Dorothy Clark: I wonder if she still remembers how I used to chase her down the school path, pulling at her pigtails.) But, as the day wore on, my attitude towards my new companion began to change: her help was invaluable when it came to tackling some knotty problems or other. Even at this early stage I had a feeling that there was something special about her, although my boyish pride would never have allowed me to admit it.

Our education at first was fairly basic. Our first year was spent scratching away on slates and learning to read from simple illustrated books. Words were spelled out laboriously and tables chanted in unison. So we ploughed on, under the watchful eye of Miss Ermison, until at last it was felt we could be trusted with pen and ink. The sheets of paper we were issued with were ruled on either side to allow for a wide margin wherein remarks and comments by the teacher could be written, in red ink – and I must admit that at times my margins showed more industry than the main copy. Each letter had to be carefully formed, and woe betide any unfortunate pupil who caused an ink blob to appear: this was considered an unforgivable sin, usually punished by caning.

At playtime we congregated in preordained corners of the playground where we played our games and teased and chased the girls to add spice to our mundane existence. At lunch times those of us who lived locally returned home, leaving less fortunate companions to sit in the classrooms and unwrap lunches from metal boxes. Then in the afternoons, with school over, we made our various ways homewards, some to fetch the milk from the dairy, some to help on farms, and some to wend their leisurely way across the fields to isolated cottages.

Once having learned to read and write, I found a whole new world opening up to me. From the school library I borrowed books which were read and re-read, one in particular being entitled *What Katie Did*, the author of which I have long since forgotten. The pleasure to be got from between their covers sustained me on many a dark winter's night when, with chin cupped in hands, elbows on the table, I pored over them in the soft lamplight until, unable to keep my eyes open any longer, Mumford would light the candle and guide me, half asleep, to bed.

Even at this early stage Kathy must have had a special place in my affections, for I remember taking her the odd bunch of flowers, always kept well hidden under my jacket, in order to escape the inevitable ribbing from the rest of my unruly acquaintances. In response she would often, in the playground, pass me hastily scribbled notes which, as soon as read, would be deposited down the boy's toilet for the same reason that I concealed the flowers.

At this time however, larger events and new innovations were beginning to touch us in our daily lives. Mr and Mrs Lewis who lived at, and administered, the village stores, became the proud possessors of a one valve wireless set, and villagers were invited into the sanctity of their front parlour to sample the delights of this twentieth century miracle. It boasted two sets of earphones so, by releasing the individual ear pieces from the headband, four people could listen at once. How we marvelled at the crackling sound which came from so far away! Failing to grasp the mechanics of the thing, I often wondered just how the voices managed to travel from far beyond Broadway and find their way into Mr Lewis's front parlour.

It was not long before Mumford had her own crystal set, made for her by Mr Davis up at the power house. Now of an evening she would sit with a look of rapt attention on her face and earphones clamped tightly to her ears. What a task it was to fiddle the 'cat's whisker' tuning on the crystal until the best reception was obtained! I must confess that there were times when, without thinking, I burst into the cottage, letting the door slam behind me, thus dislodging the tuning and sending Mumford into a perfect frenzy as she struggled to get the station back again.

The power house, so called, had been built and equipped to provide electric light for the Hall across the park, as well as for the church, dairy, stables and village hall, a facility which, until the coming of the national grid scheme, was denied to the rest of the village. Harry Davis, an ex-naval man, was in

charge of it, and he and his able assistant, Jack Sallis, kept the
two large oil-powered engines running. These engines were
housed in a white-tiled building behind which were sited the
banks of open cell batteries which when fully charged supplied
the electricity. Watching the machinery at work was a never
ending source of wonderment to me and, when allowed, I
would stand for ages at the entrance while the huge flywheels
rotated and Jack Sallis, oily rag always at the ready, busied
himself wiping off an oil smear here and there, all the time
keeping a wary eye on the prominently mounted dials. I say
'wary eye', for Jack only had one good one; in spite of which,
there was very little that he missed either in the care of the
machinery or the antics of us young lads, who at times would
tend to become a little too venturesome. Then he would
threaten: 'I'll make thee hop like a frog, so I will,' and, believe
me, we did hop when he got aroused.

Harry Davis and his wife Ivy had an adopted son named
Geoffrey, a lad of my own age who for some obscure reason
rejoiced in the nickname of Bumper. He and I spent many
happy hours playing under the glass roof covering the car wash
area where Lady Monsell's Rolls Royce was garaged. We
floated our toy boats along the ditch which ran the length of
the lane up to the dairy and, loading our clock-work lorries
with mud and sticks, sent them speeding across the smooth
brick floor of the garage forecourt. Our greatest joy, though,
when no one was about to interfere, was to play on the estate
fire engine which was housed nearby. In its turn it served as a
pirate ship, stage coach, and many other roles as fancy
dictated. Of course, it did not always stand idle. There were
times when it was required to perform its intended duties –
occasions like its annual inspection when it would be put
through its paces under the watchful eye of a very important
gentleman from London. What a scene that was! First the
horses, which were usually supplied by Albert Fisher, had to be
caught and harnessed, one to each side of the long pole which
protruded from the front steering axle. This being done and
when all the crew had been assembled and accounted for, the
engine with its full complement would proceed at a steady
gallop up to the Hall, where the water supply would be laid on
and hoses unrolled. With three or four men ranged along the
bar which stretched the length of the engine on either side,

pumping would then commence – an operation which always seemed to cause some difficulty, and much delay, before any rhythm was achieved. At length, the water would come squirting out, minus, of course, a considerable amount which escaped from holes in the hose pipe. Meanwhile the gentleman from London, notebook in hand, waited patiently to one side until the hoses were ready to be directed at a prearranged aiming point. Then the fun would start. Out came the jet of water, going everywhere but at the target, and more often than not the poor old doves in the trees around would receive the full benefit of the firemen's efforts, not taking too kindly to being washed out of house and home. However, with honour at last satisfied, the hoses were rolled up and stowed away in the lockers and all made ready for the return journey – during which, if we were lucky, we would be allowed to ride on the engine back to the power house, where it would quietly rest until its next call out.

In those days, life in the village seemed to revolve around events which occurred regularly in their due season. One great social highlight of the year was the garden party up at the Hall, usually held to support some good cause in which Lady Monsell had a personal interest. Here in high summer, the villagers gathered to spend a pleasant afternoon and evening walking the grounds and sampling the delights of the many stalls and attractions provided. There were bottle stalls, tables laden with home-made produce, bowling for a pig, races for the younger ones and the wheel of fortune. This last was usually looked after by Mumford – an arrangement which left me more or less to my own devices.

On one particular day, having explored all that was on display, I found myself beside the large ornamental lake, home to a multitude of breeds of ducks and wildfowl, the care of which came under the personal supervision of Lord Monsell. Feeling bored with things, I sought amusement by skimming flat stones across the surface of the water, a pastime known as Ducks and Drakes, this being very appropriate in view of what happened. Apparently unobserved, I continued with the game until, to my horror, just having launched a stone on its way across the lake, a passing duck got in its way, the missile striking it in the neck. Before my eyes, the poor bird keeled over to float lifeless on its side on the water. Appalled, I panicked and then, realizing it was time to make myself scarce, I raced across the park to the safety of the power house, fear lending speed to my feet as I ran. Out of breath and near to tears, I hid in an outside toilet, where I remained until found by Mrs Davis on her return. She, after piecing together my tearful story, took me back to Mumford's cottage. No sooner was I inside than panic struck again, causing me to seek refuge under the bed where I stayed until she came home. No amount of threats or promises would induce me to forsake my sanctuary, so there I stayed all night, dreaming of the awful retribution which would overtake me the next day.

Sure enough, early the next morning Mr Pyke-Nott, the estate manager, called and I was hauled before him in the parlour. Mumford sat in her chair, face as black as thunder, while I, standing before them, hands clasped behind my back and head hung low, recounted the incident of the duck, all the time wishing that the ground would open up and swallow me. As my story unfolded, I began to feel worse and worse, particularly when I learned that the bird I had so prematurely sent to its Maker appeared to be one of a breeding pair of a rare species highly prized by his Lordship. Looking back, I feel convinced that only the fact that my act had not been intentional saved me from being dispatched to the colonies, a fate which at the time seemed highly probable. However, after a severe reprimand from Mr Pyke-Nott, and a letter of apology and regret from Mumford, the matter was closed. I don't think I shall ever forget it, though, as even now, each time I see a duck swimming or hanging from a hook in a butcher's shop, a feeling of guilt creeps over me.

Thankfully, such occurrences came only rarely to disturb the tranquillity of life in the village. Small happenings did, however, generate their own excitement. I remember once how, on returning from Evesham, we learned that an aeroplane had landed in one of Hulbert's fields down by Bulman Coppice. All agog, Mumford decided that we should view this marvel and so, the next day, armed with picnic basket and flasks of tea, we set off. From early morning to late evening, we sat admiring the biplane, examining it from end to end and sheltering under its wings when the rain came, but, alas, it remained earthbound, and late in the day, we returned home with curiosity unsatisfied. The following day we heard that it had gone, so the chance of seeing my first aeroplane take to the skies was lost.

There were, of course, other events which filled our calendar. On Wednesday mornings the lads and I would gather at the top of the village outside Charlie Staight's butcher's shop to witness and occasionally assist in the slaughter of cattle. Sitting on the top rail of the fence, we viewed the proceedings with awe. The unfortunate beast, which had been held for some days in the fasting pen, was led into the yard where a rope, passed through an iron ring, was tied around its neck, the loose end being taken up by us boys. With much pushing it was pole-axed, stuck, and bled. Now, all this may seem very brutal, but that was the way of things then. Incidentally, we were never paid for our efforts, the only reward being a large slice of home-made cake which Mrs Staight handed to us out of her kitchen window.

At other times we attended a pig killing, which took place in the yard at the back of Fred Walker's cottage. Here, watching from a safe distance, we saw the pig, finally cornered, being laid on the sacrificial bench. Squealing and struggling, it would fight savagely, its efforts to escape sometimes proving too much for its executioners. Free for a while, it would charge round and round the yard hotly pursued by Fred and his helpers, egged on by our cheering. Eventually, however, the deed being done, it was carted off up to the dairy where, in the yard, it would be singed to remove all the bristles from its hide. When it had cooled it was hung from a hook and opened up. There was always great competition to get the bladder, for this, once cleaned and dried, made an excellent football. Strange how we seemed to take all this in our stride, particularly as the death of a small bird could reduce us to tears.

By reason of their individuality, some of the animals in the village attracted our personal attention. This was especially the case with Miss Hayworth's cat Clarence, a formidable beast, who, thoroughly spoiled and arrogant and seemingly devoid of any affection for the human race, was wont to sit on the wall outside her cottage glowering at anyone who dared to approach. It had a nasty habit of allowing the hand to get within inches of its person before, with a speed that defied the human eye, it lashed out, claws extended. Badger, who had an ongoing feud with Clarence, decided one Saturday that enough was enough, and that some positive steps should now be taken to resolve the situation. Borrowing a wicker basket, a length of rope and a short piece of broom handle from his father's shed, and a half-consumed tin of sardines from his mother's larder, he prepared to put his plan into action.

At the rear of Miss Hayworth's cottage was a large lawn which faced on to Grinnel's Orchard. Here on warm sunny days the cat liked to lie and sun himself, while Miss Hayworth took her usual afternoon nap in the parlour. Badger, timing his approach to perfection, having waited a while until he was sure that all was quiet, came creeping round to the rear of the cottage to set his trap. First the wicker basket was placed at a distance, its lid propped open with the piece of broom handle to which he tied one end of the length of rope. Then, trailing the loose end, he withdrew behind a large laurel bush and sat down to await events.

For a while all was peaceful and calm. Clarence, lying flat on his back, all four legs extended, was enjoying the feel of the sun on his tummy, completely unaware of what was in store for him. With eyes closed in ecstasy, he sniffed the air around – until suddenly he picked up the scent of the sardines which Badger had placed in the bottom of the basket. Slowly he rose to his feet and stood, whiskers twitching in anticipation. At length, discovering the source of the tantalizing smell, he cautiously approached the basket, stalking round and round it, as if puzzled how to proceed. Badger, watching from his hiding place, gripped the rope tightly, hardly daring to breathe. Finally the cat, unable to resist the temptation any longer, dived in for the sardines; Badger gave one sharp pull, down came the lid and his victim was well and truly caught.

From here on events moved quickly. The lid was secured with a peg, the rope and broom handle thrown over the fence into the orchard, and basket and cat whisked away in the same direction through a gap in the fence. Still, for a few moments, all was quiet. Then the cat, beginning to realize the predicament it was in, started to scratch and spit, and tear round and round the walls of its prison like a rider on the wall of death, emitting the most horrible sounds of frustration. Badger, making what haste he could, though the basket was heavy and slowed his pace, got at last to the church where, after making sure that the coast was clear, he opened the door and went in. The cat, perhaps sensing that it had entered on holy ground, ceased its frantic struggles to escape and stood with claws extended and fur bristling, peering through the wicker work of the basket. Meanwhile, Badger, hunting about for a suitable hiding place, eventually decided on the vestry, where he hid the cat behind a stack of discarded boxes in a dark corner. With one last look around he retraced his steps into the churchyard and, taking care to close the door securely behind him, made his way home, intending to return later in the evening and set Clarence free.

Unfortunately, events did not turn out as planned, as an unforeseen visit to an aunty in Alderton prevented him from returning. Darkness fell and, failing to see just how the animal was to be liberated, he gave up, and decided to leave matters in the hands of fate.

The next morning an agitated Miss Hayworth, alarmed at the disappearance of her beloved cat, walked the village calling out its name. Badger, on his way to church, passed by on the other side hoping against hope that he would be able to resolve matters before any members of the choir arrived. Thwarted once more, he resigned himself to the inevitable, carrying out his choral duties with an angelic look on his face which hid the apprehension he felt inside.

The vicar mounted the pulpit and the congregation waited in silence for the sermon to follow, the only sounds being the shuffle of feet and the rustle of hymn and prayer books as they were placed on the shelves in front of the pews.

Suddenly, and without any warning, all hell was let loose. The cat, what with the noise of the organ and the singing, had worked itself up into a frenzy. Over went the basket, out came the retaining peg and Clarence, not stopping to question his new-found freedom, fled into the nave where, with every hair standing on end and spitting venomously, he stood for a moment confronting the amazed congregation. What happened next is history. Members of the choir, forsaking their seats, chased the cat round and round the stalls, the parishioners who joined in only adding to the confusion. The vicar, from the safety of his pulpit, clasped his hands and looked to heaven in disbelief.

Round and round went Clarence – up to the altar, where it knocked over the silver candlesticks – into the organ loft where Charlie Richardson crouched behind his seat hands over his head, then back into the aisle where his feet scrabbled desperately on the smooth tiles as he sought a means to escape. Some of the more timid ladies present had climbed on to their pews by this time, where, with skirts raised, they watched the scene of pandemonium going on on all sides. All efforts to secure the offender were in vain until, sensing that the church door had been left partially open, Clarence shot through the six inch gap with the speed of light, and was last seen perched in the topmost branches of a willow tree in the churchyard. There, with his fur still bristling and eyes wide with terror, he sat endeavouring to regain some of his lost dignity.

Strange to relate, the instigator of the incident escaped scot free, having, in the confusion, been able to secrete the basket, which he recovered some time later when things had died down. Clarence still continued to sit on the wall outside Miss Hayworth's cottage, but whenever Badger passed by, he would beat a hasty retreat. As for his owner, she could never understand why her pet would go berserk whenever a tin of sardines was opened.

# 2

*We drain the mill pool and learn a*
*valuable lesson, go haymaking,*
*sample the delights of the flower show*
*and indulge in a spot of carol singing.*

There were times when having exhausted all other forms of amusement, we turned our attention to our two arch enemies – Mr Hawkins, the head groom at the Hall stables, and Bristol Lyes, who was responsible for keeping the driveways and paths neat and tidy. Mr Hawkins was a man of sour disposition who was for ever chasing us out of the area around his stables. He had gained the nickname Dolly Legs on account of the two spindly extensions which supported his body, so bowed that it was extremely doubtful if he could have 'stopped a pig in a passage'. Unhorsed, he lacked staying power and, therefore, we found it comparatively easy to escape his clutches. He was for ever reporting us to Old Thunder, our headmaster, who would administer the inevitable punishment; however, we considered the caning we received a small price to pay for the joy of seeing Mr Hawkins, riding crop in hand, puff and pant his way round the churchyard, where we would lead him a merry dance in and out of the grave stones.

Bristol Lyes was another matter altogether. He was a slow, elderly man who was rarely seen without his old pipe firmly rammed in the corner of his mouth. They said that the nickname Bristol had been give to him on account of the particular brand of tobacco he smoked, but I suspect that there must have been another reason. In the autumn, with the leaves falling, he spent hours sweeping them up into tidy heaps with his besom. Watching from the shelter of the plantation, we would wait until he was out of sight before creeping out to scuff them back over the driveway, causing Bristol on his return to chase us, besom in hand, over the adjoining park. I suppose it was pretty senseless behaviour on our part, looking back, but at the time we thought it great fun. He did, however, manage to corner me once, and then I received such a beating across my backside that I decided that for the small entertainment I got out of tormenting him, it would perhaps be better if I left him severely alone. I never harboured any bad feelings towards him – in fact, he was always one of my favourites – and now that he is no longer with us, I sincerely hope that if there are autumn leaves in Heaven, they do not, when swept into neat piles, attract horrid little boys to come along and kick them about.

Some people are a constant presence in one's childhood, others appear only fleetingly, but some event connected with them causes them to be stamped indelibly on the memory. Such a one, with me, was Ivy Maxfield. Mumford had provided a swing at the bottom of the garden, an innovation which gave us endless hours of pleasure – that is, until Ivy came to play. She was staying for a short holiday with Ernie Bishop who lived a few doors away, and Mumford thought it a good idea to invite her round for an hour or two, as company for me. Ivy was a thin, gangling girl, much older than me and, being a born organizer, and used to having things her own way, it wasn't long before she began to make my life a misery. One morning whilst I was enjoying myself on the swing, one hand holding on to the rope, while with the other I grasped a small tin trumpet upon which I was blowing lustily, this awesome female suddenly appeared, ordered me off, and proceeded to take the swing for herself. Standing in front of her as she swung, I blasted away on my trumpet in annoyance, but failed to notice that her long legs, sticking straight out in front of her, were getting nearer and nearer my face. The result was inevitable. With one mighty heave as she swung forward, her legs hit the trumpet, ramming it halfway down my throat and knocking me backwards in the process. Seeing me lying there, apparently unable to get my breath, Ivy panicked, took to her heels and disappeared into the safety of Grinnel's orchard; and it was left to me to stagger back into the cottage where Mumford found me and managed to extract the offending instrument. On the doctor's orders I was put to bed where for the next few days I lay in agony, unable to eat anything solid, and existing solely on a diet of milk and custard.

Ivy left the village, much to my relief, but it was months before my throat finally healed. For years afterwards, whenever I heard the expression 'To blow your own trumpet', I remembered that day and became very cautious whenever tin trumpets and skinny girls with gangling legs were concerned. However, my throat seemed to be fated as some time after this, when running down the garden path, mouth open as usual, a wasp flew in and stung me, resulting in another prolonged diet of milk and custard.

By this time Kathy had been more or less accepted by the gang, and often accompanied us on our forays into the dairy rickyard to persecute George Nurden, or to climb trees in the plantation. This latter pastime involved a test which tradition demanded should be undertaken by all of us. The plantation, which occupied a considerable space between the power house and the churchyard, consisted mainly of old yew trees whose tightly knit upper branches served us well in our many games, and also provided a safe refuge when being chased by one or other of the estate workers. The test, for want of a better word, was to climb the first tree by the power house and then to pass from tree to tree without putting a foot to ground until the churchyard wall was reached. After several failed attempts Kathy was excused, due consideration being given to the fact that she was a girl, but in spite of this we taught her how to find the nesting wren and robin and climb the tall trees in the park, to gaze in wonder at the tiny finches' nests woven precariously on the furthermost tips of the branches.

Her love of all wild creatures impressed me deeply. One day whilst playing our games in the lane at the back of Bank Farm, we came across a young chaffinch lying in the roadway, pitifully fluttering in its last desperate efforts to cling to life, its tiny wings beating as it struggled to rise. For a while we stood watching it until Kathy, unable to bear its suffering any longer, ran forward and picked it up. Tears welled in her eyes as she held the tiny thing to her breast. Soon it was still, the spark of life quenched, and a thin trickle of blood stained its beak which Kathy wiped away with the tip of her finger. During all this time we stood watching her in silence until at last, gently taking it from her, I carried it to the roadside. There in a mossy bank strewn with wild grasses I buried it; no doubt it still rests there, I hope so. Strange that in later years and under very different circumstances, I was to remember that small bird and its untimely end.

There were times however when Kathy would forsake us to engage in more feminine pursuits with dolls and prams: and it was on such a day that tragedy nearly overtook us. Titch and Lofty Harris, Ernie Lane, Badger and I had found our way across the fields to the old mill, a veritable paradise in which to pass away the long daylight hours. Tired of chasing the ducks on the pool nearly out of their feathers, wading in the shallows of the slow running stream in search of moorhens' nests and climbing the gnarled willow trees for suitable bow and arrow material, we decided to paddle in the swifter waters which ran down the concrete sluice from the mill pool. Now, the sluice was as slippery as a greased pole and as yet none of us had managed to traverse its whole length standing on our feet; more often than not we finished the journey flat on our backs, ending up in an undignified entry into the shallow stream at the bottom; and today was to be no exception. Badger had just commenced the perilous descent when, with a noise like an express train, a wall of water released from the sluice gate above came rushing down, sweeping him off his feet and depositing him in the swirling pool below.

We guessed at once what had happened. Lofty, who had been experimenting with the winching mechanism of the gate, having found out how to raise it, had been unable to slip back the catch which activated the lowering gear, and so shut off the flow of water. Luckily the rest of us were within easy reach and, after getting over the shock of seeing Badger's arms flailing as he was swept down stream, we raced to a point where it narrowed and grabbed him as he floated past. Heaving him out on to the bank we flung ourselves down, exhausted, while Badger, now full to the brim with mill water, lay coughing and spluttering on the grass.

Lofty, meanwhile, realizing the enormity of his escapade, had begun to make tracks for home and safety. Unfortunately, his path crossed that of Stiver Griffiths, a worker at the mill who, no doubt, having heard our cries for Badger's safety, was on his way to investigate. Clutching Lofty by one ear, he marched him back to where we still lay, too tired out to think of flight.

'Well, you young varmints,' he said, 'I reckon as how Mr

Spencer will want a word or two about this 'ere.' The 'this 'ere', we gathered, referred mainly to the emptying of the pool rather than to the plight of poor old Badger who, now having regained his breath, stood dripping like a drowned rat.

Mr Spencer was the estate under manager, a man held in high regard in the district, and especially feared and respected by us younger ones. Seeing that we had caused the great creaking mill wheel to grind to a halt, we had very little doubt that he would take a serious view of things, and I must admit that life at that moment seemed fraught with unknown retributions. Following Stiver, who was still holding on to Lofty's ear, we tramped on to the Mill House and were conducted into the large kitchen where Badger, who had suffered most, stood shivering and trailing mill water over the polished stone floor.

Stiver had gone off to report: we could hear, along the dark passage, the murmured rise and fall of his conversation. Then a pause; and the slow measured tread of authority; the next moment the awe-inspiring figure of the mill manager was confronting us.

He surveyed the six dejected figures that stood before him, all the while tapping the sides of his brown leather riding boots with the short hunting crop he held in his hand. 'It would appear,' he said, 'that not only have you nearly caused the death of one of your companions, but you have by your actions drained the mill pool dry and by doing so brought the mill to a complete standstill. If there be any possible explanation for your conduct, I should be pleased to hear it.'

This brought home to us the enormity of what we had done, and excuses failed us: we just hung our heads, feeling the shame. How long that silence lasted I cannot remember, but at the time it seemed an eternity.

Then Mr Spencer spoke again. 'As it appears none of you has a tongue in his head, it is my intention to give each of you six of the best in an area which will cause extreme discomfort when sitting down, at least for the next few hours. You, sir,' he said pointing at me, 'will follow me into my study and, when you have been dealt with, Mr Griffiths will send the rest of you in one by one when called for.'

The humiliation of those six strokes, administered while I lay across the arm of a leather chair, was hard to bear: it was not the actual pain which worried me but the indignity of it all.

When it was over, I made my way back into the kitchen, all the time fighting hard to hold back the tears that welled into my eyes. One by one the others were directed to the place of execution until, justice having been done, and having been seen to have been done – particularly by a gleeful Stiver – we stood awaiting dismissal. Then Mr Spencer reappeared and, summoning the housekeeper, he bade her see to it that Badger had a warm bath and that his clothes be dried, after which we were all treated to thick slices of bread and jam, and cups of hot sweet tea.

So ended a miserable day. Thoroughly chastened and with sore backsides, we made our way back to the village determined, at least for the time being, to give the mill and its occupants a wide berth.

Returning from the dairy the next morning, I chanced to meet Polly Fisher, our post lady who, although she by now must have known about our escapade of the previous day, never said a word about it. Post bag swinging from one shoulder, she stood looking me up and down, her gaze finally coming to rest on my freshly polished boots. Then, passing round to the back of me, she remarked: 'A good soldier never looks behind,' and continued on her way down the street. Long after she had gone I pondered her remark, and it was only when I reached the cottage and examined both boots carefully that I realized what she had meant: toes and sides were polished to a near mirror finish, but the backs had been overlooked. Here was another lesson well learnt, as even today I always pay particular attention to that area, compensating for the oversight of long ago.

Polly was a respected member of our community, and she made a very impressive figure in her navy blue uniform edged with red piping, the long skirt of which reached almost down to her ankles, partially covering her calf length button up boots. This, together with a piece of headgear reminiscent of an Australian bush hat, which had one side turned up and pinned to the crown, gave her an air of authority. Her ever cheerful nature was infectious. Postcards would inevitably be read by her long before delivery, and their contents be transmitted verbally to the recipient. Postmarks and individual styles of writing were a special study of hers, enabling her to deduce the situation and identify the sender and form a shrewd idea as to the information contained. However she was a kindly soul who was never found wanting when help was needed.

The love of her life, or so it was said, was Charlie Richardson who played the organ up at the church, a mild inoffensive man who was known in the village as Gadget. Most of his courting of the elusive Polly was conducted in the plantation where from vantage points in the old yew trees, we watched his amorous advances, occasionally hiding his bicycle after first letting the wind out of both tyres. These activities lent spice to summer and winter evenings when, with little else to do, we unwittingly interfered with the course of true love.

Thinking back, the servants of the Post Office must have suffered quite a bit from our attentions. One post man daily cycled the six miles each way from Evesham to Dumbleton to bring and collect the mail, and between journeys he would rest in a galvanized tin hut erected for the purpose in Grinnel's orchard. Here, gaining respite from his duties for a while, he brewed up and took a short nap before pedalling back to Evesham. Regretfully, however, I have to say that we often disturbed his slumbers by throwing stones on to the roof. Jacketless and half asleep, this would bring him storming out of the door, only to find the orchard as quiet as a grave: how was he to know that the perpetrators were by then safely concealed in the branches of a large walnut tree that stood nearby? Luckily he was a fairly tolerant man, for never once did he complain to higher authority. No doubt, if he had done so, we should have found ourselves in very serious trouble.

At regular intervals Mumford and I visited Mrs Kirkcaldy, who lived all alone in a cottage down at Little Cheltenham on the Evesham road. Off we would go after lunch, through the orchard and past the smithy, where we often paused to pass the time of day with Mr Pulley the blacksmith. Then out into Long Meadow, me carrying the hurricane lamp which would give us light on the return journey long after the sun had set.

Mrs Kirkcaldy was a small, frail lady of some eighty years of age who never ceased to fill me with wonder. How anyone could get to be that old and still manage to be so bright and chirpy was beyond my comprehension. Somehow she reminded me of the sparrows who daily congregated on the roof our our cottage and who, with all their fussing and business, never seemed to achieve anything in particular. The curtains of her little cottage were always kept drawn to exclude the daylight from the furniture and fittings, and it made me feel that if I had dared to shout or make a noise, it would awaken echoes of long gone inhabitants, who, roused from their slumbers, might well appear from dark shadowy corners to raise their hands in disapproval. The mantelpiece above the fireplace was covered with dark velvet cloth from which hung fluffy green tassels, and antimacassars graced the backs of all the chairs. On the walls, sepia photographs hanging in dark maple frames, showed family groups standing around pianos, or posed in upright cane chairs, surrounded by aspidistras in large china pots. The wallpaper had long since lost its freshness and there was one place where the original colour of it could be seen, a picture having been taken down and never replaced. It was I suppose, one of the last outposts of a dying Victorian-Edwardian way of life.

After a glass of home-made ginger wine and a sugared bun, of which Mrs Kirkcaldy seemed to have an inexhaustible supply, I would retire outside into the garden, leaving my elders to chat and exchange confidences over cups of tea, the best china having been brought out specially for the occasion. Quite content with my own company, I then made my way down to the small stream which meandered nearby where I would sit watching the antics of the ducks and wild fowl – never I may add, interfering with them, as I had not yet forgotten the incident up at the Hall. With jerky inquisitive movements the smooth-feathered moorhens steered themselves busily amongst the tall reeds, stopping now and then to peck at some unseen titbit below the surface of the water; while a busy blackbird, which had its nest in a low bush overhanging the stream, flew backwards and forwards bringing food to its eager throated young. Occasionally in a flash of colour, a kingfisher shot by, so swift in its flight that I could hardly follow its progress. And so I sat dreaming and watching, creating in my mind a wonderful world of fantasy in which all these things had their place. Regretfully, in later years they were to be destroyed by reality leaving a void never again to be completely filled.

Soon however it was time to leave, and in the late evening with the shadows beginning to wrap themselves around us, Mumford and I returned home, the light from the hurricane lamp bobbing and weaving as we walked.

And so the seasons came and went; winter turned to spring and life in field and furrow stirred to meet the new days. On the still pond behind the cricket pavilion ducks, busy with nesting arrangements, quacked and paddled amongst the marsh marigolds at the water's edge while from branches in the overhanging trees green shoots beginning to burst their way out, were festooned with raindrops which hung like tears. Birds busy with courting chattered like old fishwives and the early daffodils hung their shrunken heads in shame for loss of golden glory. We played our games of make-believe, searched hedgerow and tree for birds' nests, fought our way to the tops of prickly hawthorn bushes to view the roofed homes of the magpie, and chased the rabbits round their warrens for the sheer joy of seeing their bobbing white tails disappear down the holes, only for them to reappear, poking out twitching noses to sniff the air for danger. How they ever managed to turn around in such confined spaces was always a mystery. Soon the young fledglings would be leaving their nests and the cuckoo be readying himself for his long flight to warmer climates, while the little blue tit which had nested at the bottom of Mumford's garden, fetching and fussing done, relaxed and made ready for the long days of summer.

As in all villages we had our cricket team of whom we were justifiably proud, and all we youngsters had our heroes amongst the players. The ground, in its setting among the trees in the park, was a quiet haven where on summer afternoons the villagers gathered to relax and enjoy the game. I can call to mind the names of many of the players even now: Freddie Lucking from down at the brickyard, Harry Stratford, the head gamekeeper's son, who had shoulders like a barn door, and who could and often did, hit a ball well over the top of the tall elm trees that lined the ground, and whose fearsome bowling put the fear of God into many a visiting batsman. Charlie and Ronnie Griffin, father and son; familiar figures for many years, these two, and always to be relied upon to notch up a good score. The Hopkins' boys, Victor, Leslie and Eric; Jim Collett; and, of course, Dicky Pike-Nott, the estate manager's son, who, after appeals against him on the field, would turn and glare at the umpire as if to say, 'Give me out if you dare.' Not many did, seeing that most of the players and

On the still pond behind the Cricket Pavilion, ducks busy with nesting arrangements, quacked and paddled near the water's edge,

46

officials were employed by the estate; it would have been a brave man indeed who would have ventured to have dismissed him for anything less than spread-eagled stumps.

Matches were played on Saturdays with an occasional mid-week fixture, and it was only much later that Lord Monsell allowed any activity on the Sabbath – and even then the game was only permitted to continue until the sound of the first bell being rung for evening service drifted across the park, when stumps would be drawn and the match abandoned. In the early days the grass was cut with a gang mower drawn by Teddy Hopkins' horse, its hoofs encased in leather shoes to avoid damage to the pitch; and it was the rule that such operations had to be carried out before anyone was about, so as not to disturb the inhabitants of the Hall above. The large side screens gave notice of a similar concession. Painted white on one side and green on the other, they would always be moved to the far side of the ground at the end of each game, where they would be positioned with their green side facing up to the Hall, thus ensuring that when viewed from that angle they did not offend the eye.

Away matches were also attended, the players and supporters being transported to them by horse drawn dray. On the return journey, triumphant or otherwise, they called at numerous pubs along the way, the consumption of liquor being more or less equal to suit either contingency. And so it was that, long after darkness had fallen, the dray and its merry occupants travelled the village street, dropping off players at gateways where understanding wives and mothers waited to guide them to bed.

Home matches took precedence over all our usual activities on those days. Gathering at the entrance to the ground, we eagerly awaited the arrival of Mr Capaldi, an ice cream vendor of Italian extraction, who came from Evesham in his pony cart. This colourful vehicle had the four corner supports for its canopied roof painted with red, white and blue bands, the crimson and gold lettering around its sides giving it a real carnival appearance. Crowding round it, we consumed as many halfpenny cornets as pocket money would allow, before climbing to our vantage point in the flat-topped yew by the dairy. At the tea interval there was always a rush to volunteer to fetch the tea urn and milk from the dairy, as this gave us access to the pavilion, a treat normally forbidden. Once inside, there was the added bonus of cakes and cups of tea, though these, of course, were not available until the players had finished their meal. Then, as the shadows lengthened, we chased around the edges of the field, lending a helping hand to retrieve cricket balls which had been hit into the fish pond. Swallows and swifts darted in and out amongst the players, hunting ceaselessly, while we, hardly less agile, ended the day by scrabbling under the pavilion in search of empty cigarette packets with the cards still in them, or to pick up the odd coin which had somehow fallen from the players' pockets as they sat on the verandah above.

Soon it was haymaking time, when foxgloves gave colour to bank and hedgerow as they swayed and nodded in the warm sunshine. A time of stillness and sultry evenings when the year rested before beginning its slow journey towards autumn. The farmer walked his fields, the long sweet grasses, dried and bleached by the sun making a carpet for his feet. Proud white moon daisies cut down in their prime, lay mingled with clover and meadow sweet and as he walked he would pause to take a swathe in hand and smell it to see if it was ready for gathering. We, the young ones, eagerly looked forward to when, free from school, we could wend our way down to the meadows to romp and chase in the hay – from near dawn to dusk at weekends – helping now and then to fork it on to the high waggons. Many a sip of home-made cider we shared with the farm workers as they sat for their meal breaks under the shady trees, they taking great delight in seeing us lose our legs after a few cupfuls. But the greatest treat of all was to be hauled on top of the loaded waggons and allowed to ride back to the rickyard. From our lofty perches we surveyed the world as it passed by – a world that looked very different than when viewed from the ground level. Then, with hay forked from waggon to rick, to enjoy the return journey to the field, bumping and lurching along the rutted cart tracks with much chasing and hanging over the sides to be grabbed, perhaps at the last moment, when it seemed certain that we must fall head first overboard.

At the end of the day, with dusk settling, horses were unhitched and waggons left shafts down until the morrow. Then, after roping the great horses behind the lead mare, one of us would be allowed to sit astride her broad back where we clung for dear life. How sad that these lovely creatures no longer grace our fields! Not once did I see or hear of any mishap in their handling. Straight as an arrow they made their way back to the stables, there to be unharnessed and led into the quiet of their stalls where feed could be pulled from the iron racks and munched, accompanied by much flicking of tails and stamping of feet. Each had its individual rack to which it would be tied – a task we were sometimes allowed to carry out and which necessitated passing from one horse to another under their great bellies – yet never once did they protest.

With haymaking done our thoughts would turn to what was always one of the main events of the year, the annual flower show. Weeks before the event, preparations would be discerned on allotments and in cottage gardens. Potatoes, cabbages, beetroot and parsnips would be jealously guarded and prize blooms tended and fussed over; in kitchens, home-made jams and preserves, cakes and other delights were planned and made ready. Seemingly by tradition some of the awards were almost foregone conclusions; Mrs Seymour's flower arrangements usually swept the board, whilst old Ben Hardacre's onions were the talk of the district, or at least as much of it as came within verbal communication.

At school we had our own small plots adjacent to the school house, which we dug and planted under the supervision of Old Thunder the headmaster. My efforts always seemed doomed from the start, flowers and vegetables dying from diseases as yet unknown to science – and this in spite of the ever loving administrations of Kathy who had taken it upon herself to be my chief adviser and helpmate. Hearing the expression Green Fingers talked about by the grown-ups, I often studied mine, wondering if and when they would change colour but they never did; consequently I never managed to get an entry accepted for the show.

In the days before the event we impatiently awaited the coming of the huge steam engines which drew the loaded waggons that contained the attractions for the accompanying fair. On the day they were due to arrive we gathered at the bottom of Nut Meadow, straining eyes and ears for the first sight and sound of them. Sitting on the parapet of the stone bridge we waited impatiently until at last they came into view, engines puffing and straining, brass and paintwork gleaming, the chains which steered the wheels, clanging and bumping, the steam hissing and enveloping the drivers in a misty white cloud. From the tall black chimneys whose tops were fitted with spark guards, looking for all the world like ladies' hair nets, grey smoke puffed out to go rolling across the nearby fields. Metal buckets slung beneath the vehicles clanged and banged against the ironwork and sweating drivers, their faces blackened with coal dust, leaned and peered over the sides of their cabs as they spun the small steering wheels.

Following behind came the gaily painted waggons whose sides bore the magic words Scarrot's Amusements, and behind them the living vans from whose curtained windows creatures with brown elf like faces peeped at us. What a fussing and snorting, pushing and pulling took place as they eventually swung into Dairy Lane on their way up to the cricket ground! Swarthy young men, seemingly at great risk to themselves, jumped on and off the towing bars shouting instructions to the drivers who spun their steering wheels backwards and forwards. Exalted by it all we ran and stood and dashed about, always taking great care to keep out of harm's way. This was one night when we were allowed to stay up late, and we made the most of it. Then, as darkness fell, we wended our separate ways homewards, tired, smoky, but completely happy to eagerly await the coming of the following day.

I cannot recall a flower show that was spoiled by the weather. No doubt there were such times, but memory being what it is, perhaps I chose to forget them. There would be no lingering in bed on this of all mornings; no time to bandy words with George Nurden, or tease the ginger tom cat at the dairy, no time to dally at the timber yard or visit my friend the frog. The milk collected, I would tear up to the cricket ground where the rest of the gang had already positioned themselves in the flat-topped yew tree. Below us, strange men were to be seen busily erecting the swing boats, side shows, and the steam-driven roundabout with its prancing painted horses and gleaming brass twisted suspension arms. In a corner of the field near the entrance gate, the large marquee in which the judging of the flowers and produce would take place, was up with trestles and tables already in position inside. Men in shirt sleeves fetched and carried, stopping occasionally to chat one to another, while harassed villagers furtively made their way inside the tent, their offerings, the culmination of so much hard work, wrapped or clutched close to their chests. In the centre of the field, proudly decked in red, white and blue bunting, stood the newly erected bandstand, all ready to receive the Alderton Village Band, who seemed to have an unsigned but accepted contract for the event.

Oh, how the sight and smell of it all lingers still. Sitting there, I craned my neck this way and that so as not to miss the slightest happening below. Borne on the soft breeze, the smell of warm steam from the engines and the scent of freshly trodden grass, mingled in our nostrils. The men from Scarrot's, busy making last minute checks on swing boats and rounda-bouts, cast hungry glances towards the parked living vans where their womenfolk were preparing the midday meal, and soon it was time for us to leave too, to dash home, bolt down our dinners, and wash and change into Sunday best.

At two of the clock, fearful that the whole thing might start without me, I swung on the gate of the cottage to await the arrival of the band, which would begin its processional march from the bottom of the village. The afternoon, warm and sultry, caused every sound to hang on the still air as if reluctant to leave. Small knots of parents and friends were making their way towards the cricket ground, but the younger ones were not among them; they waited like myself.

At last, faintly at first, I could hear the opening number as the Alderton men put their best foot forward, the blast of which, should you be down at the bottom end with them, used to send Mr Bodie's two black retrievers barking and straining at their chains. Louder and louder rose the music. What tune they were playing I neither cared nor listened for, the steady beat of the big drum being all the rhythm needed to start my feet tapping. On they came, past the school entrance, past the Post Office where Stacey Launchberry, our postmaster, having forsaken his charge of the King's Mail for a while, stood contentedly puffing his pipe and beating time with one hand on top of the yard gate. On they came, the drum weaving from side to side to enable its diminutive player to observe which way he was going – I half expected him to continue straight up the street after the rest had turned into Dairy Lane. They may not have been the best of bands, but who cared about that? Their names, when viewed from the distance of passing years,

51

At two of the clock, fearful that the whole thing might start without me, I swung on the gate of the cottage to await the arrival of the band.

52

read like a roll of honour: Fred Agg, Fred Bessant, Peﾑcy Cashmore, Harry Wlliams, Fred Clark, Dick Green, Harold Hobbs. Surely it is only right and proper that those of us who were privileged to enjoy such rural delights should remember them with pride?

Taking my place with the followers I was soon joined by Kathy in best Sunday dress, her face aglow with excitement and long hair brushed until it shone: this was how I was to remember her in the years to come. Holding hands we pranced and danced to the music like the children of the Pied Piper, enticed all the way to the cricket field. Arrived there, the band, now thoroughly out of puff, installed themselves on the bandstand, where they were served with plentiful supplies of cool beer from the nearby refreshment tent. As the day wore on, each member was to be heard playing the tune of his choice, regardless of arrangement or conductor, but no one bothered about such a minor detail.

In the show tent, the air was thick with the scent of flowers, vegetables, home-made cakes and preserves, some with blue cards, some red and some white, showing that judging had already taken place. Proud winners stood by their exhibits to accept the congratulations of their fellows, whilst those who had not succeeded were consoled with the remark that 'there's always next year.' The sun, beating down on the slackened canvas of the tent, turned the interior into a hot house, causing jackets to be discarded and ties and collars loosened, while outside the air was filled with the chatter and laughter of the crowds. Music from the steam organ competed with the offerings from the band, and young and old squealed with delight in the gaily painted swing boats. Gamekeeper, parkkeeper, and estate worker rubbed shoulders with their betters for, on this special day, class had no part in things. Lady Monsell, with young Joan, Diana and Patricia in tow, followed at a distance by their nanny, toured the side shows, pausing now and then to effect a purchase or to exchange words with a respectful villager. Meanwhile, in the more secluded parts of the field, sweethearts happy in their newly found love walked hand in hand, the girls demure in their finery and giggling with embarrassment when asked for a kiss. The young lads, in their stiff white-collared shirts, their necks browned from work in the fields, vied with each other for the honour of escorting the prettiest ones, leaving the youngsters, who as always refused to be left out of things, to spy on and tease their elders.

Soon it was time for the culminating event of the afternoon, the great cycle race, which took place on a course around the outer perimeter of the field, and attracted riders from far beyond the village. The local contingent, however, always gave a good account of themselves. Leslie Hopkins was memorable as, mounted on his old bicycle, which boasted one fixed gear, with sleeves rolled up and flat cap peak at the back fixed firmly on his head, he hotly pursued the more experienced riders in their club colours, heads bent low over their sleek machines.

Kathy was in her element. She stayed close to me all day, prattling away merrily, while I endeavoured to give the impression that she was merely being tolerated – but no matter, for secretly I was happy in her company. Then, towards the end of the afternoon, we wandered to the edge of the field, where, on a bale of straw set under the cherry trees, we sat holding hands and dangling our legs over the side as we munched away at sticky toffee apples. After a silence, turning and looking me straight in the face, she asked with the simplicity of youth: 'Are we sweethearts, and shall we get married when we grow up?' I wonder how often that question has been asked, and the answer given without any thought of commitment. Fixing my gaze somewhere in the region of my boots, I mumbled a reply of sorts with which she seemed satisfied, as immediately she started to chatter away about other things as young girls are apt to do. So for the moment the matter was left unresolved, and many years were to pass before that question was asked again.

Afternoon wore into evening and youngsters whose bedtime was long past, clutched the trailing skirts of parents and were dragged, half asleep, round the circuit of the now illuminated stalls and amusements. In the centre of the field the bandstand stood deserted, stacked with discarded instruments, the players – red of face from their labours having left to mingle with the now thinning crowds who, loath to leave the magic of this one day, were beginning to make their way homewards. Kathy and I stayed to the very last minute until, with darkness closing in, we made our way on tired legs down Dairy Lane.

The following morning, with chins cupped in hands, we sat

by the roadside to watch the departure of Scarrot and his amusements, staying well into the afternoon until the sound of grinding wheels and the steady puff and beat of the steam engines had faded into the distance. Up at the cricket ground teams of men were busy dismantling the show tent and clearing away the debris of the previous day in readiness for the cricket match a week hence. In a few hours all was silent again; no trace remaining to tell of the activities except the deep ruts the heavy vehicles had made. Thoroughly dejected we returned to our play, filling in the gaps until our next great adventure, harvesting.

The fields were now at their best, the long stalked crops, intermingled with soft yellow corn marigolds and brilliant red poppies, swayed and danced in the soft breezes. Harvest was a time when everyone available, including women and children, gathered to help. Families wended their separate ways down the lanes to join the menfolk who had been at their work since early daylight, bringing baskets of food to sustain them and the workers during the long day ahead. With errands done, I slipped through the orchard to the fields at the rear of the smithy, where men had already started to cut a passage round the edge to enable the horse drawn reaper to operate, their brawny brown arms keeping up a rhythmic swing, pausing only to wipe the sweat from their brows or to hone a blunted edge with the whetstone which each carried tucked into his broad leather belt. As they advanced, conversation drifted between them until the task completed, they gladly downed tools and walked to meet wives and families, and to enjoy a breakfast laid out in the shade of the nearby trees.

Soon, however, it was time to start again. Away went the reaper and the helpers followed, gathering up the corn into sheaves, which they expertly tied with straw ropes: there was an art, too, in the stacking of the stooks. Finally, only a broad band of uncut wheat remained across the middle of the field. Into this haven all the rabbits, confined by the circling of the reaper, had gradually retreated; now, amid the shouts of the work people, they were driven from cover, chased and when caught, despatched with one sharp blow behind their ears. How pitiful they looked lying so still in the stubble, their eyes glassy and unseeing.

I well remember my first attempt at killing, and even now

the memory of it pains me. They were cutting a field on the Beckford Road where, after chasing many poor rabbits, who fortunately could run and manoeuvre much better than I could, I chanced on one which was crouching behind a stook. No doubt petrified by all the noise and activity, it lay with legs outstretched, ears flattened along its back, nostrils twitching with fear. All but tripping over it in my excitement, I grabbed it by the back legs as I had so often seen men do, and clouted it smartly, but to no avail. Eventually, worn out and frustrated by my efforts, and deciding that this was just not my day for killing rabbits, I gave up and started for home.

Now, it's all of two miles from Beckford to Dumbleton and I swear that I stopped every hundred yards or so to give the poor thing another clout. At last, reaching the cottage and still clutching the bewildered rabbit, I staggered indoors to present it to Mumford. She took one look at it and promptly let it go free in the orchard at the bottom of the garden. Away it scampered as large as life, no doubt with one of the worst headaches it ever had or ever would have, and wondering just what it had done to deserve a two mile thumping from a small boy.

After the reaping came the threshing, and in the rickyard all was ready. Shirt-sleeved men with pitchforks in hand, fed the ever-greedy conveyor, which lifted the sheaves into the threshing machine driven by a stationary steam engine. Rats in the ricks there were aplenty and before long the terriers were busy. What brave little creatures they were! Darting in and out, they caught the fleeing rats and swung them high in the air, sure that their victims would be dead long before they hit the ground. Then, at the end of the day, the silent grey bodies were heaped on straw and burnt.

All too quickly the long days of summer began to shorten as the first signs of autumn spread their mantle over field and woodland. The leaves, now tinted and brown, hung silent, waiting the coming of the winter frosts, and high in the horse chestnut trees the 'conkers' in their prickly cases were ready to fall to earth where they would be gathered and used in our play. Chattering swallows, looking for all the world like morning coated wedding guests discussing the brides mother, gathered on overhead wires and we raided the orchards for the few remaining apples which hung precariously from bare branches. Before long it would be time for sprout picking when the Arctic wind, sweeping down from the north, would search the fingers of yesterday's snow which sulked in hollows and under hedgerows and send the fallen leaves scurrying to hide in dark damp corners. For us it was the time of cheerful log fires and warm mittens when spinning tops, Dutchmen tall and slim and Boxers small and fat, all decorated with blue and red bands, would be lashed from one end of the village to the other. Iron hoops too, invariably made for us by Mr Pulley the blacksmith, were bowled at a furious pace down the street until, on reaching Mr Bodie's house, they were let go to crash into the railings at the bottom.

Meanwhile, in the dark woods above the Hall, preparations were afoot for the annual pheasant shoot: this was an occasion not to be missed. Eager-eyed, we made our way across the park to where guests, suitably dressed and gunned, and attended by estate gamekeepers, stood in pre-selected positions along the sloping meadows beside the big house.

Soon, in the distance, the shouts and stick banging of the beaters would be heard as they drove the unsuspecting birds before them. We would see the pheasants from our safe vantage points, break cover and come flying and squawking into the open. Round would swing the guns, puffs of smoke followed by the sharp report of twelve bores filling the air, each salvo sending the game plummeting earthwards, to be gathered up by the gun dogs and taken back to their masters. When the day's sport was over, our own retrieval consisted of searching the ground for the empty cartridge cases with their bright brass ends, which we used in our fantasy games.

The annual shoot was always followed by a ball and feasting up at the Hall and Mumford would be called upon to assist in the kitchens. Late in the evening, with hurricane lamp swinging, I walked the half mile or so to escort her home, helping to carry the wrapped basins of dripping and any other tit bits left over. Never since have I encountered such dripping as that: spread thickly on rounds of toast and eaten in front of a glowing fire, its taste defies description. I can recall, when the last crumb was eaten, carefully licking each finger before wiping them clean on my jersey front, leaving very little for the cat, who invariably sat beside me with a look of expectancy on its face.

Another event which demanded my attention at this season, was the meet of the North Cotswold Hunt. One frosty crisp November morning with the autumn sun lighting up the jewelled spiders webs that hung and swung gently in the hedgerows, Titch, Lofty, Ernie, Kathy, Badger and I gathered around the entrance to the Hall stables to watch the comings and goings. Ladies in long black riding skirts and shiny top hats, accompanied by their menfolk in hunting pink, were to be seen checking harness and saddles, and issuing instructions to harassed grooms, their breath hanging in misty clouds in the cold air. The Master of Foxhounds, mounted on his chestnut mare, with the white blaze, was wheeling amid the milling hounds who surrounded him in a forest of wagging tails and eager eyes. Bouncer, Bonny, Ranger, Trotter – the names were rapped out like staccato bursts from a machine gun, as he called the more venturesome of them to order.

Then, when all was ready, and with much prancing and snorting from the horses, no doubt as keyed up as the rest, they wended in jumbled procession up to the Hall where the stirrup-cup would be drunk. There is something very English about a hunt moving off into the countryside, riders jogging and chatting, hounds sniffing and exploring about the Master, all raring to be off and to pit their wits against the quarry who, even then, was probably crouched deep in some covert with ears pricked to catch the first sound of their approach.

Soon they were in full cry, the riders dispersing to various vantage points from which they could take up the chase. We, meanwhile, sitting on the exposed side of Branstead Wood which overlooked the rich, ploughed fields, awaited events. In the distance could be heard the incessant baying of the hounds, and the trumpeting of the Master keeping them to their task.

Suddenly the fox shot out of the dying bracken away to our left and ran, tail streaming out behind him, across the first of the fields. The hounds, picking up his scent, broke out behind him. A half dozen or so of the horsemen who had forced their way through a thickly wooded covert followed. Digging booted heels into their horse's flanks, they came charging down the hill in pursuit, taking a low thorn hedge in their stride – that is, with the exception of one rider whose mount, refusing at the last moment, catapulted its unfortunate passenger head first into a muddy ditch.

High up as we were, our cheeks glowing in the frosty air, we kept the whole chase in sight, watching every artful dodge and manoeuvre of the fox. Judging by the way he twisted and doubled back on his scent, he was obviously an old hand at the game, and we could both see and anticipate his every move, until he abruptly made his escape via a shallow ditch and drainage pipe, the hounds massing and circling in frustration in the centre of the field.

Kathy, with her soft ways and love of animals, greeted this result with a sigh of relief. She rose from amongst us, brushing herself down, and I, realizing that it was time to leave, got up too. Hand in hand we returned together through the dark woods, leaving the rest to find their own way home. Now and then we would pause to retrieve a fallen branch with which to strike at trees and bushes as we passed, or Kathy would run ahead, but she always came back to me and took my hand again: her absolute trust in me was touching. And so another day passed, bringing us one step nearer to the realities we would ultimately have to face. For now we lived each day as it came, little realizing that in the autumn of our lives we should tread the same footpaths together, searching in vain for those lost golden days of youth.

One useful addition to Mumford's income which I took a great delight in participating in, was the gathering of blackberries and their eventual transportation to Evesham market. These expeditions usually lasted a whole day, beginning immediately after breakfast when, complete with flasks of tea and sandwiches, and a supply of empty baskets, we made our way up to the Warren, a large hill overlooking the village. The steep climb behind us, we would sit for a while admiring the panoramic view which spread itself below. The church nestling in its churchyard, thrust its tall tower above the trees while, on the line of the village street, smoke curled from cottage chimneys to go drifting over thatched and slated roofs. From the timber yard in Dairy Lane would be heard the restless whine of the saw, and from Hulbert's Farm, a sheep dog barking excitedly. There were to be seen the mellow cottage where George Stratford, the gamekeeper, and his son Harry lived, and the rectory hard beside the church, from where the Reverend Ashwin ministered to his flock. It was a truly rural scene and one at which I never tired of gazing, each familiar landmark of which is etched on my memory. In later years, when far away in a land which was then only a name, the mental picture of it sustained me during many lonely hours.

Now, the Warren was estate property and the cultivated blackberries growing on it were for the exclusive use of the Hall below. However, by gleaning from the bushes on the far side, we could be reasonably sure of an uninterrupted day: on those rare occasions when one or other of the gamekeepers chanced by, on recognizing Mumford they usually turned a blind eye and continued on their way.

Inevitably I would commence operations by stuffing myself with the luscious fruit, while Mumford got on with the serious business of filling the baskets. She always started on the higher branches, guiding them towards her with the aid of the crook of her walking stick. Then gradually she worked her way down the bush explaining as she did so that this was the correct way, ensuring that the hardest part of the gathering was done first. Tiring as the day wore on I would curl myself up on a shady bank to sleep while Mumford picked on steadily. At length, with baskets now full, she would wake me up to wend our way homewards through the park and down Dairy Lane.

The days and weeks passed quickly and soon Christmas was upon us, that magic time of the year when fact and fantasy became immersed in a feast of wonderment and delight, a time when the ritual of carol singing was always faithfully observed. As always our first call was up at the Hall where, complete with carol books, lanterns and shining faces, we offered the household our sometimes tuneless renderings of most of the old favourites: our 'Winter's Fuel' at the end of the first verse of *Good King Wenceslas*, drawn out and unnecessarily prolonged, would have done credit to a pair of mating barn owls. With repertoire duly completed one of us would raise the heavy knocker on the great oak door, it was a duty which I, truth to tell, when called upon to execute it, derived more pleasure from than the singing. Then we would wait until suddenly the door would open, throwing a shaft of warm light into the darkness and revealing, with the familiar leather pouch in one hand, the portly figure of the butler. His was an impressive presence, and as he stood smiling down at us, I almost expected him to produce a rabbit from his pocket or wave a hand to conjure up a genie, but alas, he was only human. Then followed the usual speech in which he informed us that his Lordship and gathered company had enjoyed our festive offerings and wished us one and all the compliments of the season. Now, whether his Lordship ever bothered to listen to our singing I shall never know, though I like to think that he did. However, this was a minor detail compared with the monetary reward we hoped to get. So we stood, our arms outstretched as we awaited the customary inspection of hands, clean or otherwise. After due consideration the butler selected the person with the smallest ones, drawing their owner towards the door where the leather pouch filled with coins was held open and proffered. Only one take was allowed, and I must admit that it took us a while to fully understand the significance of this annual event: eventually, however, it dawned on us that perhaps he did far better out of the deal than we did.

The payment having been made, we were then conducted to the kitchens, where the cook filled us to bursting point with mince pies and other Christmas fare, and regaled us with glasses of lemonade and ginger wine.

Well fortified with cake and coin, we made our way back to the village to give the inhabitants the benefit of our seasonal greetings. Starting at the top end, we invited the long suffering occupants to hearken to the herald angels singing and the shepherds watching their flocks by night. And if the rendering of the carols grew more lusty and our progress a little more unsteady as the evening advanced, this was due in no small part to the tots of home-made wine offered and imbibed on each doorstep.

Meanwhile, in the side room of the village stores, a transformation was taking place. Behind the tinsel and streamers in the windows, stockings hung down filled with sweets and other good things, and toys of all descriptions packed the shelves. Ranks of green bottles of wine, a phalanx of comely plum puddings in white basins, a counter full of boxes of figs, dates and preserves, and biscuit tins and caddies of tea adorned with pictures of royalty and views of Buckingham Palace, tempted the eye and the appetite.

Elsewhere in the store it was business as usual. Buckets, pots, and pans and other household goods were crowded on hooks near the planked ceiling, while sweets in glass jars ranged themselves around the walls. Invading the floor space, brooms and mops stood beside sacks of corn and bran each of which had its neck neatly rolled back, each with scoop to hand. Above the preparing counter sides of bacon and hams, wrapped in muslin, hung all ready for cutting while on the white marble slab beneath, blocks of fresh yellow butter stood waiting.

Mr Lewis, in starched white apron, busied himself behind the counter stopping now and then to serve a customer and deposit the money in the large ornate brass till. Percy Wood the stores assistant handyman, in smartly cut jacket, flat cap, and highly polished brown boots and leggings fetched and carried from store room to shop, weighed down with boxes and paraffin containers which he loaded into the back of the old model T Ford van in the street outside. What a joy it was to stand and watch the tea, sugar, and other commodities being weighed on the great brass scales, and to marvel at the deft way the packets were crimped and folded by My Lewis! Surrounded as it was by the smell of paraffin, oil, corn, maize, and fresh polish, it was to me a veritable paradise in which a small boy could spend a fascinating half hour if the errand upon which he had been sent had little urgency. In all this however, the collection of cigarette cards was of prime importance. Standing outside on the pavement I would waylay the menfolk to request the crisp new cards. Cricketers, footballers, stars of stage and screen, railway engines, ships of all nations, and many other absorbing subjects were covered by their colourful pictures, all to be admired and exchanged as necessity dictated. They gave us access to another world far removed from that of our experience, firing our imaginations and adding to our knowledge of things.

In the cottage Mumford too was busy making preparations. Sprigs of holly and mistletoe were lodged behind pictures hanging on the wall, paper chains and lanterns strung between the rafters of the high ceiling. On the sideboard bowls of apples and oranges, boxes of figs and dates, kept company with the black marble clock which had been presented to Grandad by Austin Chamberlain when he left after serving for many years as a gardener. On the window sill beside the door, displays of hyacinths, some white, some blue, added their fragrance to the very special smell that Christmas has – a smell of fruit, plum puddings and small wax candles flickering on the festive tree.

Around the cottage mysterious parcels were hidden away in cupboards, on the tops of wardrobes and under beds, in company with net string stockings filled with sweets, tin whistles, folded children's books and chocolates. How sad that the delighted feeling these things evoke should fade from us as we grow older, becoming enclosed in a world we have left behind!

And so to Christmas Eve. I was off to bed early, though first making sure that Mumford had left a glass of milk and a slice of cake on the parlour table for my expected visitor. Late into the night I tossed and turned, worrying myself with problems beyond my mending. What if Mumford had left too much fire in the grate, what if the venerable old gentleman got himself stuck in the chimney? The possibilities for disaster seemed endless; each sound in that clear silent night my imagination turned into sleigh bells, but at last, worrying done, I fell into a fitful sleep, eager that the night should pass as quickly as possible.

Christmas morning: and wonderland, strange how memory always dictates that such days should be snow covered, frosty and crisp, but that is as it should be for what would Christmas be without them? Outside the village was quiet and still as it rested under its white mantle, no footmarks as yet having marred the glistening carpet that covered road and hedgerow. At the bottom of the garden a few solitary birds fluttered and perched in the old hawthorn tree, each movement by them sending cascades of white powder earthwards, while in the orchard beyond the trees groaned under their heavy glistening load. With bated breath our little world waited for the commencement of the festivities. Under thatched roofs where icicles hung outside frosted windows excited children leapt from their beds eager to open and explore the gaily wrapped parcels which had mysteriously appeared during the long night of waiting, while all down the village street lights appeared as lamps were lit and fires rekindled as busy parents readied themselves for the long day ahead.

Roused by the first shafts of weak sunshine filtering through the window, I made my way into the parlour where, sitting in front of the fire which Mumford had already got going, I unwrapped the neatly packed parcels – the contents of which, I may add, were not to be seriously played with until later. Lead soldiers, fresh from the darkness of their cardboard box, were arranged in battle order in the hearth and fruit and sweets put aside with strict instructions that they were not to be eaten until after breakfast. Breakfast! Who would worry about such a mundane thing on this of all days?

One present which I remember well was a small toy gramophone whose yellow painted sides were adorned with flowers and dancing elves and fairies, the only record that came with it being *The Ritual Fire Dance*, a work then far beyond my comprehension, but there who cared, and I played it over and over again marvelling at the sound that came out of the flimsy tin horn.

Born on the still air the bells rang out their festive message summoning one and all, old and young, to the morning service. Suitably gloved and wrapped against the cold I was dragged unwillingly out into the street to join others making their way churchwards. However, once outside I broke away to scuff through the snow and roll snowballs until at last we reached the church where, with cheeks glowing and hands tingling we entered, each to sit in favourite pews. Perched on the hard seat I remained as quiet as a mouse, marvelling at things which as yet I did not fully understand the significance of. The Reverend Ashwin, solemn as befitted the occasion, made his way to the altar preceded by the choir in their white surplices, candles flickered with each cold draught that blew in from the many chinks and crevices, and the congregation, hushed with expectancy, waited for the service to begin.

At the back of the church the Monsell family, accompanied by visitors staying at the Hall, sat still and remote in their pews, unreachable in their everyday life but somehow drawn together with us on this special morning. The Hall staff, or at least as many of them as could be spared, bowed their heads in their seats in front, knowing that just before the sermon commenced, they would be required to leave by the side door to dash back to complete the dinner arrangements – this they did discreetly, though indeed, if it had not been done so, no one would have dared to comment.

In my place beside Mumford, I fell to wondering how God would be spending His Christmas. Would Be by now have unwrapped all his presents? If He had, judging by the size of His family, where would He have room to put them all? These childish thoughts and many others to which not even the grown-ups seemed to have the answers, went through my mind as I sat there in the semi-darkness. Above the altar, shafts of sunlight penetrating the stained glass windows threw multicoloured patterns on to the tiled floor beneath, and a small bird, having found sanctuary inside, flew backwards and forwards, chirping excitedly as the choir and organ gave full voice. Then, having explored all avenues of escape, it took refuge in one of the branches of evergreens with which the church was decorated, where it sat, tiny head cocked to one side, preening its feathers and viewing the carryings on below.

After the service, the congregation filed out into the churchyard, to gather in small knots, stamping their feet and blowing noisily into cupped hands to restore circulation. We young ones free for the moment from parental control, chased about in the snow stopping only to discuss the presents we had been given or to make plans for the morrow when we could meet and play with our new toys.

Then it was back to the cottage for turkey and plum pudding, and all the delights which toy soldiers, crayons, paints and pencils could bring, to be followed by Mumford's reading of the books which had been amongst the gifts. As the day ended, full to the brim with Christmas cake and other good things, I lay sleepily on the hearth rug, while Mumford dozed in her chair by the fire; and the cat, well padded out with turkey, licked his paws and cleaned his whiskers with satisfaction, before settling down.

All too soon it was over and we were getting ready to greet the coming of the new year. On the night before that, however, old Harry Lock would start his one man crusade. Commencing at the top of the village he visited each cottage in turn, to offer his tuneless rendering of *The Miner's Dream of Home*. As at each call he was treated with glasses of home-made wine, he soon got merry, and indeed was never known to have completed more than half his journey – being found, more often that not, standing on his head outside Arthur Tandy's cottage, still singing lustily.

Harry was only one of the many characters who lived in the village, whose colourful escapades, told and re-told, entered the folklore of the district, to be handed down through the generations. In a cottage down by the school lived Herbert

Greenwood, one of the estate gamekeepers. He was married to a most formidable woman whose pet aversion was his old pipe. Admittedly, she had reason, for when he stoked up on his rounds through the woods, you could see Red Indian type smoke signals rising above the trees. The secret of all this was the black twist which he sliced and fed into his pipe with his pruning knife. It was said that his wife spent most of her day and sometimes nights, seeking out, finding and destroying the offending baccy, a pastime of which her old man was fully aware.

Eventually, however, he got the whole thing figured out. In order to preserve an emergency supply he kept a short length of it tucked into the case of a cartridge from which he had removed the shot – but not, as events were to prove, the powder. Out one day in the woods on vermin patrol, the gun tucked under his left arm in true keeper fashion, he met the squire and his lady who were out walking. Touching his forelock in the approved fashion, he paused for a while to engage in conversation with them on matters relating to young pheasants and game in general. Suddenly out of the brush not twenty yards away stepped an old dog fox, a pheasant grasped firmly in its jaws. For a brief moment man and animal froze – until the squire, sizing up the situation, grabbed Herbert's gun and, unaware that the left barrel was for shooting and the right for baccy, let fly with both. Now, from here on, truth becomes stranger than fiction: the fox leapt into the air, fell back and after a few twitches lay still. Herbert, knowing full well that the squire had missed with the left barrel, as was evident by the bark stripped from a nearby tree, couldn't believe his eyes. The alternative didn't bear thinking about, but sure enough, on examination there it was, a couple of inches of black twist sticking out behind the animal's left ear. It is said that the squire never really believed what he saw, and prudence decreed that the story was not related in his presence. Herbert, for his part, would neither confirm nor deny it and, whenever the subject was raised, he would grin sheepishly and turn the conversation to other matters. However, there is an interesting footnote. Shortly after the incident, it is said, he had the village carpenter cut a neat patch box in the stock of his gun and fit it with a secret spring, the whole arrangement being all but invisible to the untrained eye. From then on his wife was never allowed to touch the firearm, and there in safety his emergency supply remained, its hiding place being known only to Herbert and the village carpenter.

Further down the street and not far away from Herbert's cottage, lived Cocker Edwards and his brother Allen. They were bachelors both, and rarely seen out of each other's company. Once a year it was their custom to visit Alderton Fair, a journey which necessitated a long walk through the woods above the Hall. Needless to say, during the day at the fair, they partook freely of the local cider, so that by nightfall they were well in their cups and, returning, found it necessary to lean on each other for support. It is asserted that on the way they spent a great deal of time and effort striking matches to locate glow worms, so as to put out their lights, an occupation which lasted well into the early hours. Exhausted by their labours, and being by then in need of a rest, they seated themselves on a fallen tree to discuss the day's events, always concluding with the immortal words: 'Well, it'll be eleven months two wicks (weeks) and a fortnight afore us comes this way agen,' – an accurate if somewhat redundant computation, it might be thought, but nonetheless typical of Gloucestershire philosophy.

These two were once troubled by an unwelcome visitor to their cottage, a venerable old owl who each evening would insist on perching on the roof to begin its nightly serenading just about the time the brothers wanted to retire. No amount of banging and stone throwing seemed to discompose him, and so one hot summer night they decided to take more drastic action. Grabbing an old muzzle-loading shotgun from the rack above the fireplace, where it had lain unused for years, Allen primed it with powder and shot and, after ramming the charge well home, went out through the back door to deal with their friend on the roof, who by this time was in full song. The light outside being poor and in order to steady his aim, Allen stood on an upturned bucket, leaned against the rainwater butt and took careful aim. The old gun, having seen better days and being weak in all departments, went off with a bang as he squeezed the trigger, sending a cloud of black smoke skywards and splitting at the breach as it did so. Propelled by the explosion, Allen shot backwards against the wooden rainwater butt which burst open, sending him and the contents into the kitchen garden, much to the amusement of the owl, who, hooting fit to bust at the comedy of errors below, fell off the roof and broke its neck. Such is the stuff of which all good folk tales are made.

Two trades, of all those carried on in the village attracted my keenest interest: the blacksmith's and the wheelwright's. The latter's workshop was next door to the Post Office and there, depending on the mood of the workmen, I was sometimes allowed to sit out of the way and watch them at work. Mr Launchberry, who was in charge here, was adept at many other jobs, carrying out when necessary the repair of waggons and traps, the making of coffins, and even furniture restoration now and then: in fact, any work which required his expert knowledge of wood. Surrounded by the tools of his calling, he worked ankle deep in freshly cut shavings from near dawn to dusk, applying the skills which had been handed down through generations; skills which relied not so much on mechanical aids as on a trained hand and a keen eye.

The fashioning and building of a wheel was one of the most demanding of all trades. Hubs, or naves as they were traditionally known, were lathe-turned out of elm, this being preferred on account of its twisty grain which made it less likely to split. Spokes were shaped by hand from cleft rather than sawn oak, which was cut from the wood according to the lie of the grain, great care being taken not to cross it. Each spoke was so designed that, on assembly, it would fit snugly into the recess provided in the hub and felloe, or outer ring of the wheel (these felloes normally being made from ash on account of that wood's flexibility.) Waggon beds, front rails, outer rails, coupling poles and all the hundred and one parts which went into the making of a waggon were conceived and made here to the highest standards of craftsmanship. Every stage of the process was a joy for me to watch, but for the drama, I suppose I loved the final operation, the sweating of the great iron band on to the finished wheel, best of all. From the workshop all the shavings and odd bits of wood were gathered and a fire set going in the yard outside. Then, when it was well alight, the iron hoop was placed on it and left until it was nearly red hot. At precisely the right moment it was grasped in tongs, placed over the wooden rim of the wheel, and quickly tapped into position, before being doused with cold water in order to make it shrink, thus ensuring a tight fit. Clouds of hissing steam enveloped the leather-aproned workmen as they went about this task, and, as I sat there watching, I became more determined than ever that when I grew up I too would become a wheelwright and join Mr Launchberry in his workshop.

And so to the blacksmith, George Pulley, whose smithy, at the bottom of Callow Lane, was as much an established part of things as the village church. Here, in a smoky darkness lit only by the glow of his forge, he made and fitted shoes for the great cart horses and hunters, as well as parts for cart and carriage, and gates with delicately twisted stems and lengths of chain. A king in his own right and master of his establishment, he was, in my eyes, almost a being from another world, who but rarely emerged from his lair on working days, save to take short breaks in the fresh air outside. George Pulley was far from resembling the traditional blacksmith of poem and legend, for he was short of stature, but in his sinewy arms and slightly drooped body he held the strength to wrestle with the great shire horses he shod, and endure the long hours in the heat and smoke of his forge. On Sundays, clad in his best attire, he made his way twice daily to the church to sing in the choir, unrecognizable in his clean white surplice.

He too is no more: he lies at rest beside his wife hard by the door by which he entered and left for so many years. I often visit the smithy, but it is not the same now. There is no sound of hammer striking metal, no pungent smell as the hot shoes are held firmly down on great hooves. The place is quiet and deserted, but even so there are times when I can still see George Pulley standing there, gazing thoughtfully out across the meadows, as I had often seen him do when I was a boy.

Still more slight incidents and occurrences float back into my mind from that distant past as I write. These were the small change which, joined together, made up my life.

On rare occasions a hen or chicken would be required for the pot and usually, when such a sacrifice was demanded, one of the men from the village would oblige, deftly performing the task in the fowl house at the bottom of the garden. However, at times no such help was available, and Mumford, particularly desirous to see the victim plucked and safely deposited in the metal oven above the oil stove, would decide to despatch the bird herself. Looking back, I can only assume that her chosen method of execution was instigated by sheer necessity and desperation. Having coaxed the hens into a corner of the hen house with handfuls of tasty corn, she selected the one bound for the pot. With apron flapping and reddened face, she dived straight for it amongst the now startled birds, causing great confusion, much squawking, beating of wings, and a general scattering in all directions. Seated on a chopping block nearby, I viewed the proceedings in amazement, all the time trying hard to guess which one of that frightened flock would be chosen. Round and round the pen went Mumford and the hens until, in their panic, they made an undignified bolt for the small opening which gave access to the orchard beyond. All jamming through together, by sheer weight of numbers they at last broke through to freedom, their alarm gradually subsiding as they strutted there out of reach. But Mumford had already secured her victim, and brought it to the place of execution.

What happened next I relate with much misgiving. Grasping the hen in one hand, she laid its head on a block of wood and with one swift blow from the chopper, which she had taken from the tool shed, severed its head from its body. The bird, now released, dropped to the ground where for a brief moment it lay flapping its wings. Suddenly, it was on its feet again and wildly charging round the garden, with Mumford in pursuit, hatchet in hand. Two full laps of the garden it made until with a last flutter it collapsed and was still. In all the excitement and in attempting to follow events, I fell from the log I had been sitting on. Flat on my back and with eyes covered, I lay there waiting until the body had been collected and hung with feet tied together on a nail protruding from the tool shed door. Then, slowly getting to my feet, I staggered to the privy door where I was violently sick. Duly plucked and seen to, the headless corpse finally reached the metal oven as intended, but my thoughts during the ensuing meal returned constantly to the bird's untimely end. It occurred to me that had it been the large cockerel who dominated the hen house, and who had taken a dislike to me right from the first day it arrived, I should perhaps have felt better about the whole incident.

Another escapade in which I was involved could well have had disastrous consequences.

We were sitting one morning on the brick wall of the disused village pump at the top of Callow Lane, Ernie, Lofty, Titch, Badger and I, considering how best to spend our Saturday freedom. George Pulley, leading a horse to the smithy, paused for a moment to cast a suspicious eye over us, but deciding that at least for the moment we were not up to any mischief, went on his way. Idly we kicked our heels against the parapet, and hurled the odd pebble at Louise Clark's cat, which crouched watching us from the shelter of a row of cabbages in her garden.

Then suddenly Ernie broke the silence: 'How about thick Buzzard's nest up by Hulbert's Farm? Reg is allus saying as how he reckons he could get to un'.'

For a moment no one spoke and I, hoping that one of them would find a good reason why I should not accept the challenge, hesitated to reply; but as no easy escape seemed to offer, I agreed at last and off we went. At the top of the village we were joined by Kathy who, unknown to us, had been waiting outside the butcher's shop.

'Us don't want thee along of us,' said Badger, having taken it upon himself to act as spokesman, though he was careful not to look her straight in the eye.

'Bet you're up to no good,' she replied, at the same time looking at me in obvious appeal.

I weighed the chances of my losing face before the gang, as against hurting her feelings; but when I saw her eyes beginning to fill with tears, I could hold out no longer. 'All right,' I said, 'but if we have to run for it, you'll have to keep up or get caught.' That was all the confirmation she needed. Happily she tagged along, chatting away to one or other of us, only to be greeted with stony silence, as is the way of things when small boys are saddled with unwanted female company.

At last we reached the site of the nest in question which was perched in the high branches of an elm tree at the edge of Hogsleasow Wood. Viewing the challenge afresh, I couldn't help but experience a sinking feeling at the pit of my stomach. However, it was too late to back out now so I heaved myself up into the lower branches and commenced to climb upwards.

The nearer I got to the top the more frightened I became; only a stubborn streak, fuelled by sheer desperation, induced me to continue. I didn't dare look downwards at the tiny upturned faces below. Kathy, watching my every move, shouted words of encouragement but by then I was too far away to hear them. Up and up I climbed, the freshening wind swaying the topmost branches alarmingly. In something approaching sheer terror I clung to the stout trunk as I stared across at the nest, now only a few feet away. The fledglings strained their scrawny necks, beaks open, no doubt taking me for a parent bird returning with food. Gingerly I edged forward, but before I had gone any distance at all, one of the adult birds, which had seemingly been observing my progress, swooped down, claws extended to protect its young: the swish of its wings as it passed over me was far too close for comfort. Shutting my eyes tight, I clung face down on the branch wishing with all my heart that I had stayed on the ground. Three times the bird swooped, and on each attack I felt that my end was near. At last, deciding that honour was satisfied by my having reached the nest, I thought it time to beat a hasty retreat.

It was then that I discovered that all the strength seemed to have gone out of my limbs; I simply hung there, unable to move either up or down. Believe me, in those few moments I lived through a nightmare.

Luckily, however, and unknown to me, Charlie Dones, one of the gamekeepers had seen my plight from the coppice where he had been patrolling. He now made his way to the foot of the tree where, after shouting advice, none of which I could hear – or if I had, would have been unable to act on – he unshouldered his game bag, propped his gun up against the trunk and, with strict instructions to those below to stay well clear, started to climb upwards to where I clung. Slowly he guided my feet, branch by branch, foothold by foothold to safety. When we finally reached the ground, I sank to my knees, overcome with relief. Charlie then gave us all a good lecture on the dangers of tree climbing, emphasizing the point by way of a smart cuff around the ear for me, being the chief offender, after which he gathered up his gun and game bag, called his dog to heel, and set off back to the coppice, leaving me to get over my fright.

For a while we just sat there until, feeling that some reaffirmation of leadership was called for, I challenged the rest to a race to the bottom of the meadow. Kathy, last as always, came and took my hand in hers, making me promise never to do such a stupid thing again. I gave her my word gladly, for I wouldn't have climbed that elm tree again for all the candy twist in the village store.

That evening Mumford and I went to call on Mrs Leigh Sallis who lived in a thatched cottage set back from the village street, approached by a winding path overhung with apple and pear trees. It was here, seated at her green baize table, that she spent many happy hours playing cards and exchanging the gossip of the day. The French windows were open to the garden, and, taking my fill of cake and ginger ale, I watched the night-flying moths, attracted by the light of the oil lamp, come fluttering in to hurl themselves against the hot glass chimney. Singed or exhausted, they fell into the brass well of the wick holder, there to slowly die, an end for which I could see no reason.

In the lulling softness of the night, a nightjar could be heard making its churring call as it flew, while a faint rustle now and then in the undergrowth told where some small creature was moving through.

Sitting there, I thought of the elm tree and my eventful climb, wondering if the Buzzard had gotten over its encounter with the pale-faced intruder by now, and if Charlie Dones would relate my adventure to Mumford when next they met. I fervently hoped not, as grown ups never seem to understand the ways of young people and were apt to come down hard on their occasional follies. Growing up, I was beginning to question everything, finding the answers were legion.

Some days later Charlie Dones did call. To my relief he did not mention the tree climbing incident, suggesting instead that I might be allowed to accompany him for a short while on one of his nightly patrols through the woods. Mumford didn't take too kindly to the idea at first, but after being assured that I should be well looked after and returned at a reasonable hour, she finally gave her consent.

The following evening we set off. It was a clear moonlit night and as we walked the shadows seemed to turn themselves into the shapes of witches and hobgoblins, a fact which caused me to cling closer to Charlie and his two dogs. In spite of this, to me, it was sheer magic, another world, where creatures of the night moved silently about their business. As we made our way through the woods, Charlie explained their habits and showed me where a fox had crossed our path not minutes before, and where, in the branches of the low fir trees, dopey pheasants sat roosting. Crouching in the cover of an overhanging bush we watched an owl swoop silently down and take a small rodent in its extended claws, the only indication of its presence being the silent swish of its wings as it bore its victim away.

Straining my ears I listened to the night sounds around me. Across the valley a vixen's eerie cry rang out as she called to her mate, the sound causing the short hairs on the nape of my neck to prickle. Then, whilst making our way through the dense undergrowth we came upon a small clearing where I witnessed an encounter, the memory of which kept me awake on many a dark night. In the moonlit arena a rabbit sat on its haunches while around the outer edge a stoat, belly to the ground, circled it. The poor creature seemed to be hypnotized; following the stoat's every move it seemed unwilling or unable to make its escape. Silently and without taking its eyes off its intended victim, the predator, its circuit gradually decreasing, moved in. The rabbit, sensing that its end was near, emitted a series of unearthly screams, and just at that moment I could have turned and ran but Charlie kept a firm hold on me. Suddenly it was all over, and death must have been almost instantaneous as the crouching brown creature leapt at the rabbit's throat. We withdrew and left him to his feast.

Nature seemed very cruel at that moment, but as Charlie explained, that was the way of things in the wild: the stoat had only killed to eat, and not out of any bloodlust. But I can't say I was convinced. I dreamed about that rabbit for a long time afterwards, and woke in the night still able to hear its terrible screams.

# 3

*In which I learn the facts of life, leave Dumbleton
and enjoy a short stay in Wiltshire*

And so I grew up, moved from junior to senior class at school
and reached the age when I began to realize that there was
more going on between grown-ups than holding hands and
kissing.

It was about this time that I developed a childish infatuation
for Phyllis Reynolds, a comely young lass some twenty years of
age. Much to my dismay she flirted with all the eligible lads of
the village and tended not to pay much heed to me; I fear that
she was inclined to regard her junior admirer as a mere
nuisance on the occasions when, content to worship from afar,
I followed her up the village street. Of necessity my adoration
of her was operated strictly from a distance. However, I did
run errands for her when asked so to do, hanging on every
word when she deigned to speak to me.

Looking back I can only assume that it was all part of
growing up, an experience which, at times, I found very
painful. However Phyllis did have one steady boy friend. His
name was Bert Sharp and he worked in the timber yard up
Dairy Lane. He was a strapping young chap who doted on her
and, although I resented his attentions, I sometimes delivered
messages between them. For this service I was always given the
odd coin, but on the whole considered myself well rewarded by
the smile of thanks which the young lady bestowed on me.

One Saturday evening after the cricket match had ended, I
decided to return home by way of the plantation where,
kicking and scuffing my way through the undergrowth, and
not paying much heed to the direction I was taking, I suddenly
became aware of voices coming from a shallow dell surrounded
by bushes. For a moment I stood still, uncertain what to do

75

next; then, curiosity getting the better of me, I crawled stealthily towards the sounds, to be confronted with a sight which, to say the least, utterly confounded me. Phyllis and her lusty boyfriend lay side by side in the hollow, their clothes scattered around them. It was the first time I had seen a naked women other than Mumford on bath days, and for a while I couldn't make head nor tail of things. Locked in each other's arms, they lay kissing and writhing, completely unaware of my presence. Scarcely daring to draw breath I watched, fascinated, until at last they were still, the game, if such it was, apparently over. For a while they remained entwined; then, with much giggling and slapping, they stood up and began to dress. Eventually they made their way into the churchyard where they disappeared, still talking and laughing.

For a while after they had gone, I sat trying to sort the whole thing out. In a strange way I felt excited, but was too young to understand why: suffice it to say that the episode disturbed my thoughts for quite some time, while my affection for Phyllis withered and died. Whenever we met in the street after that, I would look at her and picture her lying up in the plantation with her young boyfriend; and somehow I could never feel the same about her. In later years I was to realize that such encounters were not always confined to darkened bedrooms with curtains drawn, but that in the wider world there were many secluded dells where, safe from prying eyes, young people sought and found each other.

☆ ☆ ☆

There comes in all our lives, the inevitable turning point dividing the past from an incalculable future; and that moment duly came in mine. Up to now my life with Mumford had continued in its tranquil way with very little happening to disturb it; to accept each passing day as it came had seemed the most natural thing, and was sufficient. But then one morning, Mumford received a letter from my parents in Hereford and as she sat in her chair reading it, I could tell from her worried expression that it contained bad news. All that day I sensed that events which somehow involved me were taking shape; when she had come to terms with them herself, she took me aside to explain.

It appeared that my parents had decided that it was now time for me to join them and my elder brother, and that arrangements were to be made to deliver me to Hereford within the next two weeks. The blow was a bitter one, for knowing little of the rest of my family, I had come to regard Mumford as my only parent. She tried hard to explain that my proper place was now with them, and it was only when I saw the tears in her eyes that I realized how upset she was.

Rushing out of the cottage, I ran down to the bottom of the garden where, crouching against the wall of the hen house, I cried until there were no tears left – my little world was collapsing about me and I was frightened of what lay ahead. Mumford came and led me back indoors where for the next few hours I clung to her for support; she did her best to pacify me, but I was inconsolable.

The next two weeks passed all too quickly. The gang took the news in silence, and all the life seemed to have gone out of our play. Kathy, when I told her, stood for a while not wanting to believe that I was leaving. Putting her arms around me she kissed me lightly on the cheek; then, still sobbing, she turned and ran from my sight, leaving me near to tears myself.

It was a bright spring morning when I took that last ride to Evesham on Bill Wood's carrier cart; even Rafnalley looked more dejected than usual. The battered suitcase containing all that I possessed in the world lay at my feet and, as we journeyed down Nut Meadow, I turned in my seat to take a lingering look back at the village nestling under its wooded hills, wondering if I should ever see it again. Ernie, Lofty, Titch and Badger had gathered at the top of the street to see me off, but Kathy was uppermost in my thoughts: her absence would leave a gap in my young life, not to be really filled, as it happened, for many years. All this was long ago, but I still remember how miserable and lost I felt as, sitting beside Mumford, I watched the familiar landmarks slipping by; it seemed the longest journey I had ever known that took us into Evesham and down to the railway station. Crouching in the corner of the carriage as the train steamed slowly out, all I was aware of was that each turn of the wheels was widening the gap between the known and the unknown.

On reaching Hereford I was duly delivered into the care of my mother who fussed and tried to make me feel at home, but to me she was a stranger; in my uncertainty I clung tightly to Mumford's hand, not wanting to be parted from her. She stayed for a few days in order to see me settled, but at last the time came for her to leave. How I wished, with all my heart, that I could have chased after the train that was carrying her away from me and out of sight! But, powerless to do anything about it, I was at last forced to accept the inevitable and be literally dragged from the station.

I cannot dwell with any degree of certainty or clarity of mind on the events of the following few months. Displaced and ill at ease, I tried hard to fit into my new way of life – at first with very little success. My parents, no doubt with the best of intentions, set about moulding me into the son they thought I should be. My elder brother's example was kept constantly before me: he was by then firmly established as the academic of the family and had already won a scholarship to the local high school. My own feet were put on the first rungs of the ladder in Lord Scudamore's school in Friar Street, an establishment very different from that in the village where I had received my early education. In due course, I too was nominated for possible entry into the high school to join my brother but, as events were to prove, I never made it. Taking the first part of the entrance examination, I passed easily; but when the time came to take the second part, I flatly refused to do so. Perhaps the sight of my brother sitting at night with endless homework had some bearing on my decision. A more likely reason though, was that the more I felt I was being pushed, the more I became determined to pull the other way. In spite of long lectures and veiled threats I stood firm, until at last the subject was dropped, never, I fear, to be forgotten or forgiven. From that time onwards I had the feeling that I was in some ways taking second place, as my brother's schooling became an obsession. I was not worried; it meant that some of the pressure was taken off me, leaving me to jog along and look forward to the time when, education over, I could leave school and – my hope was – eventually return to Dumbleton where my heart remained.

My parents, as was the custom at the time, believed in catering for our spiritual needs, which was odd really, seeing that my father was a self-professed atheist. Nevertheless, I was duly enrolled at St Nicholas Sunday School and later in the church choir, an arrangement which, I gathered later, as it served to keep my brother and myself out of the way for most of Sunday, had been designed more for our parents' benefit than for any excessive interest in our spiritual needs.

Often we would arrive at the church at the very last minute, dashing into the vestry to don our cassocks and surplices, just before the service began. Then, bored by the tedious sermon, we wiled away the time flicking pellets of wet paper at the boys in the pews in front, more often than not earning a sharp tap on the head with a hymn book from our elders in the seats behind. We spent our collection money on sweets at the little shop up Friar Street and quickly mastered the art of putting non-existent pennies into the collection plate as it was passed around. From our lofty heights in the choir stalls we ogled the girls sitting in the front rows of the congregation, singing like angels whenever the choir master's eye fell on us, and generally treated the whole occasion with a degree of levity which only youngsters can.

Armistice Sundays, for some reason which then I failed to understand, made a great impression. On cold November mornings, just before eleven o'clock we gathered round the war memorial in the churchyard where during the two minutes silence we stood bare headed to remember. We, the young ones, although aware of the sadness of the occasion, had no personal memories unlike the older members of the choir and congregation who stood clutching their wreaths of red poppies. Many of them had lived through those terrible years and still bore the scars. As we stood in silence the world around us was stilled. Only the few remaining leaves on the trees above, rustled by the chill wind, seemed to have life.

With the sounding of the maroons which marked the end of the two minutes we opened our song sheets and, led by the vicar, sang 'Oh God our help in ages past', 'Time like an ever rolling stream bears all its sons away'. Little did I then realize that in later years and in a setting far removed from that peaceful churchyard, I was to think back and remember those few lines that I had sung so innocently, and at last realize their full meaning.

Mr Pritchard, the verger, suffered constantly from our high-spirited pranks, and on the whole bore our tormenting with great forbearance. However, there was one incident which resulted in my being suspended for six months, a fact that was kept from my parents until years later, by which time it was too late to exact retribution. At the top of the stone steps leading down to the stoke hole where the church boiler was situated, stood a large metal dustbin. One evening, having balanced it on the top steps I gave it a push just as, unknown to me, Mr Pritchard was emerging from the door below. Down it went, hitting the verger and scattering the contents all over him. It was a stupid and thoughtless act which fortunately did very little physical damage, but certainly offended his dignity. Hauled before the choir master, I was told in no uncertain terms that my services would not be required for the next six months. As a result, for the duration of my sentence I continued to attend church, but occupied a pew at the back, keeping well out of sight. One advantage of this was that just before the sermon commenced, I was able to sneak out and disappear. Unfortunately, Mr Simcox the organist, who seemed to have eyes in the back of his head, soon cottoned on and ordered me to sit in the front pews where, from his seat at the organ, he would keep an eye on me.

Sunday school in the parish hall in Breinton Road I treated in like fashion. Seated in small groups we were instructed in the mysteries of the
Good Book and saying prayers to a deity very remote from us, whose likeness gazed down on us from the painted walls. We sang of a 'green hill far away', which to me conjured up a vision of some great white city perched high on a green mountain where, bathed in eternal sunshine, a golden-haired Jesus waited with outstretched hands. Many a time I stared in wonderment at the picture of him which hung above where I sat. This showed him standing in an emerald green meadow knee deep in colourful flowers, while around him, some standing and some kneeling, were children of all nations looking up at him in adoration. Black, white and yellow, they made a great impression on me, as I tried to puzzle out who they all were and where they came from. It brought to mind another picture which used to hang above my head in the bedroom at home, showing Jesus standing by a doorway, wearing a crown of thorns and holding a lantern in his hand: it was entitled, as far as I can remember: 'The Light of the World'. He looked so sad as he gazed down at me; however, I was grateful for his company, particularly through the long winter nights.

All these spiritual activities I fear were only tolerated in anticipation of the summer outing – an event not to be missed on any account. Packed into the coffee-coloured solid-tyred City Charabancs, we made our way out into the countryside where, in the lush meadows, we ran our three-legged races, juggled with eggs on spoons and chased the girls, sticky bun in one hand and bottle of lemonade in the other. At the end of the day, tired and dishevelled, clutching the orange and bar of chocolate which the weary helpers handed out to each – glad, no doubt, to see us homeward bound – we boarded the charabancs for the return journey through the gathering dusk.

But even this did not complete my search for spiritual guidance, as on Tuesday evenings in the winter months I attended the Barton Hall. This was a chapel institution, and so was apart from the ordinary line of my religious education; I fear that, here too, the prospect of another summer outing drew me in. I know that I always took great care to ensure that the card with which I had been issued on enrolment was stamped with a purple cross in the appropriate date square, this being the passport to those pleasures to come, as one had to have a certain number of attendances recorded to be included. Seated in hard pews in the tall gaunt chapel building, we always started the evening by singing our song. As far as I can remember it went something like this:

'Come to the Children's Meeting
Held in the Barton Hall.
Come every Tuesday evening:
All are welcome, all!

All girls and boys invited,
All who are over seven,
Come then to learn of Jesus,
And the way to heaven!'

Strange how these insignificant things stick in the mind never to be forgotten. Looking back, I suppose that my attendances at these various religious institutions were prompted more by thoughts of rewards to be gained than by any desire to improve my soul: however, it did no harm, and perhaps some of the teaching rubbed off on me. With the perversity of youth, and more to embarrass than to seek knowledge, we often asked the meaning of such words as 'breasts' and 'carnal knowledge' when read from the Bible. I doubt though if we ever received much satisfaction from our strait-laced young teachers, who had a way of carefully avoiding direct answers to such questions.

As time passed I grew to accept the inevitability of my new way of life, and to adjust to it. The council estate where my parents lived, built shortly after the First World War, proved an ideal playground, a popular gathering place being under the street gas lamp which stood at the end of the cul-de-sac, near to our house. Here on cold winter evenings, we congregated to play our games of marbles and indulge in youthful horse play. There was never anything wilfully vindictive or destructive about these activities, other people's property being respected. However, as so often happens, one or the other of us would occasionally step out of line and, being no saint, my turn soon came.

At the end of the estate some new houses were being built and the bricks, planks and half completed structures exercised a strong fascination. Although forbidden to enter the area we often succumbed to the temptation, and had great fun chasing and playing hide and seek, while at the same time keeping a wary eye open for the approach of the Law. One Saturday afternoon when the workmen had gone, we were thus engaged when, unknown to us, our local policeman happened along on his bicycle. Now Constable Morris, or Jigger as he was more affectionately known, was one of the old timers: he sported a large drooping walrus moustache and had hands like dinner plates; and, as we often found to our cost, he could show an exceptional turn of speed when required. Two of us he caught that afternoon, myself and Chicken Perkins, and we both received a belting on our backsides from these large hands, administered I may add, while he held each of us in turn across his knee. Never once did we learn of him taking any official action, punishment delivered on the spot proving far more effective than a trip to the magistrates' court. He knew us all by name and in happier times would stop and enquire if we were behaving ourselves – always, of course, receiving the obvious answer. Then he would dive his large hands into the pocket of his tunic and bring out sweets for all of us. When caught and punished by Jigger, it would be no use running home and complaining to our parents as they would instantly proceed to give another dose of the same, to warm up where he had left off.

Memories being what they are, we are apt to recall those events which for one reason or another were wont to make a great impression, forgetting the minor pleasures that filled the gaps between. High among these must be reckoned the times when we went picnicking. On fine summer Sundays when excused from church and Sunday school, three or four families combined for a day's outing to Breinton Springs, a local beauty spot on the banks of the river, some three miles away. In the early morning we made our way into the country, a caravan of chatting parents and noisy children, with food and necessities for the day packed in wicker cloths baskets slung beneath the cross bars of the men's bicycles. With the sun growing stronger every minute to chase the shadows from under tree and hedgerow, perspiring elders called and cuffed the more venturesome who would insist in getting underfoot while inquisitive cattle in the fields bordering the roadway congregated at gateways to poke snuffling noses through the bars to see what all the noise was about. On we went, skipping and chasing and doubling back, past Warren Farm, until at last we reached the picnic spot. Here we had great fun negotiating the steep path to the water's edge. Not for us the longer and more sedate way which our parents took, but slipping and sliding and grabbing at bushes to steady our progress, we scrambled down, with torn trousers sometimes resulting.

The spring, after which the site was named, issued from a cleft in the high bank, and made its short journey into the river by way of a channel which it had carved for itself over the years. This we spent hours damming up, watching the water rise higher and higher until at last, forced to release it, a tidal wave burst in the river below. At meal times, chequered table cloths were laid out on the grass and held in place with stones at the corners. Kettles steamed away on wood fires replenished with fuel gathered from the coppice above, and with sandwiches, cakes, pots of jam and other good things, we feasted to our heart's content. Strange how food eaten in the open air always seemed to taste better than when consumed at home from a table; perhaps it was the informality of the occasion which accounted for this. Our greatest joy, however, was when, with boots and socks discarded and trousers rolled up above the knees, we paddled in the shallows of the river. How cold it sometimes was, obliging us to return often to the safety of the bank to restore lost circulation in hands and feet! But this never distracted us from our main pursuit, and the thrill of lifting mossy stones to see if some Bully Head was lurking beneath. Carefully lowering a hand into the water, we scooped the unsuspecting fish into a waiting jam jar to be held up and admired. Even today when I revisit the spring, as I often do, memories return to urge me to roll up my trousers and seek those elusive fish which still lurk beneath the mossy stones. Oh youth, how desperately we reach out for you in later years, only to find that you have passed away with those long gone summers! Late into the evening we sat around the dying embers of the fire, watching as the mists settled over the waters and crept along the banks. Then, after the last cup of cocoa, tired and grubby, we set off homewards, the sleepy ones being carried on the broad shoulders of parents while the rest, heads down and grumbling, trudged along behind.

Soon, however, I was to be uprooted again, my parents deciding that I should spend a holiday with my father's brother in Devizes. I didn't take too kindly to the idea, particularly as only now was I beginning to get over my enforced move from Dumbleton; but, bowing to the inevitable, I was put on the train in charge of the guard and despatched south.

Uncle Stanley, the youngest of my father's brothers, ran a small grocery shop situated on the corner of New Park Street opposite Wadworth's Brewery. It was a family business which he managed with the help of his wife Vera, and it was she who met me on my arrival at Devizes station: luckily, I took a liking to her from the start. Her warm welcome helped to dispel the home sickness that I had felt on the journey down and, seated in the small flat above the shop, munching cake, I soon began to feel more at home.

My grandfather lived in Sidmouth Street, a short distance away. He was also in business, being the proprietor of a cutlery shop where, in accordance with his calling, he sharpened knives and scissors, repaired umbrellas and sold a multitude of odds and ends pertaining to his trade. He was well respected in the community and carried on with pride the calling which had been that of his father and his father's father before him.

His nickname of Cutler I too was to adopt when later I started school in Devizes.

I soon made many friends among the younger children who lived near to my uncle's shop and, released from the immediate supervision of my parents, and the need to compete with my elder brother, began heartily to enjoy my holiday. However, as things turned out, I was to stay much longer than I had anticipated. When the time approached for me to return, my parents suggested that I remain a while longer. I agreed and so, in due course, the question of my schooling arose. With this in mind, Aunty Vera led me one morning to St Peter's along the Bath Road. Dressed to kill, I was conducted through the dark Victorian building, its sombre atmosphere causing me to take an instant dislike to the place. Finally, no amount of persuasion would induce me to stay, and so back home we went. Next it was decided to try Southbroom School down by the Green, and close to Grandad's shop in Sidmouth Street. Here, as luck would have it, a distant cousin took me under his wing. It was a lovely old building standing in its own spacious grounds having at one time been a private residence; and I took to it immediately.

On my first day, I was greeted in the hall by an elderly teacher who, no doubt feeling sorry for my doleful appearance, asked my name and where I was living. Pausing for a moment to digest the information given him, he then told me that he had taught my father when he was a lad, and added that he hoped that I should turn out as good a pupil as he had been. At the time I entertained grave doubts as to that possibility; however, I soon settled in, determined, if only for the sake of my father's reputation, to put my mind to my studies.

Uncle Stanley and Aunty Vera, it has to be said, were an ill-matched couple in many ways, and always seemed to be at loggerheads. Either she was blamed for not puling her weight in the shop, or he was off on some hairbrained scheme, leaving her to cope. Somehow Uncle never seemed to have grown up – I suppose being the youngest of the family he had been spoiled – but in spite of this they treated me well, and I soon learned to keep out of the way when trouble was brewing.

I helped in the shop after school, weighing up tea and sugar and generally making myself useful. At first I did this gladly, but as time wore on I realized that work was beginning to interfere with play, and my efforts to escape out into the street via the back door often got me into trouble. Even so, there were compensations. When no one was about I could help myself from the jars of sweets which stood in rows on the shelves – to such an extent that before long I couldn't face them, though they were handy to take to school and trade for other things. Each new delivery of cigarettes enabled me to open the packets and swap the cards within; thus I was always the first to get a complete set of any new series.

One chore that I was never happily reconciled to was the making of ice cream. The equipment for this laborious operation consisted of a small wooden tub having a separate metal container which, once filled with the necessary ingredients, was placed inside the outer tub and packed around with ice. The lid was then tightly secured, the rotating handle of which, when operated, activated the wooden paddles within which stirred the mixture. Not daring to stop, I would sit in the semi-darkness of the store room turning the handle until my muscles ached. It was not the sort of occupation a lad would choose on a warm summer's day, but I had no choice; though I'll admit that it nearly put me off ice cream for life.

At weekends I acted as errand boy, delivering groceries: on Saturday nights this meant working until nine or ten, as in those days there was no such thing as early closing. Strangely enough, however, I enjoyed it and soon learned to find my way around the dark alleys in New Park Street where most of Uncle's customers lived. One of my favourite calls was on Mrs Stapleton, an elderly lady, who lived in Orange Court. She had great difficulty in walking, so I was employed to collect and deliver her order. She was a dear old soul who treated me like a son and, when I could spare the time, I liked to visit her and listen to the stories she would tell of her youth, when she had been in service. She smoked endless cigarettes; indeed I cannot remember ever seeing her without a fag in her mouth: her little house reeked of nicotine and the ash trays in her parlour were always overflowing. Uncle Stanley told me once that she had 'steep feet'. This amazing piece of information so fascinated me, that when I thought she wasn't looking I used to study them, trying to figure out what he meant as, to me, they always looked perfectly normal, encased as they were in a pair of well-worn slippers.

Fortunately, however, life was not all work and school. There were occasions when, the shop being closed on Sundays and excuses made to Grandad as to why I would not be attending chapel, we went picnicking, usually accompanied by the family from next door who had three daughters of about my own age. Our favourite spot was up on Roundway Downs, where we raced and chased to our heart's content through the long summer days. At other times, in the proper season, I liked to go fishing down by the canal. There I would spend hours trying, but as far as I remember, never succeeding, to catch something. Nevertheless I managed to fall in the water a few times, which resulted in a quick dash back to the shop to change into dry clothes and face the wrath of Uncle Stanley. He would promptly ban me from further visits to the canal, though I fear to little effect.

Life with Uncle and Aunty was, to say the least, never dull and there was one memorable moment when things between them really boiled over. That morning Aunty decided to have a lie in. Uncle, busy downstairs getting ready for the day's business, must have realized this for, his shouts from the bottom of the stairs receiving no reply, events suddenly took a new turn. The next thing I knew, he had filled a bucket with cold water, taken it upstairs and, pulling back the bed clothes, poured the lot over Aunty. She, of course, as soon as the water hit her, jumped up and emitted a most blood-curdling scream, the sound of which caused me to dive under the sheets and hide. The row that followed was a real beauty; the language was awful and I'll admit that I learned a few swear words that day that I hadn't heard before. For the best part of an hour the argument went on until at last, Aunty having risen, dried herself and dressed, packed her belongings and went back to her mother in Fish Pool Street – not for the first time, I hasten to add. However, after a few days she returned and they carried on as if nothing had happened.

Whenever I could, I visited my grandparents at their shop in Sidmouth Street. It was to me a fascinating Aladdin's Cave, its walls hung with sober rolled umbrellas and bright sun shades, its glass-topped show cases harbouring a host of things dear to any boy's heart. Gleaming pocket knives and pruning knives were housed there, along with more tricksy ones, whose multiple blades folded delicately and were contained by a polished bone handle.

Grandfather and Grandmother also had a feud going, but she, being older and wiser than Aunty Vera, had long since learned how to get her own way without her partner being aware of it. Thus, if she wanted a new hat, she waited for an opportune moment and took the money from the till: my own pocket money, too, was frequently supplemented from the same source. I never wanted for a new penknife or a supply of comics: these last, incidentally, Grandfather banned from the house, he being a pious member of the Plymouth Brethren, who did not look too kindly on what they called 'The Devil's Literature'.

On Sunday mornings and evenings, dressed in my best clothes, I would accompany them unwillingly to chapel, a stark building in Canal Lane. The meeting room was on the upper floor and access was gained by a flight of stone steps on the outside. I remember thinking when climbing them that perhaps this was what heaven was like, the large empty room underneath representing the alternative which Grandad was always preaching to me about.

But the cold interior and the extremely uncomfortable wooden pews we occupied soon shattered any illusions I may have had. There was no organ or music of any kind and the assembled congregation sat in silence with heads bowed until Charlie Maslin, a gentleman with a long white beard who must have been all of eighty years of age, struck up a hymn in a loud quavering voice – upon which the rest joined in. Sitting wedged between my grandparents, with no means of escape, I listened to the wailings and viewed the mournful faces around me with a kind of wonder as to what religion could be all about; the people seemed to get so little pleasure from their devotions. I know that, for myself, I was mightily glad when the service was over and I could scamper down those heavenly stone steps and into the daylight.

On his return to Sidmouth Street, Grandad would step through the back of the shop and climb the ladder to the loft above his workshop. There, well concealed from prying eyes, he kept a quart jug. This he would produce and hand to me, together with the necessary money. Then I would go out through the back entrance to have it filled with beer at the pub across the road, returning by the same devious route and being careful not to spill any on the way. Down would come Grandad and take a long swig, after which he reascended to the loft, carrying the beer with him. This ritual was enacted every Sunday morning, until at last I assumed that somehow it was all part and parcel of the chapel service.

He was very strict regarding other sorts of indulgence, however. Not only on the Sabbath but throughout the week, no swearing or blasphemy was allowed, no wireless set and no entertainment of any kind. Comics, as I have said before, were forbidden and prayers were said each morning and evening. Fortunately, with the connivance of my grandmother, I managed to smuggle the forbidden literature in and hide it under the mattress of the bed in the spare room where, crouched in a dark corner, I enjoyed the Devil's literature. When visitors called, usually fellow members of the chapel, I developed a very lucrative side line reciting the Lord's Prayer to them, for which I was usually paid sixpence, the pat on the head resulting being a small price to pay. I went through this performance so often that I believe for a shilling I could have recited it backwards, but unfortunately I was never called upon to do so.

Now, Grandad had a good eye for business and down at Longcroft Road he owned a row of garages which he used to let. After numerous complaints from the car owners who had their tyres punctured by rusty nails left lying about on the forecourt, he offered to pay me sixpence for every twenty I could find. Of course, I went to work with a will, realizing very quickly that I could augment the genuine article with an inexhaustible supply taken from his workshop. However, I think he finally tumbled to what was going on, as our business arrangement ceased very suddenly.

Although he followed a strictly religious life, Grandad was not above the occasional outburst of profanity. I discovered this one Saturday morning when he had roped me in to operate the treddle bar which drove the lathe in the workshop on which he did his scissor and knife sharpening. Standing beside him, foot on the bar, I had just got the thing going at a rare old speed when his foot, which had been dangling uncomfortably close, slipped and became trapped between the bar and the stone floor. Dropping the knife he had been sharpening, he hopped around the workshop holding his foot and swearing like a trooper. For a moment I just stood well out of reach until, realizing that perhaps it was time to make myself scarce, I dashed out into the back yard and hid behind a pile of boxes. There I remained until I was sure that I could show my face again, leaving Grandad still hopping and swearing.

Of all my relations in Devizes, my favourite was Uncle Fred, the black sheep of the family. He had run away to sea at an early age and was not talked about within the family circle. On the very rare occasions when his name was mentioned, Grandad would clasp his hands together and raise his eyes heavenwards, saying: 'He has strayed from the fold and learned the Devil's ways.' However, much to my delight, Uncle Fred would sometimes appear out of the blue after one of his long voyages, when the family would take great pains to keep him, as much as possible, out of sight.

I enjoyed his visits, finding in him a kindred spirit. As I sat in the back yard, listening to the tales he recounted of his many voyages, and the far flung places he had visited, my imagination would be fired – so much so, that I forgot my early ambition to become a wheelwright and work in Mr Launchberry's carpenter's shop, deciding that when the time came, I would run away to sea to join him.

Once, memorably, he brought back two parrots from South America whose vocabulary, taught to them by the sailors aboard ship, was hardy up to Plymouth Brethren standard. They were a continual source of embarrassment to Grandad, particularly when hung in their cages outside the shop as they often were, where they favoured any passerby who cared to stop and listen with their nautical observations. Soon a small crowd would gather to watch their antics, until the local policeman would feel obliged to intervene and insist, in the interests of law and order, that they be taken down and removed into the shop. I delighted in them, and fed them with anything I could lay my hands on.

Being very much creatures of impulse, they had some rather strange habits. One of these was to walk about on the table whenever a meal was laid there, picking and pecking at anything that took their fancy. They would make straight for the butter dish and promptly wade in, much to the annoyance of my grandmother who, with apron flapping, would endeavour to get them back into their cages, an exercise which always resulted in a great deal of squawking from the parrots, intermingled with a few of their choicest swear words. Eventually they both died due, it was assumed, to the quantity and variety of tit-bits that were fed to them whilst hanging in their cages outside the shop. Somehow, life without them never seemed the same.

In later years Uncle Fred quit the sea and settled down in Melksham, where he ran a transport cafe. Grandad outlived all his sons, with the exception of my father and Uncle Stanley, and when he eventually died, Grandmother sold all his considerable property and blew the proceeds inside two years. All that came to our side of the family were the garages in Longcroft Road, and a small bequest to me. The latter my parents invested, feeling that perhaps it might benefit me in later years; and how right they were.

I spent two years in Devizes and was just beginning to feel settled there when my parents decided that it was high time I returned to Hereford to complete my education. So I said goodbye to Southbroom School and the many friends I had made there, and went back to Lord Scudamore's School, leaving behind my brief spell of freedom and many happy memories.

When I first arrived in Hereford from Dumbleton, my teachers seemed to experience great difficulty in understanding my broad Gloucestershire accent, visits to the school by my parents being, I feel sure, mainly to confirm that I was indeed English. However, as time passed, I quickly learned to speak without the prolonged rolling of my 'r's', and the use of such phrases as 'Where be to', 'What bist at', 'Where bist going' and 'Thee have thick un'. Segregated into standards, and not into forms as scholars are today, pupils progressed from the lowest (No. 1) to the highest (No. 7), which was our last resting place before being let loose on the outside world. Each class had its own resident teacher who was responsible for all subjects, with the exception of art and history. These came under the direct supervision of Mr Giles, or Tec as we called him, a mild dapper little man who was always well turned out in a nigger brown lounge suit and fawn-coloured spats, which he wore summer and winter over his brown shoes. The stern elderly spinster who had charge of Standard Three, was notorious. Chastisement was meted out by her by the precise and deft application of an infamous black ebony ruler to knuckles and backside and, naturally, most of my vulnerable parts came in for quite a lot of attention. It was fortunate that in this part of the school there were only boys, the girls having their own separate establishment segregated from us by a high brick wall. This at least put a stop to any youthful romances during school hours, and ensured that we devoted our attentions to our learning without diversions. However, in the freedom of Friar Street such omissions could be, and were, speedily put right.

Our male teachers, middle-aged men of distinction and always well-dressed, commanded and indeed received respect. They administered learning and justice in equal measure. No undue familiarity was allowed, a formal 'Mister' or 'Sir' being insisted on, on all occasions. In school our behaviour and responses were organized to a pattern which was strictly adhered to. At the commencement of the day when seated in our desks, we waited in absolute silence for the classroom door to open. Then, rising to our feet, we chanted 'Good Morning, Sir', not daring to sit down until the master had taken his place at his desk. If during the course of the day our headmaster, Mr Ryder, came into the room, we immediately stood up in our places and remained so until given permission to be seated – and woe betide anyone who dared to fidget!

My Ryder was a man of some fifty or so years of age and, being large in stature and heavily built, had the misleading appearance of a cuddly bear. He rarely emerged from his private study other than to attend and conduct early morning prayers in the large hall where, standing by his desk on the raised platform, he led the singing, all the while keeping a sharp eye open for any boy not attending, or a latecomer who might be trying to sneak unobserved into his place in the assembly. Caning by him for some oft-repeated or serious misdemeanour was carried out in his study and only occasionally, and for special emphasis, would the whole school be assembled, and the victim be obliged to receive his punishment on the platform. Once, and only once, I suffered that fate for throwing a prefect in the school refuse bin. Now, whether it had the required effect or not I cannot say, but it certainly made me something of a hero amongst my mates.

Playtimes were regulated to a certain extent, and there were always three or four teachers present to keep order, the games we played being rough and tough, judged by present day standards, though I believe that in a strange way they were character building. On the railing around the playground, we performed acrobatics, mainly to impress the girls in the adjoining building who, unknown to their teachers, would encourage us from behind their classroom windows. When the time came to return to our lessons, however, a whistle was blown, upon which everyone froze; and the unfortunate lad who moved a muscle until the order was given to form ranks and march back, knew what was in store for him.

Of all the classrooms I passed through on my way up the ladder, Standard Six, supervised by the dapper Mr Giles, holds a special place in my affections; this, no doubt, was because he specialized in the two subjects, history and art, at which I seemed to excel. At the end of the year when competitions were held, I am proud to say that I always carried off the top marks. In other spheres, however, the picture was bleaker, particularly in arithmetic, where the mysteries of decimals, equations and algebra were never thoroughly mastered, so that my name could always be found at the bottom of examination lists.

Finally, I reached Standard Seven, where Mr Lloyd, the master in charge, strove in vain to improve my knowledge in these subjects: had it not been for the small slips of paper with the necessary answers written on them, passed to me by my classmates under the desk, I doubt if I should have survived. Seemingly, however, I was not as smart as I thought. During the war years, when home on leave, I ran into Mr Lloyd, and during our conversation, he informed me that he had been fully aware of the help I received, but had decided to turn a blind eye to it in the hope that I might learn more from my classmates than from him.

Empire Day was an important event in the school calendar and we, in our Sunday best, celebrated it by parading on the Castle Green, where we sang *Land of Hope and Glory*. Of course, the full significance of what we sang about was lost on us, and I doubt that at the time we felt any undue pride in the large empire we were honouring; but at least it was a day away from school and for this, if for nothing else, we entered into the spirit of the occasion. As the service ended, we soon discarded the small Union Jacks we waved, and they were trodden underfoot, much to the annoyance of our teachers who viewed this act of sacrilege with dismay. Thinking back and remembering the sea of innocent faces, I often wonder how many of those fresh-faced youngsters were called upon to make the supreme sacrifice in defence of 'Hearth, Home and Empire' in the not too distant future. Perhaps it was just as well that we could not see that far ahead.

Hereford in those days was a sleepy old market town. In Broad Street, a row of ornate wooden huts ran down the centre and gave shelter to the drivers of the horsedrawn cabs which plied for hire. Their animals stood patiently with nose bags hung, while the owners, gathered in small groups, would hurriedly spring into action each time a prospective fare approached. Mr Prosser, one of the cabbies, whose stables were in Barton Road, provided me with many a free ride to school. Concealed from view, I waited for his cab to emerge. Then, when he was well clear of the gates and out on to the road, I would run up behind and perch on the back of the slow-moving vehicle until we reached St Nicholas Church, where I jumped off and tore up Friar Street, arriving at school just in time to hear the bell ring out its last warning to late-comers.

The Kemble Theatre, once the Corn Exchange and now long since gone, provided many delights in film and variety. Here, for nine pence, an evening's entertainment could be enjoyed in the company of such stars as Hutch, the Western Brothers, and other celebrities of the day; while on the screen flickering epics like *The Covered Waggon* and *Ten Commandments* kept us glued to our seats. Another favourite haunt was the old Kinema down St Owens Street where for two pence we were treated to the antics of Felix the Cat and his companions. But it was the Palladium in Berrington Street, known affectionately as The Flea Pit, which drew most of us on Saturday mornings. Here from about ten o'clock, crowds of youngsters milled, squabbled and pushed while they waited for the doors to open – upon which there followed a mad rush to be first inside. The poor old commissionaire could never stem it and in fear of being trampled underfoot usually took refuge in the ticket office. We climbed over the backs of seats, arguing and fighting in our endeavours to make our way to the front, but, as soon as the drapes in front of the screen were drawn and the safety curtain raised, the noise gradually subsided and we sat eagerly awaiting the arrival of Elmo Lincoln, Doctor Fu Man Chu and the seemingly endless exploits of Pearl White who, at the end of each epic was either left tied down on a railway track or hanging over a cliff by her finger tips. This was the era of silent films and the dialogue which appeared on the screen was invariably read out loud, no doubt for the benefit of those of the audience whose reading abilities couldn't cope, but it all added to the fun. Villains were hissed and booed; occasionally they were shot at with small pieces of orange peel propelled from home-made catapults, which the commissionaire was kept busy confiscating, as well as sorting out the frequent fights which broke out among the rival factions. Down in the orchestra pit Mrs Alderson, the accompanying pianist, thumped away, keeping her eyes fixed on the screen, so that she could change the pace and style of her playing to suit the particular sequence shown. Only the top of her head was visible behind the wooden barricade which protected her from the squabbling, missile-throwing audience behind. The show over, we streamed out into Berrington Street, eyes puckered against the strong light, to make our various ways home, eagerly looking forward to the following Saturday when the whole noisy adventure would be gone through again.

All these pleasures we took in our stride, never questioning our good fortune or worrying about tomorrow. In the winter months, when the river, swollen with rain and melting snow, burst its banks and covered the low lying fields with a foot or so of flood water, we were in our element, making rafts out of planks of wood and empty drums which we floated between the hedgerows, engaging in mock battles with each other. What fun we had steering our home-made craft and splashing about, losing our footing sometimes! Then, at the end of the day, the painful walk home, soaking and with legs sore and chapped between the thighs where our short trousers had failed to keep out the searching winter wind: a hot bath invariably awaited us, after which we were sent straight to bed.

Strange how young boys seem to be fascinated by water. I still remember the pleasure I got from the small brook which ran alongside the road at the bottom of our avenue. I could never see its rapid flow without staying to drop sticks and empty match boxes in, and watch them negotiating their way from one end of it to the other. Finally they would land up in the large drain and disappear through the iron grating to be lost for ever; I often wondered if they would get to the sea in the end and from there to some far-away shore where another boy, with a very different-coloured skin from mine, would watch them being tossed backwards and forwards on the tide. What a beautiful world of fantasy it all was!

We had a family living next door to us who were, to say the least, accident prone. Mrs Webb, whose husband was a pastry cook working in Birmingham, was a lady of some refinement who had obviously been used to better things. As her husband only appeared at weekends, the poor woman was left to cope as best she could, a task which under the circumstances, would have daunted most wives. Billy, Harry, Violet and little Herbert, who was then still at the crawling stage, may have been manageable individually, but collectively they were a recipe for disaster. I clearly recall one occasion when, just having settled down to have our tea, we heard a tentative knock on our back door. Mother answered it and there, rather shamefacedly, stood Billy, to announce that his mother had gone out shopping and that Harry had set fire to the curtains in the living room. Dropping everything we all dashed next door, to find that, indeed, a fire of old newspapers had been lit under the window, the curtains of which were well alight, the flames almost having spread to a nearby easy chair. Father, quickly sizing up the situation, tore the blazing curtains down and stamped on them, while we, coughing and spluttering, gathered the smouldering remnants and took them, along with the cushions from the chair, outside into the garden where they were left to burn out. Billy, trying to be helpful had meanwhile fetched a bowl of water from the kitchen but in his haste had tripped over Herbert who, unknown to him, was crawling about on the floor. As for Harry, the perpetrator of the incident, feeling that it was time to make himself scarce, he had locked himself in the outside toilet and for some obscure reason dropped the key into the pan.

Eventually some sort of order was restored: Harry was released – an operation which necessitated forcing the toilet door off its hinges – the house was searched for any boxes of matches which might have been lying about, the windows flung open to get rid of the smoke and fumes, and we went back to finish our tea in peace.

They had a passion for lighting fires and, when not at school, would spend the best part of their days tearing up the garden with torches of screwed up newspaper which they lit from the gas stove in the kitchen. To vary the pattern a little, Billy managed to stick a digging fork through Harry's foot, and Violet to get her hand stuck in an outside drain. Occasionally, however, things seemed to be on the point of getting more serious. For instance there was the time when Violet turned the gas oven taps full on and Billy, needing another light for his bonfire, dashed in and struck a match to light his newspaper torch. The explosion that followed punched out the kitchen windows and blew Herbert, who was crawling about on the floor out into the passage. Luckily the other three escaped with burns to their hands and most of their hair being singed off. How they survived at all was a miracle and I often heard my father say that if there was a God, He must surely be looking after them.

Another time, Harry and Billy, in search of some diversion, started to push empty tins through the rollers of the old wooden mangle which stood in the back porch: Billy turned the handle while Harry fed in the tins. All was going swimmingly until one of the tins became stuck, upon which Harry tried to push it through with the result that his hand went in with the tin. The first anyone knew about it was the tremendous yell that he let out, a yell fortunately heard by the coalman who happened to be delivering next door. Rushing in, he managed to prise the rollers apart with an iron bar, and a chastened Harry was removed to the hospital.

And so the chapter of accidents went on. Billy, sneaking a ride on the back of one of the old Foden steam waggons belonging to a local miller, fell off and got himself run over by a following delivery van. On Regatta Day down by the river, he stepped forward onto what he thought was firm ground to get a better view of things, only to discover too late that it was a patch of floating weed. In he went and, being unable to swim, nearly drowned; indeed, had it not been for the swift action of a bystander who dived in after him he would have done.

Mrs Webb seemed to bear up remarkably well under the strain, although I do recall having seen her sitting at the kitchen table, head in hands, crying her eyes out. However, as always, there was a lighter side to things. Mr Webb on his weekend visits always brought with him a selection of cakes and buns from his bakery, and we would wait for him at the bottom of the avenue, confident that he would open his case and share out some of the contents before making his way to No. 27 and the harassed Mrs Webb.

One day, it seemed that their luck had changed. A relative had died, leaving them a considerable sum of money, enabling them to move to Birmingham and buy a house. Very little was heard of them after that – that is, until the war years, when it was rumoured that during an air raid their house had received a direct hit and that they were all killed, with the exception of Violet, who happened to be away visiting an aunt. Truly, they were a tragic family who deserved better from life; but apparently fate had decided otherwise.

At the bottom of Westfaling Street, Mrs Price's shop, installed in what had once been a private house, was liberally adorned on the outside walls with enamel signs, showing the goods that she dispensed to the surrounding district. This was the era of Robins Starch, Veritas gas mantles, Sunlight Soap and the Bisto Kids, an age which gave us the well-known Bovril poster which showed a pyjama-clad gentleman clinging to a large bottle floating in the sea, and bearing the message 'Bovril prevents that sinking feeling'. On the way to school, pocket money permitting, we were sure to stop off here, setting the brass bell fixed on to the inside of the door clanging furiously as we burst in, and bringing Mrs Price from her parlour, wafting a distinctive aroma of boiling cabbage and paraffin. In front of us, in the semi-darkness, shelves reached almost up to the varnished plank ceiling, from which hung sticky brown flypapers whose surfaces were covered with the harvest of the previous summer. Here were displayed jars of sweets, gob stoppers to be sucked and passed around to those less fortunate, sherbet fountains and dabs, locust beans, tiger nuts and lengths of black liquorice rolled into wheel shapes; while on the counter, slabs of Sharp's toffee lay in trays, all ready to be broken up with the small hammer that hung alongside. Pushing and shoving, with noses only reaching up to the counter, we would be unable to decide among the delights so temptingly laid out for us, until in desperation we grabbed the first thing which the by now exasperated Mrs Price brought forward.

Like all youngsters, we engaged in a certain amount of

horse-play. One of our favourite games was to tie a button on a length of cotton and suspend it outside a neighbour's window. Carefully attaching a further length, we would hide behind the hedge and gently pull, causing the button to tap against the panes. Out would come the irate house owner to chase us down the street where, once caught, as we often were, a box aside the ears was a powerful hint to us to continue our activities elsewhere. Another pastime, and one which required a little more planning, was White Horse Kick: perhaps it would be as well to explain the mechanics of the game. For victim we would take the most timid and gullible of our companions, blindfold him and, after turning him round several times in order that he should lose his sense of direction, we would lead him up to the nearest front door and position him with his back to it. On the command 'White Horse, White Horse, Kick', he would lash out with his feet in all directions, and inevitably make contact with the door. At this point the rest of us would beat a hasty retreat, leaving the unfortunate lad to face the consequences.

On Guy Fawkes night there was always a bonfire at the top of our garden, and in the weeks before the event we scoured the district collecting bags of leaves and sacks of crisp shavings from the carpenter's shop in Chandos Street. Some of these were used to stuff the guy, which we made from old clothes scrounged from obliging neighbours. When all was ready, this melancholy object was fixed to a pole driven down through the centre of the heaped pile of wooden boxes and discarded mattresses, where it was left contemplating the bare sprout stalks which surrounded it until its brief hour of glory came round. Then we sent our rockets soaring into the air, chased around with sparklers in hand and watched fascinated as cascades of silver stars from Roman Candles burst and scattered around us. On wooden line posts Catherine Wheels spun, throwing snake-like traces until, their force spent, they hung smouldering and dejected. As the evening drew to a close, we would sit roasting potatoes in their jackets in the dying fire, before going to our beds in rooms filled with the smell of smoke and gunpowder from discarded clothes hanging over the backs of chairs.

As in all communities, Hereford had its well known and outstanding characters, and Teddy Narraman, our local rag and bone merchant, was one of our favourites. Dressed in black morning coat, top hat and silk muffler, he pushed his handcart round the streets calling: 'Rag a' bone! Rag a' bone!' pausing now and then to apply a well worn comb to his moustache and snow-white beard. On Saturday afternoons down at the football ground in Edgar Street, he provided welcome entertainment during the half time interval when, well primed with drink, he walked onto the centre of the pitch, divested himself of jacket and top hat, and proceeded to execute what can only be described as a tribal dance. The crowd would roar, and wilder and wilder his steps would become until, collapsing, he would be carried off by the stewards and left to sleep at the rear of the stand.

At infrequent intervals another character known as Coal Black Charlie would appear. Where he came from no one knew, but he undoubtedly had a well-regulated circuit round the district. With long matted hair and worldly possessions tied in a bundle slung from his shoulder, he walked the streets knocking on doors to beg for food and water for his billy can in which, on a fire lit at the roadside, he brewed his tea. There must have been an interesting story behind Charlie and his decision to take to the road, but he was a man of few words and no doubt his secret eventually died with him.

At home times were hard, and my parents were having a job to make ends meet. Father, out of work for two years, was getting desperate, and there seemed no hope until quite unexpectedly his luck changed. He obtained work with the Shell Mex BP Company, repairing the two gallon cans in which the petrol was sold, pumps at that time being more of a novelty than an accepted fact. After this he was to be found in a small brick shed situated near to the Goods Station Yard at Barrs Court, where, lit by a single electric light bulb, he sat for hours laboriously working his way through piles of damaged cans. Once repaired, they had to be repainted in bright pillar box red and small pots of this inevitably found their way to No. 29. Mother, who was adept with a paint brush, used then to transform everything within reach, including on one occasion the seat on the outside toilet. One morning Father, having need of the facility and not realizing that the paint was still wet, sat on it. The result caused great amusement and the sight of him bending over while Mother applied liberal doses of paint remover should, I feel, have been photographed and recorded for posterity.

On Fridays when the wages were brought home, both parents sat at the kitchen table and allotted money to the various tins which, between times, had a permanent home on a high shelf. These tins were labelled according to their needs – Gas, Rent, Food, Coal, Etc. – the last one being for extras and receiving its portion only after all other expenses had been catered for. Father was also given his beer and tobacco money allowance and, when all was completed, the tins were returned to the shelf where they stood, labels carefully arranged to face outwards, until the next pay day.

Arising from this weekly ritual, there occurred one small incident which branded itself on the memories of my brother and myself. He had taken a halfpenny from the kitchen shelf which, for some reason had eluded the weekly calculations, but before he could spend it Mother had discovered it in a pocket of his jacket. When Father returned from work that evening we were both taken out to his workshop, where, after heating a soldering iron, he silvered both sides of the coin. When it had cooled he handed it to my brother, impressing on him that he should always carry it and, whenever he felt like taking something which did not belong to him, he was to take it out and remember. As far as I know he carried that coin until the day he died.

There were many other things which Father taught us. Time and weather permitting we were instructed in gardening and general husbandry, while in the workshop we learned the art of carpentry and boot and shoe repairing; I, for one, spent many hours at the bench under his supervision, soling and heeling with leather purchased from Woolworths Stores.

On Saturday mornings before receiving our weekly pocket money, we were required to perform various chores such as chopping wood, filling coal buckets and running shopping errands. Whenever I could I chose the latter, when, with the grocery list folded and tucked into my jacket pocket, I walked the mile or so to town, there to hand the order in to the India and China Tea Stores in High Town to be delivered later in the day either by horse drawn van, or cheeky errand boy on his shop cycle. Wandering back there were many pleasant diversions to be enjoyed. Standing outside Marchants Grocery shop I would savour the smell of freshly ground coffee which wafted out into the street, then, with face pressed against the small panes of the bowed window, watch the activity taking place within under the low beamed ceiling. It was a dim subdued world where elderly gentlemen in white coats and stiff starched collars, stood behind polished mahogany counters while in the corner, near the window, the shining bacon slicer went backwards and forwards depositing thin slices on squares of greaseproof paper laid ready, its operator seeming to be inches away from disaster as his fingers hovered near the revolving cutting blade.

Then on down Broad Street and King Street, skipping and staring, stopping and wondering until I reached the railway bridge overlooking Barrs Court Goods Depot. There I heaved myself up on to the parapet to watch the busy tank engines at work, shunting waggons this way and that while the larger main line locomotives, steam up, stood waiting until all their charges had been assembled. When all was ready they would start on their long journey, puffing and snorting with drive wheels spinning as they endeavoured to get a grip on the slippery rails. Slowly they eased themselves and their charges out of the sidings, waggons jolting and banging behind them, the noise of clanging buffers echoing as the couplings took up the strain. Clinging precariously to the parapet I watched as the engine passed under the bridge enveloping me in a cloud of smoke and steam, then, coughing and spluttering, to race across to the other side to watch it emerge, and staying until the rattling guards van disappeared out of sight round the bend on the far side of the rail bridge that spanned the river.

Long after the sight and sound of it had gone I would sit visualizing its progress past lush fields and under other bridges where no doubt there would be other grubby little boys waiting to watch its progress. On and on through valleys and over hills until it reached the gaunt industrial landscape of South Wales where smoke from the engine would go rolling over the grey slated roofs of the rows of terraced houses nestling under bare slag heaps, dark against the sky. In later years I often returned to visit that bridge. No need now to heave myself up for I could easily see over the top, but the noise and bustle of the shunting engines was long gone and the sidings were empty and weed strewn. However, with a little imagination I could still transport myself back to those far off days when, as a scruffy little schoolboy I had sat and watched my fantasies being carried away on those jolting waggons.

As in all well ordered homes, Monday at No. 29 was wash day, when mother would light the gas under the copper which stood in a corner of the kitchen. Shredding thin slices cut from a bar of Sunlight soap into the boiling water, she stirred until a good lather had been obtained, then added the clothes which would be agitated and prodded with a bamboo pole affectionately known as The Copper Stick. This implement, when not performing its wash day duties, had other uses, notably as a means of threatening us when for some reason or another we had stepped out of line.

Everything was washed by hand and squeezed dry through the wooden rollers of the mangle which stood in the back porch. Poor mother, with her damp hair hanging down in wisps about her face and hands coarse and red, worked in that steam filled kitchen from early morning to dusk. No time to prepare a hot midday meal; all we had were thick cold meat sandwiches, which more often than not were eaten while sitting on the stone step of the yard doorway.

She did, however, have a fairly efficient way of drying and airing the clothes. Above the gas stove hung a wooden rack which, by means of pulleys and cord, could be raised and lowered; with the clothes spread on this and the burners of the stove turned low, the drying process slowly took effect. This arrangement was not without its hazards however. One evening as we sat in the living room listening to Radio Luxembourg on Father's radio, we suddenly smelt burning. Out we all dashed to find the kitchen filled with smoke. The reason soon became apparent: some of the laundry had slipped and fallen off the rack on to the gas rings below, where it had caught alight. Mother, panicking, slipped on the smooth surface of the lino on the floor, and disappeared under the table, from where she was eventually rescued. Meanwhile the rest of us charged backwards and forwards removing the burning items and escaping with them into the garden. In truth, we did very well out of the incident as, after much soul-searching, several other items, well worn and discarded, were added to the pile, the insurance company paying out for the lot. Even now when I catch the distinctive smell of damp clothes drying on radiators I remember that dramatic scene.

There were, of course, other moments to be savoured – such as the time my brother cleared the table. One tea time at the conclusion of the meal, and being eager to be out to play, he asked permission to leave the table and, on this being granted, slipped quickly off his chair and darted for the door. Unfortunately, a worn thread in the table cloth caught on a button on his jacket and, as he went, he took the cloth and everything with him. For a moment there was dead silence; in the doorway he froze where he stood, cloth still hanging from his jacket, awaiting the explosion he felt must surely come; but all was well – my parents saw the funny side of it and burst into laughter, sending him on his way and leaving Mother to clear up the mess.

During my final years at school my thoughts often turned to Dumbleton. On rare occasions Mumford would visit us, and old memories of the life I had shared with her would be painfully stirred. On the station platform tears would be shed, and a feeling of loneliness would overwhelm me as the train bore her away once more. It was significant that I was never allowed to accompany her, even for a holiday; my parents well knew that, once back in Dumbleton, they would have had a hard job to make me return.

Time passed, and in due course I reached the age of fourteen. Plans as to my future were now discussed, plans in which I seemed to have very little say, such being the way of things in those days. It was the custom of local employers to send notification to the school of any junior posts they had available, inviting applications from those of us who had reached school-leaving age; and it happened that one such opening presented itself during the last few weeks of my stay at school. Messrs Painter Brothers who owned and ran the local steel works, required a junior office boy; my parents were enthusiastic and in due course my application, written in best copper plate, was forwarded. An interview was granted and on the appointed day, Mother and I made our way to their offices, me with my best suit on and she in her best Sunday hat; this, incidentally, she always wore on important occasions, even donning it when necessity dictated that the coalman be severely reprimanded for delivering an inferior grade of coal.

As far as I can remember the interview went very well; sitting on a chair in the corner I listened while they discussed me as if I weren't there; but I must have made a favourable impression as shortly afterwards a letter was received saying that the post was mine with a starting salary of seven and sixpence per week. My mother kept that letter for many years, no doubt to vindicate both herself and me, for in it Mr Painter had written: 'I can now understand why your son is above average' – an observation he was to have cause to regret before very long.

It should be appreciated that in those days a job carrying such badges of office as a clean white collar and black alpaca jacket was greatly sought after, as it elevated one into a social bracket well above that of the usual shop assistant or errand boy. These were the days of the late twenties and early thirties when openings for young school leavers were at a premium, and when even fathers and elder brothers found it hard to keep from joining the ever growing dole queues. In the streets of the city, out of work miners from South Wales walked the gutters caps in hand singing their songs and begging for pennies, their faces devoid of hope, looking out on a world which had all too soon forgotten the heroes of the late war. How sad it was to see men of their calibre subjected to the whims of money-grabbing pit owners and forced to beg in the streets! A time would come when we were again to have need of their services and be grateful that they were on hand, prepared to risk their lives daily in order that the wheels of industry were kept turning. Young as I was, I was aware that in the social strata to which my parents belonged, and which my father referred to as 'working class', there was a fermenting sense of inequality; perhaps it was this that laid the foundations for my socialistic leanings in later life.

In due course I took up my duties with Messrs Painter Brothers, answering the telephone, making tea, and carrying out general filing duties. The two directors of the company were a Mr Leslie and Mr Ralph, two completely different characters, the former presiding over the office staff and responsible for administration, while the latter dealt with the engineering and factory side. With Mr Leslie, who had been an officer in the late war, I got on well: he was a kindly, patient man who guided me through the first few months. Mr Ralph was a very different kettle of fish. He was erratic in his behaviour and indulged a habit of condescension which at times I found infuriating. In spite of that, he did seem greatly interested in my further education, and it was he who finally persuaded my parents that I should take a correspondence course in business management and accountancy. How well I remember the long hours I spent poring over balance sheets, ledgers and sundry accounts, one hour each morning before breakfast, and a further two hours each evening before being allowed out! Mr Ralph was also responsible for another torture to which I was subjected, my having to attend evening classes at St Owen's School – although I must admit that my growing interest in the opposite sex led me to play truant on many occasions. The omission was duly reflected in my reports and it began to be sensed that I was not as whole-heartedly absorbed in furthering my education as I should have been. One winter's evening, after a bit of 'sparking' along the river bank had absorbed the time I should have devoted to my studies, I was walking my latest girlfriend home through the Cathedral Close when I came face to face with my parents. The incident was particularly humiliating to me as, without explanation or discourse, I was ordered to return home, leaving the unfortunate young lady to disappear into the darkness.

The transition from short to long trousers had by this time been safely accomplished and with pride I wore my first 'off the peg' suit. The hairy nature of the cloth necessitated frequent stops to scratch exposed parts not used to being packaged, and the baggy trousers with their heavy turn-ups were certainly not crease-resistant, but in spite of these shortcomings I managed to conduct myself with some sort of dignity. I had moved forward a step and felt sure that at long last I was growing up.

I was with Messrs Painter Brothers for two years. During that time I made some progress, but it soon became clear that I was not cut out for office work. Letters passed between employer and parents; then one Monday morning matters suddenly came to a head. I received a minute's notice and was sent packing. I shall never forget the look on my mother's face when I told her, or the reception I got from my father when he arrived home from work. Why it should have come as such a surprise to them I couldn't imagine, as it must have been plain for some time that I was not happy in my job; however, perhaps I should explain the incident which precipitated the crisis.

The company secretary, a pompous and overbearing man, had for some reason best know to himself taken a dislike to me from the start. He was scoutmaster of our local troop, of which my mother was cubmistress, and I did learn in later years that there had been some dissension between them: this may have had some bearing on his attitude towards me. Suffice it to say that on the day in question he had been unusually vindictive at a time when everybody seemed to want everything at once. He was very short with me, ordering me to take a typewriter into his office. I cannot remember exactly the conversation which took place between us over the inter-office telephone but I would say that by the time I reached his door, tempers on both sides had just about reached breaking point. As soon as I entered, I saw he was standing legs apart, hands on hips, all ready to cut me down to size in front of his two clerks. They, no doubt having heard his side of our exchanges over the telephone, were awaiting the outcome with bated breath. Realizing that this was to be the final showdown, I stepped forward, dropped the typewriter at his feet and without a word turned and left. The rest is history; summoned into Mr Ralph's office I was informed in no uncertain terms that my services were no longer required and, with what I can only describe as a feeling of relief, I collected my belongings and turned my back on Messrs Painter Brothers for good. Thus did my feet fall off the first few rungs of the ladder of success and I was back on the ground, unemployed.

During this uncertain period of my life I visited Dumbleton several times to stay with Mumford, cycling the thirty-two miles each way. Naturally I made a point of meeting Kathy. The old days were not forgotten, and though, in growing up, we seemed to have lost a little of that tree climbing adventurousness which had formed the basis of our early relationship, we enjoyed each other's company, finding that we still had many things in common. She took me home to Manor Farm where I met her parents. They seemed pleased that we had got together again. Walking the fields and lanes we kissed and held hands as all young people do, talking of everything except any permanent understanding between us; and so we whiled away many pleasant hours, being in no hurry to commit ourselves. Cycling the miles home, I had a strange feeling that although each of us sensed the possible inevitability of our understanding, neither was prepared to put it into words. In the midst of so many new experiences, we were inclined to take each other for granted, which, as I was to discover later, is a dangerous thing to do.

Now begins that short interlude in life which my mother was fond of describing as the 'calf love' stage when romances, innocent as they were, took on a seriousness unwarranted by the occasion and when, in that uncertain limbo between youth and adulthood, we seemed to be neither one thing nor the other. Aping the fashion of the time we plastered our hair down with Brilliantine, wore navy blue shirts and white ties, and crammed our feet into patent leather winkle pickers. We made our first clumsy efforts with shaving soap and razor, and scanned our faces in the mirror for pimples and blackheads, unsure of our developing masculinity. Suits were purchased from the fifty shilling tailors, the shoulders of the jackets of which were padded out with spare handkerchiefs to obtain that square Humphrey Bogart look. In winter we added heavy Cromby overcoats belted at the waist and reaching well below our knees, the final touch being a Harry Roy trilby, worn at a rakish angle on our heads. Like out of work Hollywood extras we strolled around and, on Saturday and Sunday evenings, dressed to kill, paraded up and down Broad Street and High Town, stopping occasionally to snatch furtive kisses from girls, all done up in their weekend finery, who giggled in darkened shop doorways.

Things at home were not so good and Father, again out of work, and unable to provide for his family, suffered a loss of pride and dignity. For Mother, too, these were trying times, and I well remember the day when, having invited a friend to tea, she placed three Great Western Railway mugs on the table, the best she had to offer. Shopping for the Sunday joint, when one could be afforded, was left until late on Saturday evening, the butcher in Eign Street having in those days no deep freeze facilities, selling off his meat cheaply at that time. However, in spite of everything, the large stew pot was always kept simmering on the gas ring and into it went all sorts of bits and pieces of meat and vegetables ensuring that, if nothing else, we could always count on a good nourishing meal.

Early manhood was now fast approaching, and girls were beginning to absorb my attention, as I realized that they had more to offer than companionship. My first serious venture into this as yet uncertain world was aided and abetted by a young lady named Lillian Skinner who worked as a daily help at a house in Ryeland Street near to where I lived. How I met her I cannot remember; it is sufficient to say that in the ecstasy of callow youth I fell for her in a big way; and even now I look back on the experience with great affection. We took long walks down by the river, she with her arm through mine. Strict propriety was observed at all times, the occasional kiss being all that was needed to provide complete fulfilment to my first uneventful teenage romance. In my efforts to please and impress her I once bought her a box of chocolates which I handed to her as we crossed the Victoria Bridge on our way to the Castle Green. She, with a decisiveness which baffles me to this day, promptly threw them into the river: perhaps she was trying to tell me something, who knows? Anyway, as romances seemingly must at that age, ours petered out, she having taken up with a dashing young page boy from the Imperial Hotel. There were two other sisters in her family, Connie and Rene, and I was destined to indulge in brief romances with both of them in later years. I often think of them all, probably now with families and grandchildren, and wonder if their thoughts, in quieter moments, ever go back to those far off days and the seemingly heart-breaking hours they spent growing up.

I was nearly sixteen at the moment of my parting with Messrs Painter Brothers, and clearly it was high time that I took stock and sorted out what I was going to do with the rest of my life. Signing on at the local Labour Exchange, I reported twice weekly, for which I receive the princely sum of seven and sixpence. The rules were strict and if given a Green Card bearing the name and address of a prospective employer, you reported for an interview regardless of the type of job on offer, knowing full well that to refuse to do so would mean the termination of your weekly pittance. Several jobs came my way during the six months I was signing on, the most arduous being with the old Shropshire-Worcestershire Power Company, digging a cable trench between Hereford and Abergavenny. Here, armed with pick and shovel, and with only rare stops for mugs of tea brewed on an open fire beside the road, we dug away in all weathers, for one shilling an hour. There was no use complaining as, if you did, the walk back to the Labour

Exchange was a long one and the recriminations on arrival short and sharp. However, it did me no harm and I managed to stick it out until the job came to an end.

After that, having no fixed plan in mind, I became restless. One amongst a host of possibilities I considered was the Merchant Navy, no doubt influenced that way by the related experiences of Uncle Fred; however, I hesitated to take such a long stride towards my independence. Deep inside I remained insecure, as I had been ever since my enforced departure from Dumbleton; and my vacant hours were spent walking for miles in the country, trying to get things into perspective. Luckily, I was able to find casual employment on market days, when I would help out on the stalls, load and unload waggons, auction bunches of bananas from the back of a lorry and mingle with the farmers selling the periodical *Farmer and Stockbreeder* on commission. This was a fascinating world in which I learned how to juggle plates and saucers and talk the ladies into so called bargains, quickly learning the market blarney so necessary in such transactions. However, as the weeks passed I could see that this way of life was getting me nowhere, although at the time there seemed no way out.

Fortunately, it was not all work and worry and in the evenings I went dancing, sometimes two or three times a week. The fox trot, waltz and quickstep were the favourites then, being performed with feet encased in shiny leather shoes on maple floors liberally dusted with powdered resin. Strangely enough, it was my mother who took me to my very first dance. This was at the town hall where, unwillingly and awkwardly, I was dragged on to the floor to 'One Two Three, One Two Three' in a straight line up to the corners where an ungainly shuffle enabled me to change direction for the next lap. But I soon got the hang of things and, having been endowed with a good ear for music and a sense of rhythm, became quite proficient in the art. I served my apprenticeship, so to speak, at the Mortimer Road Rooms, a large wooden hut standing on waste ground down by the gas works. This may not have been the most romantic of venues, but for sixpence we were able to dance the evening away to the accompaniment of a modest but enthusiastic three-piece band. Well known tunes such as *The Very Thought of You, Little Man You've Had a Busy Day*, and *Moonlight Madonna* stirred the senses as we glided round the boarded floor under the glare of unshaded electric bulbs which hung from the planked ceiling. Between dances we gathered round the trestle table to drink lemonade from clumsy glasses and puff away at Woodbine, Lucky Strike and Black Cat cigarettes – not because we enjoyed them, but for the fact that in a strange way they made us feel grown up. Why we had to be continually proving ourselves is one of life's mysteries, but seemingly it was expected of us; and we gave in gracefully.

On Saturdays we flocked to the VAD Hut in Edgar Street where the band was a little more sophisticated, consisting as it did of a Scottish lady on the drums, her husband who doubled on piano accordion and two others who performed on saxophone and trumpet. In thousands of dance halls like that romances blossomed, and there must be many married couples of that generation who owe their partnerships to the stately waltz and invigorating quick step, and who, even now, cherish the memory of those blissful Saturday nights when skilfully they engineered the last dance with the partners of their choice for the pleasure of their company home. There in the semi darkness, with the slowly revolving coloured ball suspended over the middle of the floor throwing a multitude of changing patterns, we leaned against the perfumed hair of our partners as we moved as one. No need to ask the vital question as the tune invariably played was *Who's taking you home tonight*, then the long walk under street lights that threw dark shadows across the deserted pavements until at last, with destination reached, to stand in darkened doorways, unsure and hesitant, to snatch a kiss from eager lips before she disappeared, a kiss that stirred emotions of which, as yet, I was uncertain. In the half light with soft young breasts pressed against me and the provocative scent of her young body invading my senses, I looked into misty eyes so full of promise; then, as the door closed behind her, to wend my solitary way homewards through now darkened streets, a still world where, behind drawn curtains, lived others who had already passed along the growing up road but now had more pressing problems to attend to.

And so I danced the time away, falling in and out of love and engaging on mild vendettas when so-called steady girlfriends deserted me to lavish their affections elsewhere. But always, through all those years of unrequited adolescence, Kathy was in my thoughts, my feelings for her unchanged, and as deep as ever. I only wished she could have been there to share those carefree days.

In the early weeks of May, Hereford celebrated with its annual fair, and roundabouts, helter skelters, cake walks and dragon rides came to town, together with innumerable side shows on the outside of which scantily dressed ladies shamelessly exhibited their charms and invited us to step inside and enjoy more. High Town, Broad Street, King Street and Commercial Road overflowed, while beside and behind the amusements steam engines puffed away as they drove the generators which supplied the lighting and power. For three whole days and nights we lived in a world of perpetual delight, when five shillings provided an evening's admission to wonderland. Climbing the tall helter skelter tower we slid down the polished surface of the runway on coconut mats, to finish up at the bottom in undignified heaps; watched the fearless riders on the Wall of Death as they rode round and round on their motor cycles; threw wooden hoops for goldfish; and fired air guns at metal ducks passing along the backs of stalls on conveyor belts. Throughout, we tried to look suave and impress the girls with our proficiency, while all around the noise from the steam organs mingling with the incessant chatter and laughter of the crowds, filled the air.

This was but an interlude, however. Soon we were preparing for our summer camp at the Butts Wall where, from early May until the first mists of autumn came, we lived under canvas. Our tented homes were, by camping standards, lavish, having boarded floors, proper beds and adequate cooking arrangements, all of which added to the comfort of our semi-Spartan lives. On Saturday nights, on my way back from the evening's activities, I called in home to collect the box of provisions made ready for me for the week. It was good to have parents as tolerant and helpful as mine were, in an age when many of the older generation were what was termed 'chapel minded', and firmly of the opinion that they knew what was best for us. Released from such close supervision, we swam in the river, roamed the woods, and played our nostalgic Bing Crosby records on portable wind-up gramophones well into the night.

It was in this setting, as it happened, that fate decreed that I should take my first tentative steps into a hitherto unknown world. She was a charming girl named Yvette, a nurse from the General Hospital. Being some years older than me, she was well versed in the intricacies and pitfalls of love-making – which was just as well as, although verbally competent, I had as yet to put my theories into practice, a state of things which seemingly is the way with young men floundering in the uncertain depths of early manhood. For a while we asked no more of each other than a mutually shared friendship, but right from the start her dark vivacity had captivated me. Each time I held her the longing to possess her was undeniable; and it wasn't long before the storm broke.

It was a warm sunny day and we had swum the river and walked the banks hand in hand. As the night drew on we sat on the bed making small conversation, each of us eager but hesitating to take the first step. It was one of those magic moments when, thinking back, I find it hard to remember just when we came together. Suffice to say that in the still of that summer's night, our young bodies pressed together in the warmth and intimacy of youth in its searchings, the world exploded in a million flashing lights as we took each other in the act of love making. I see her now, dark eyes giving the answers to many as yet unanswered questions, the full red lips, soft and provoking, and the rise and fall of her firm young breasts as she lay beside me. It was not lust that powered us that night but a loving intimacy which for a while shut out the world of reality. Long after it was over we lay in each other's arms, hardly daring to breathe in case the magic of that moment should be lost. The power that had lain dormant within me for so long had been released, and I was at peace.

We were to make love many times after that, but nothing could ever match the revelation of that first encounter. Eventually, as is the way of things, as we came together so we parted, never to meet again. But I shall always remember and be grateful that it was she who had guided me through that perilous moment; grateful that I had not succumbed to the coarse searchings and fumblings of inexperience that is the lot of so many seeking to discover the secrets of love.

And so the months passed, and I found employment at last as a stores assistant with a firm engaged in the business of renovating and repairing commercial vehicles. It was not the kind of work my parents had envisaged for me, but by this time, I fear, they had come to regard me as a family misfit, and were concentrating their attention on my brother, who was now established in a respectable job with the county council. I was content with that, and I thrived in that oil and grease environment, where I spent nine happy months. The Stores, a corrugated building, was warmed in winter by a solitary coke stove which reminded me of the one which used to stand in the hall in the school at Dumbleton. The mechanics were a great bunch of lads. Though time has erased many of their names from my memory, one I do remember: Rupert Thompson. He taught me to accept life as it was, and to make the most of it.

It was during that time that I bought my first car, an Austin Seven. This remarkable little vehicle cost me, as far as I can recall, £18 and, after being overhauled by my mechanic friends, gave me hours of pleasurable touring around the countryside, being particularly useful when attending out of town dances.

I remember during one of these outings in particular when things got a bit out of hand. There were four of us in our little mobile gang, and we had organized a run out to a village dance some miles from town. As the evening wore on, becoming bored with the dancing, we decided to indulge in our favourite pastime of Follow my Leader. All our vehicles, souped up in one way or another, and with very imperfect silencing systems, made a grand noise, particularly when in convoy. So off we went chasing the leader along the winding country lanes and roads until, by chance, we landed up in the grounds of the local vicarage. By this time the village policeman had been alerted and, mounted on his trusty bicycle, had come to see what all the row was about. Round and round the garden we roared, in and out of the shrubbery, with the bobby who had by this time caught up with us, himself involved in the mad chase. The vicar meanwhile, clad in pyjamas and dressing gown, stood in the doorway with hands raised to heaven: perhaps he was endeavouring to attract the attention of the policeman, who was still pedalling furiously round and round after us. At length, as we swung out of the driveway and on to the road, I caught a glimpse of the law, by now out of the running, firmly wedged bicycle and all in a clump of bushes. It was a stupid escapade on our parts; however, some days later we partially atoned by organizing a collection amongst ourselves, the proceeds of which were forwarded anonymously, together with a letter of apology, to the vicar, in the hope that it would help pay for any damage we had caused.

Time was slipping by and our small pursuits had more savour in them, to our eyes, than the momentous events which were shaping in Germany across the Channel. Jobs were still hard to come by and my father, still out of work, scoured the countryside for employment, but with little success. Thankfully, however, things took a turn for the better for him, and at last he secured work with an assurance company. On Tuesdays in all weathers he did his country rounds on his bicycle, and each evening sat at the kitchen table seeing to his book of work, but although the hours were long, at least there was now a steady wage coming in.

At home, the stringent conditions in which we had lived were eased somewhat. In the living room we had carpet to replace the bright green lino which had served us for so many years, and a new wireless set was installed to which we listened to programmes from Radio Luxembourg and *Talks on Tower Hill* given by the Rev. Donald Soper, a great favourite of Father's. Mother, now able to afford small luxuries, sent away for a cuckoo clock which she had wanted for a long time. At length it arrived, in pieces, through the post; she unwrapped it and left the assembling for a later date. Unfortunately, however, we found that she had thrown most of the vital parts away with the wrapping. A frantic search through the dustbin finally brought them to light, and the clock, dignity restored, ticked away merrily on the living room wall. There it remained for many years until at last, one of its bellows having given up the ghost, it had a resounding 'Cuck' but no 'Ooh'.

During his travels round the countryside, Father chanced upon an old motor cycle, lying abandoned under a heap of nettles in a farmer's orchard, and after negotiating with the owner, he finally purchased it. With the help of a friend it was dragged out and brought home, much to the consternation of my mother who viewed the subsequent repairs and its impending use with much apprehension. It was an old Royal Enfield with sit-up-and-beg handlebars, its two gears being operated by a handle very similar to that used on tram cars. In addition to using it for his rounds, Father would sometimes taken Mother for a spin. Our spaniel dog greatly looked forward to this occasion, and was in the habit of accompanying them. At a steady fifteen miles per hour he trotted along behind, ears flapping, while Mother, her arms tightly wrapped around Father's waist, clung on for dear life, getting very little pleasure from what should have been a great experience.

# 4

*In which war breaks out and I
get my first taste of army life*

It was about this time that, through the influence of a friend of my father's, I obtained an interview with the Post Office Engineering Department and much to my surprise was taken on as a trainee. My parents were greatly relieved, as a job with a government department, ensuring guaranteed employment and a week's paid holiday a year, was considered as a big step up the ladder. My years with them up to the outbreak of the Second World War passed all too quickly, but I cannot dismiss them without brief mention of some of the characters and amusing incidents which took place along the way.

Joe Cain will be the subject of many of these anecdotes. He was much older than me, slow but with a Liverpudlian's quicksilver sense of humour. Short and thin as a rake, he wore the same old flannel trousers and odd sports jacket day in and day out, and was rarely seen without an inch or so of ash hanging from the ever-present Woodbine in his mouth – a habit which caused great consternation in many carpeted homes we found ourselves in when fitting telephones. Once, we were working in a room where a dear old lady was confined to her bed, when he suddenly dived under it. Hardly had his legs disappeared when there came the ominous sound of screwdriver contacting china. Out the other side he wriggled, ash still clinging stubbornly to his Woodbine, and clutching in his hand a half-filled chamber pot. With a 'What shall I do with this, missus?' he started to make his way to the half-open window, and was only restrained from emptying the contents on to the garden below by swift intervention on my part. Another time, we were working in the basement of the head post office in Broad Street where, high on the wall at pavement level were two or three iron grilles. Unfortunately, it was at this spot in the street that the stamp vending machines were situated and it often happened that customers' dogs, having nothing better to do for a few minutes, would cock their legs against the grating – resulting in a greater part of their efforts being received below, on the work bench on which we working. Joe's ingenious solution to this problem was effected by wiring up the grille to the electricity mains through a transformer which gave out about twelve volts. This was not enough to do any lasting harm, but sufficient to give our doggy friends a sharp reminder, and to send them charging up Broad Street, after doing their stuff, to get as far away as possible from the stamp machines and their owners.

Joe, never the diplomat, dropped another clanger when we were carrying out some work at the residence of a retired admiral. One morning he breezed into the room and, seeing the old gentleman – who must have been all of eighty years of age – sitting enjoying the sunshine coming through the French windows, remarked: 'Well, Admiral, soon be time to get the mothballs out of the old uniform,' a reference, of course, to the rumours of war which were then circulating. The old boy spluttered in disbelief and furiously rang a small handbell for assistance, whereupon Joe, realizing what he had done, beat a hasty retreat, leaving me to cope with the situation as best I could.

Poor Joe, he had a spartan home life and many a time I have called for him in the early morning, and waited, constantly hooting on the van horn. At long last he would emerge, tucking his shirt into his trousers with one hand with the other feeding himself with a thick jam butty. He was invariably late when reporting for duty at the depot and his excuses were always, to say the least, imaginative: our inspector, Norman Davis, who was usually on hand at signing-on time, soon came to accept that being late was a part of Joe's normal routine.

Driving with him was an experience in itself. Being rather short-sighted, he tended to sit hunched forward with his face pressed up against the windscreen, allowing just sufficient room for the inevitable Woodbine cigarette to operate. Early one morning, when negotiating High Town, he managed to knock over all the empty dustbins which stood along one side of the street, causing such a noise and commotion that windows were raised in alarm on all sides. But in spite of his eccentricities, he was a true friend and a wonderful craftsman, and I had the highest respect for him. When he eventually passed on, the world lost one of its great characters.

In complete contrast there was Jack Daffurn, a good friend, who guided me through the intricacies of automatic exchange working. He will no doubt remember the incident at Tenbury Wells when I became involved in a steamy relationship with the local blacksmith's daughter, a relationship which did not appear to meet with the approval of the girl's father. One lunchtime, when seated comfortably with her on the edge of a cornfield, I was rudely diverted by the sight of him charging down the lane brandishing his blacksmith's hammer. Not stopping for explanations I took to my heels and disappeared into the cornfield, with the irate parent in hot pursuit. Fortunately, he never caught up with me, and it was with a great sense of relief that the next day we were moved on to another job, leaving the lovesick maiden with her virginity intact.

From Tenbury Wells we moved to Llandrindod Wells in mid-Wales, and here I met up with Bill Brace. I shall always remember Bill with great affection. Slow and dignified, I never knew him to panic, although there were times when it would have been in order to do so. Such a one day was the day the new automatic telephone exchange was put into commission. It was to be a local event of some magnitude, and all the civic dignitaries had been invited, together with several prominent representatives of the postal and engineering side. Under strict instructions to make ourselves appear busy during the opening ceremony, I, spanner in hand, climbed on to the cable runs in the ceiling, where I lay watching the events below. By some mischance, just as the entourage was gathered immediately below, I dropped my spanner across the main battery bar causing a shower of sparks to descend on to the unsuspecting visitors, one of whom was wearing a fur coat. Her companions flew at her, trying to brush off the sparks which by then had begun to smoulder, and eventually, thoroughly ruffled, the lady was rushed to the head postmaster's office. I lay doggo, and just hoped that no one had seen me. Whether or not the Post Office were ever charged for a new coat, I cannot say, but I assure you that the incident took a lot of living down.

In the early days, our method of transport was by motor

cycle and sidecar, and Bill and I often travelled around the country in such a conveyance. It is not a way of getting about I would recommend, particularly in the winter months with snow on the ground and icy roads to contend with. One day, returning from Knighton, I was in the wicker sidecar muffled up in a heavy overcoat, flat cap on my head, and hands encased in thick woollen gloves. As we sped along the country roads, I felt the need for a cigarette and, reaching for the matches, struck one. Unhappily, as soon as I lit it I dropped it, and it was not until I saw the smoke issuing from beneath my feet that I realized where it had gone. By then it was already too late. We chugged down Bleddfa Pitch, with smoke billowing out behind. At last, pulling to a halt, Bill calmly announced: 'I think we're on fire, mate.' By this time things were well alight and I made a hasty and undignified exit from the sidecar, scattering its contents right and left as I landed in a ditch. Bill, after shutting off the petrol supply to the bike, proceeded to put out the fire. The sidecar was almost completely gutted and some of our stores had gone up in smoke as well; however, somehow we managed to nurse the remains back to the garage. There we were confronted with hours of form filling by way of explanation, and it was many months before the powers-that-be let the matter drop.

This incident was shortly to be followed by another. Having by now lost our beloved motor cycle combination, we had been issued with one of the new Morris Minor vans and were able to travel in comfort. One afternoon, we were negotiating the same stretch of road when Bill quietly remarked that a wheel had passed us. I looked and there it was, speeding merrily down the road in front. We drove on for a bit more in silence, until it dawned on us that, as there was no other vehicle in sight, it must be one of ours. Sure enough, on coming to a halt, the van keeled over coming to rest on its rear axle. Had it been one of the front ones, the outcome might have been more serious.

Climbing the telephone poles entailed the use of climbing irons, or 'scratchers', as they were affectionately known. Strapped one to each leg, they had a spike attached at the instep which, when driven into the pole, provided a foothold. Needless to say, long hours of practice were required before any sort of proficiency was obtained. At first the only results of my efforts were sore and aching ankles and blistered hands full of splinters, but, under Bill's guidance, I began to get the hang of it. There were times, with the poles wet and slippery, that I wished they had never been invented; but the art, once learned, was never forgotten, and before long I was able to shin up and down with ease. I found it exhilarating to stand with feet on the top steps of a thirty foot pole, and my safety belt securely fixed around my middle, surveying the world around.

And so I journeyed on, enjoying life and making the best of things. Weekends and holiday times saw me back in Dumbleton to visit Mumford, and Kathy too, if she happened to be home from her finishing school. She was grown up now and in my eyes was more beautiful than ever. Of course, she flirted with all the village lads, though without showing preference for any of them; but our relationship remained as non-committal as always. Moving away from the simplicity of our childhood days, we had both developed in outlook and experience, and in those long days spent in each other's company, we gradually came to see that the time for playing games was over. For my part, I sensed, instinctively, if you will, that any undue familiarity between us would destroy something we shared and which was precious to us; so I kept such feelings at arm's length, never allowing the situation to get out of control. It was a trying time for both of us, but I knew that, had she given herself to me, the respect that we had for each other would have vanished, never to be regained. Like a startled deer, she would have shied away, thus severing the ties which, although not binding, at least gave some hope to a more permanent understanding. So I thought, but as time passed this self-created barrier between us wrought its own division. We kept in touch by letter, of course, but it was obvious that we had reached a crisis point where neither of us felt able to declare our true feelings. Time, I feel sure, would have resolved all these difficulties; and all would have been well – but time was precisely what we had not got.

It was the summer of 1939. War was in the air and Territorial and Army reserves were being called to the colours. Ministry pamphlets giving instructions on what action to take in case of air raids appeared through letter boxes, civilian gas masks were issued and stirrup pumps and buckets of sand were positioned at the foot of stairways and other strategic places. Hitler was irrevocably drawing the nations towards war, and in spite of the assurances of Neville Chamberlain, storm clouds were building ominously over Europe. All eyes were on the flashpoint, which was the Danzig Corridor, and when on 1 September German troops entered it, the die was cast. We all knew what must happen now, and in a strange way the tension was relieved when the prime minister made his historic broadcast to inform us that once again we were at war with Germany.

Father gave up his job with the assurance company, and he and my mother joined the workers at the local munitions factory. My brother enlisted in the Army Pay Corps, and many of the Post Office engineers were called up. Others, who were continuing with vital work, were to be exempt from military service. I was not to be included amongst these, and I was glad about that: I knew that sooner or later I should be drawn in. Preferring it to be sooner rather than later, I volunteered, and one cold wet January morning presented myself at St Peter's Church Hall for medical examination. And it is from this point that the story of my war effort begins.

We stood in rows naked as the day we were born, striving all the while to cover up our most private parts with hands hopefully as big as dustbin lids, while the medical officer probed and prodded us over. There was nothing personal in his examination as he passed from one to the other tapping and grunting; and I remember someone once telling me that if you were warm you were in. This must have been so in my case as, before long, I found myself confronting a seated officer. He, completely impassive, and not even bothering to look up, asked if I had any preference as to which arm of the services I would like to honour with my efforts. Now, in all truth, I hadn't given the matter much thought, but in a rush of enthusiasm I decided on the Tank Corps. Heaven knows why! Perhaps I thought I should be safe in one of those mobile steel garden sheds. The officer sucked hard on his pencil, turned over a few pages of the file in front of him, and then calmly announced that, as I was a Post Office engineer by trade, there was no other choice for me but the Royal Corps of Signals. I must say, this decision took me slightly aback; the last thing I wanted in my new career was the job I had been doing in civilian life. However, forced to accept the inevitable, I dressed and set off for home, leaving the rest of my late naked companions at St Peter's Hall to sort out their own problems.

One morning soon after, the official-looking envelope containing my call-up instructions, arrived. I picked it up from the hallway and, with mixed feelings, took it into the kitchen, where my mother was busy working. For a long time I sat with that letter unopened before me. Finally, realizing that there was no point in putting things off any longer, I slit the envelope and so learned that I was to report to the Corps of Signals at Harrogate in two weeks time.

When the day came for my departure Mother packed a few necessities in a suitcase, shedding a few tears whilst doing so. Father shook me by the hand at the same time giving me some good advice which was 'Never volunteer for anything, keep your eyes and ears open and your mouth shut', and so, on a wet January morning I stood on the platform of Hereford station looking uncertainly ahead to an unknown future. Seated in the corner of the carriage, face pressed against the window, I watched as the platform moved silently away, all the time struggling to get a last glimpse of familiar surroundings now slowly disappearing from view. The steelworks where seemingly so long ago I had placed my feet on the first rung of the ladder, the squat tower of the cathedral barely visible through the rain, and the tall spire of St Peter's Church standing alone at the top of St Owens Street. I wondered how things were in Dumbleton on this grey wet morning. Mumford, by now having received my letter, would no doubt be thinking of me and wishing me well, and what of Kathy to whom I had also written, would she be sparing me a thought?

The long journey to Harrogate is now but a dim memory. As I recollect it, my fellow travellers and I played endless games of cards using the tops of our suitcases and engaging in periods of speculation about the future, all the time trying hard to make light of things but secretly dreading what lay ahead. On the way the train stopped at dreary stations where, on cold platforms, small knots of people clustered around embarrassed and apprehensive young men clutching battered suitcases. Leaning from carriage windows they held hands up to the very last moment until fingers slipped apart and they were alone.

Sadly the wives, mothers, and sweethearts turned and walked away. The older ones had seen it all before in another age when similar fresh young faces had crowded the windows to wave their goodbyes. Sadly many of those departing travellers had not returned and were now only fading memories with row upon row of white crosses in far off places to honour them and tell of the stupidity of war.

The rain lashing against the carriage windows ran down in rivulets while outside the dreary countryside drifted by an endless panorama of sodden fields and misty hills over which the rain clouds hung like shrouds. We sped through dark satanic mill towns with their endless rows of huddled terrace houses whose slated roofs were grey and wet and where, in oblong back yards set with makeshift pigeon lofts, wooden rollered mangles awaited the next wash day side by side with tin baths and metal dustbins.

On bare allotments stood scatterings of huts where, on Sunday mornings, the menfolk gathered to discuss football or rugby, seeking refuge from busy housewives and the Sunday dinner preparations. To me it was a strange and different world where tall brick chimneys thrusting upwards, sent clouds of dark smoke hurrying down the valleys, a world peopled by strangers who were now united to face the struggle ahead.

As I sat viewing all this I tried hard to get my thoughts into some sort of order, and to control the emotional upheaval going on inside me. As the hours passed, the clickety click of the carriage wheels as they passed over the rail joints and the protesting and swaying as the train charged over the points, lulled me into a fitful sleep. Most of my companions had left by now and I was alone with my thoughts until eventually, in the darkness of the winter's night I arrived at Harrogate, there to alight on to the dimly lit platform the unfamiliar surroundings causing me to hesitate before slamming the carriage door shut, an act of finality that I felt would irrevocably seal my only means of escape.

At the station exit, to which uncertainly I had directed my steps, I made my first contact with my new life.

He stood in the doorway looking me up and down, in his hand a list clamped to a board with a rusty bulldog clip. Briefly he was silent, but then in his best parade ground voice, he demanded to know my name and why the hell it had taken me so long to arrive. His name was Martin, Lance Corporal Martin, an ex-regular soldier. Later I was to find out that he came from Northampton, but my immediate reaction was that I didn't take too kindly to his attitude. However, remembering the advice given to me by my father, I held my tongue. Still complaining he ushered me out to a small canteen near the station where the rest of the unfortunates were gathered, drinking tea and talking amongst themselves. I muttered a few hellos and retreated to a corner, not at that moment wanting to become involved, but before I could order the cup of tea I was gasping for, events were rudely interrupted. A three ton truck drew up, and into this we were all unceremoniously bundled. With the tailboard lifted and secured we were driven to Penny Pot Lane Camp where, after having our names again checked by the incomparable Lance Corporal Martin, we were deposited in a large empty wooden barrack room, there for the moment to be left to our own devices.

My first impressions of my new home were, to put it mildly, unfavourable. Along each side were placed rows of iron-framed single beds, each with three blankets neatly positioned at the head, and with a large wooden locker standing beside. At the end of the room, near the doorway, some empty fire buckets took the eye; they had been polished until they gleamed and I wondered if they ever had or ever would be used for the purpose for which they had been intended – the answer to this would come much later when the strange ways of army life were revealed to me.

By now my companions had thawed out a little and we sat on the beds, chatting and handing round our packets of cigarettes. I suppose we felt that, as we were all in the same boat, it was just as well to try and make the best of things. However, we were not left in peace for long, for our friend Martin reappeared and marched us off – rather raggedly, as I recall – to the stores, where we were issued with linen palliasses which then had to be filled with straw. This being done, we returned to the barrack room where beds were allocated and our straw mattresses deposited. Then off we went again, this time to the mess room to be served with mugs of hot cocoa and bulky cheese sandwiches. By now we were beginning to get the hang of things, and we were not unduly surprised when the five foot nothing of our friend showed up to march us back to our

125

barrack room once more. This time, after checking that we all had somewhere to lay our heads, he left us with the parting instruction to get settled in and prepare ourselves for the morrow, when our real army life would begin.

I sat on my bed after he had gone and viewed the situation with a certain amount of misgiving. I'm sure it was the same with the other lads, and that we were all of us trying to put off until the last minute the opening of our suitcases and the display of multi-coloured pyjamas which had been so carefully packed for us. The three coarse blankets with which each bed was provided seemed quite inadequate a covering for the night's rest. I soon found how they tickled and itched and the straw pallaisse rustled alarmingly each time I moved. How I missed my clean white sheets and pillow cases and the familiar surroundings of the bedroom back at No. 29! After lights out I lay for what seemed an eternity, listening to the snores of my companions and wondering what in God's name I was doing in this place. No satisfactory answer had presented itself by the time I finally managed to get to sleep.

Early the next morning the 'wakey-wakey-wakey' of a strange NCO stirred us into some sort of action. Hurriedly we donned our by now crumpled civilian clothes, which incidentally felt decidedly damp, and made our way to the communal wash house, where we carried out our ablutions with extreme difficulty. Waiting our turn in the doorway we stood until one of the wash basins became vacant, then, after cleaning it to remove the tide mark left by the previous user, we searched around for somewhere to hang our shaving mirrors. Nothing being available, we finished up shaving by touch, dodging and ducking to avoid the weaving arms and elbows of the people either side of us.

Ablutions completed we returned to our barrack room only to be ordered out again and marched to the mess room where breakfast was being served. Proferring the two halves of the issued mess tin, we received porridge in one half and bacon and eggs in the other then, porridge disposed of, we rushed to the washing up trough where, if one was lucky, the water would be reasonably warm and clean, depending of course on how many people had used it before., With the free half rinsed out, we dashed back to the serving counter to have it filled with strong sweet tea; unfortunately by this time the bacon and egg were stone cold. The meal over, back to the trough we went to swish the mess tins and utensils about in the greasy, lukewarm water and dry them with one's handkerchief before carrying them back to the barrack room.

In the next bed to mine was a lad from Wolverhampton named Allen with whom I struck up a friendship. He was a quiet chap, inclined to be rather shy, but we soon found ourselves exchanging confidences and before long he showed me pictures of his girlfriend to whom he had recently become engaged. She was a striking looking blonde and it was obvious that he was very much in love with her. As I sat on the bed with her photograph in my hand the thought struck me how lucky I was not to be saddled with any permanent commitment to one of the opposite sex, particularly now in war time. I did however tell him about Kathy and my hopes for our future together. He made no comment but I knew that he was puzzled as to why I was dragging my heels in the matter. Even if he had asked me I think I would have found it hard to explain.

In those first few days of insecurity we drifted, each reaching out for something solid to hold on to, lucid ones and silent ones, all struggling to come to terms with the new way of life. Head on we met the challenge, secretly missing our old ordered way of life where wives and parents fetched and carried, fed us, and made us feel secure in the little niche they had created. Still, as this feeling was common to us all, it brought us closer together, and it was not long before we found ourselves helping each other along the way.

Conducted to the quartermaster's stores, we were issued with battle dress uniforms, denims and all other items of kit donated by a grateful government. Each man also received a rifle with strict instructions to memorize its serial number and never to forget it on pain of death. Our names, now prefixed with our regimental numbers, were carefully written in Army Pay Books, and details of next of kin entered: from that moment on, the former were our only means of identification to be delivered without fail whenever challenged to do so. Heavily laden, we staggered back to the barrack room to try on our uniforms, and to parade the result in a row down the centre of the hut, where we awaited inspection. Some had trousers reaching half way up the leg, others had inches to spare in both length and width. Some had greatcoats which trailed around their ankles, while others were only afforded protection to knee height. And our forage caps looked equally ridiculous rammed on top of our heads. In many cases these were only prevented from slipping down and obscuring all vision by the ears which carried the weight, and which, pressed downwards, resembled a taxi cab with both doors open.

The inspecting officer, passing down the row, tried hard to stifle the amusement which showed on his face. His sergeant followed behind, clipboard in one hand and stick of white chalk in the other, and with this he marked lines on the clothing for the guidance of the regimental tailor.

Within a few days, though, we not only began to look like soldiers but indeed to feel like them. We soon became adept at assembling webbing equipment, at packing large and small packs and, most important of all, mastered the stripping and cleaning of our rifles which, once attended to, were carefully placed at the head of our beds. We blancoed and polished and learned the army way of doing things; laid out our kit for inspection, scrubbed the barrack room floor and buffed the fire buckets until they shone. However, for the second time in my life, my boots caused the most consternation – due in no small way to the fact that on trying them on I discovered that I had been issued with one size six and one size seven. The quarter-master refused to accept the possibility, and suggested that my feet would soon adapt themselves. In despair I consulted the company officer. He soon resolved the problem, but I had the feeling that the QM never forgave me for complaining. Had I been more versed in the ways of these guardians of the King's stores, I should have realized that their main function in life was to keep equipment intact, and never to change anything unless pressed to do so, as this necessitated a certain amount of paperwork. The thought did cross my mind, though, that somewhere out there, some poor solider, was hobbling about trying to get his feet accustomed to boots of two different sizes.

Within two weeks of my arrival I went down with influenza and, running a high temperature, was admitted to the Royal Artillery Hospital across the way. Weak and pale, I finally returned to duty to find that our old straw palliasses had been replaced with standard issue 'buscuits': these, although hard, were a definite improvement. We had now shaped up suffi-ciently to be let loose on the barrack square, where we trained in foot and rifle drill. The first few days of this were chaotic: some found it impossible to keep in step, while others seemed unable to distinguish between civilian and army left and right – not that there should have been any difference, but we managed to make it so. Two of our squad just couldn't swing their arms and legs independently, preferring to motivate right arm with right leg and left with left, a procedure which resulted in an ungainly shuffle. The drill sergeant, luckily, was very patient and bore all these indignities with great restraint, informing us that his mother had promised him some wooden soldiers and now, by God, he had got them.

One lad who hailed from London had made up his mind that he was not suited to army life, and right from the start he was determined to work his ticket. He was to be seen at all hours, roaming around the camp, picking up imaginary bits of paper and refusing to put on his uniform or take orders. We all admired his pluck, for it must have taken a great deal of courage to stick it out, and we were not surprised when one day we learned that his ploy had succeeded and that he was being returned to civilian life. On his last night in barracks he confided in us how he had managed it, and it was with a feeling of envy that we watched him walk out through the main gates the following day.

As soon as I had learned how to conduct myself like a soldier, the time came for my first guard duty, which I cannot claim to have been an unqualified success. It was a bitter night and, standing alone in the darkness, clad in ankle length greatcoat, ill-fitting boots, and with a civilian gas mask in a cardboard box strung around my shoulder with a length of string, I pondered on what I should do if suddenly confronted by a German paratrooper. As yet I had not even fired my rifle, my only knowledge of it being that the bullets went in one end and came out of the other. The camp, dark and deserted, was full of moving shadows which caused me to grip my rifle more firmly and cast anxious glances over my shoulder. Summoning up what dignity and courage I could, I sloped arms and paced up and down in the approved fashion, determined to do the right thing should an emergency arise.

At about twelve thirty pm, the orderly officer of the day appeared out of the darkness and stood awaiting my challenge, the correct words of which I had by that time forgotten.

Feeling that some sort of communication was required, I called out: 'Halt! Who are you and what do you want?' – a challenge, which, delivered in a meek voice, was not in any way calculated to put the fear of God into an intruder. For a moment the officer did not move, obviously unable to believe his ears; then, having assessed the situation, he came forward and asked, very kindly, how long I had been in the army. I suspect it came as no surprise when I told him 'only a few weeks.' Had it been otherwise, there is no doubt that I should have been in very serious trouble. After instructing me in the correct procedure he stepped into the guard room and, shortly afterwards, I was whipped inside and told to keep out of sight for the remainder of the duty – an order which, I assure you, I obeyed with alacrity.

As the days passed we persevered with our foot and rifle drill, learned how to salute longest way up and shortest way down, were introduced to the gymnasium and physical training, and were taken out to the rifle range to perfect the art of killing. All this we accomplished with varying degrees of success. However, shooting on the range was the biggest thrill and I well remember my feelings as I fired my first rounds at the target, knowing that I now possessed the power of life and death over some unknown adversary. There was something seductive about the mechanics of firing – the click of the bolt, as the round was driven smoothly into the barrel, the soft pressure on the trigger, and the recoil as the bullet sped swiftly towards the target – it seemed to induce the killer instinct. Probably it was meant to do so, as without it I doubt if I should have made a very good soldier.

During the course of our training we were instructed in the art of firing five rounds rapid when, between each shot, the rifle had to be lowered from the aim and brought up again. The secret of this was simply a matter of rhythm which, unfortunately, one of our squad was found to lack. Bringing the rifle up, he pulled the trigger before he had got the butt firmly tucked into his shoulder – the recoil caused the brass butt plate to smash into his mouth and break every one of his teeth off at the gums. I shall never forget his scream of agony as he collapsed beside me, poor chap. I dropped my rifle to grab hold of him, but there was little I could do. He spent months in hospital after that, until eventually he was invalided out, thus becoming the second member of our little squad whose military career was cut short.

By this time our mail was coming through regularly, and I had letters from Hereford and Dumbleton. Mumford kept me up to date with events in the village, but made no mention of Kathy who had not yet answered the two letters I had written to her. In the world beyond the camp perimeter, the country was rapidly being put on a war footing. Blackout after dark had become the order of the day, and petrol restrictions had emptied the streets of all but essential traffic. Women were being recruited to take over from men on the land, in factories, and in the armed forces, and they soon proved their worth as ambulance drivers, bus drivers and in a host of other ways. In thousands of back gardens up and down the land, steel Anderson shelters appeared, as protection against the expected air raids, while our boys in the RAF dropped leaflets over Germany in a vain attempt to effect a change of heart at the last moment. News from Poland gave no grounds for hope and elsewhere in Europe it seemed as if everyone was waiting, not yet fully roused, for the explosion to come.

We, in Harrogate, continued to train and march with unending guard duties, pickets, cook house fatigues, dental checks and inoculations filling the days. Eventually our first seven days' leave came round and with it the opportunity to briefly revisit our homes. Still in my ankle length greatcoat, and clutching the civilian gas mask in its by now battered cardboard box, I travelled to Hereford where, in due course, I presented myself at the front door of No. 29. My father greeted me with the now immortal words: 'God, son, what have they done to you?' Then Mother, dashing from the kitchen, took one look at me and burst into tears: all things considered, not a very auspicious homecoming. Neighbours shook me by the hand and wished me well, and everyone asked: 'When are you going back?' adding that seven days of Mother's cooking and some good night's rest would go a long way to restoring me to something resembling my former self. So much for the return of the conquering hero, I thought. In a way it was a strange sort of leave, for feeling and looking as I did, I stayed indoors most of the time, fearing that, if I went into town I might meet some of my former mates and so have a great deal of explaining to do.

All too soon I found myself once more on the platform at Hereford station with the journey back to Harrogate before me; but at least this time I knew what I was returning to. A change of trains at Leeds gave me time to stretch my legs and, passing a cinema, I gave a glorious salute to a commissionaire standing outside, adopting the maxim that: 'If it's wearing gold braid and looks anything like an officer, salute it.' The fact that he acknowledge it only served to confirm that my assumptions were correct.

No transport was available at Harrogate, so I was obliged to walk the miles back to camp. On arrival, I found our barrack room buzzing with excitement. Our section had been ordered to stand by and make ready for service overseas, and the next day was spent checking and re-checking equipment, swapping leave stories and drinking endless cups of tea in the NAAFI canteen. Officers came to give us pep talks, others to lecture us on the evils and dangers of consorting with foreign women; but the high point of this busy period was the issue of regulation army gas masks: at long last I was able to be rid of my faithful old cardboard box, which by then was on its last legs.

The day before we were due to depart, fate stepped in and took a hand in things. The regimental sergeant major came in to the barrack room and enquired if there was anyone who could operate a typewriter. Hesitating, as I was mindful of my father's advice, I raised a tentative hand. No one else volunteered, so I was rushed off to his office where trays full of army bumf awaited attention. I must have made a fair job of things for, during the afternoon, I was taken out of the Line Section and installed as personnel clerk to the RSM. Naturally, I was disappointed at the thought of being parted from the lads with whom I had shared those first few weeks, but secretly it was a relief to know that at least for the time being I had escaped the possible danger of active service.

On the day my old section were due to leave, I obtained permission to see them off at the station. Allen, who had become a good friend, seemed to have a premonition of impending disaster, his last words to me as the train pulled out, being: 'Cheerio, mate, I doubt if we shall ever meet again, as I have a feeling about this trip.' Poor Allen, how right he was! For within a few weeks of their landing in France, the section was ambushed and nearly all of them were killed or taken prisoner. I never did get to know how he fared, but one thing was certain: had it not been for a quirk of fate, I could well have been one of the casualties.

I enjoyed my days in the RSM's office and was especially grateful for the exemption it gave me from guards and pickets, and all the other irksome duties which our young officers thought up to keep the men busy. In time, however, I was transferred to headquarters to join the orderly room staff where, under the watchful eye of Sergeant Pask, I settled down to make the best of the war.

Things were not going well across the Channel and although a strict censorship operated, there was a feeling that great events were soon to take place. Only now was the country beginning to realize that we had taken on a job for which we had been ill-equipped and, more importantly, ill-advised: the collapse of France brought the danger very close to home. In the camp you could feel the tension in the air.

Our first inkling that evacuation of our troops was under way was when volunteers were called for to drive a fleet of buses which had appeared on the parade ground overnight. Not wanting to be left out of things, I volunteered and soon found myself seated in the cab of a single decker. I viewed the next few hours with a certain amount of apprehension, but, after much crashing of gears and near misses along the narrow country roads, I managed to reach Harrogate station where, lying in a siding, a troop train packed to capacity was waiting. All through the night we ferried the new arrivals back to camp. I can see them now, unshaven, their faces drawn, some without boots, shirts or greatcoats, but still clinging to their rifles which, in spite of all the horrors they had endured, they had refused to part with. The experiences of the last few days had affected each man differently – one would be silent, another with forced gaiety striving to lift his comrades out of the pit of despair into which they had fallen – but one and all were greatly relieved to be back in England. Sitting in the barrack room we shared our cigarettes and listened as they told of how they had stood for hours waist-deep in the cold sea water on Dunkirk's beaches, waiting to be rescued. The vivid pictures they drew us made us realize how remote, so far, the war had been from us; and in a way it made us feel guilty. Helping where we could, we posted their hastily scribbled letters to loved ones who, no doubt, would be eagerly awaiting such news; but within a week, re-kitted and pride restored, they were sent on fourteen days' leave, after which they were returned to their respective units.

As in all organizations, we had our characters who stood out; and one of these was Albert Room. He was an old soldier, a sort of misfit really, who had been assigned to the company stores where his loosely defined duties gave him ample scope to pursue various unorthodox activities. The most important of these for him were his visits to Harrogate, which he made as frequently as possible, so that he could drown his sorrows in the local public houses. Unfortunately for Albert, we had to 'stand to' at dawn and dusk in full marching order, because of the invasion scare current at that time. On his return from his visits to Harrogate he was never in any fit state to cope; consequently he would be hastily helped into his kit and placed in the centre rank of the parade where we could keep an eye on him, this arrangement being vitally necessary as, due to the amount of liquor he had consumed, he was quite unable to stand unaided. As he swayed forward the man in front would gently ease him backwards, and as he continued his progress in that direction, the man in the rear rank propelled him forwards again: thus, from a vantage point at the end of the line, all that was visible was Albert gently swaying backwards and forwards, eyes closed and a blissful smile on his face. Our Adjutant Captain Watts was much amused, and occasionally drew the attention of his brother officers to Albert's efforts to keep upright.

Just as we were beginning to feel that we should be in Harrogate for the duration, orders came for us to vacate our cosy barracks and move to life under canvas in the wilds of North Yorkshire. Our destination proved to be a large country house, in peacetime the home of a retired admiral, which stood in its own grounds close to Gilling West. In tents scattered about, we made ourselves as comfortable as possible, while in the outbuildings the stores and company headquarters were set up. For a while I carried on my duties in the orderly room, sleeping at night in a bell tent with five other lads one of whom was a chap named Sunter – but more of him later. Then quite out of the blue I was promoted to lance corporal and put in charge of the regimental post office which had been set up in a wooden hut in the grounds. Again I seemed to have landed on

134

my feet and soon rigged up pleasant sleeping quarters in my new home, my duties being to collect and deliver the mail from Darlington in the Austin pick-up which had been allocated to me. Mail from home was spasmodic; news from Dumbleton filtered through in letters from Mumford, from one of which I learned that Kathy had left her finishing school and had returned to the village to help her father on the farm. On impulse I wrote to her, and eventually received a reply which, although noncommittal, did not close the door on our relationship. And with that glimmer of hope I had, for the moment, to be content.

For the next few months we sweated it out, waiting for the threatened invasion which never came. At night the German bombers passed overhead on their way north, the steady drone of their engines being heard long before and after they had flown over us – we were too minor a target to merit their attentions.

One evening I was summoned to the orderly room where the duty sergeant gave me instructions to proceed to Darlington to pick up two officers who were attending a party at a local hotel. As my postal truck was short of petrol, I was allocated a staff car and was soon proudly on my way, sitting at the wheel of a large Humber Estate waggon. Making what haste I could, but not getting a lot of help from the masked headlights which only threw a thin beam of light ahead of me, I finally reached the hotel, only to find that the two officers had left an hour or so before. Fortunately the hall porter had been informed that they had gone to attend a private party in a small village some miles away, the address and location of which he gave me. Off I went, having only a vague idea where the village was, and needless to say, I soon got lost. However, after extricating myself from numerous farm yards and dead end lanes, and nearly driving into a pond, I reached my destination, which turned out to be a large house standing in its own grounds and approached by a long tree-lined drive.

On the way up I managed to knock over three large flower tubs, and a statue of some Greek god who had, in my opinion, been placed too near the edge of the drive for his own good. The house was in complete darkness with not a sign of life to be seen, but feeling sure that my approach must have woken up the inhabitants if there were any, I plucked up courage and rapped loudly on the front door. Suddenly a light appeared in one of the upstairs rooms, followed soon after by the protesting squeak of a sash window being raised. A tousled head, thrust out, demanded to know what the hell all the noise was about. Surprised, I came to attention and explained that there was a flap on, and that all the officers had been recalled to camp. Down went the window and another light came on in an adjoining room. Silhouetted figures began to be seen, pulling on items of clothing; then the front door opened and two officers, hastily buttoning up their tunics, emerged. In the dimly lit hall behind them, I glimpsed two young ladies in night apparel, dressing gowns drawn around them.

'How the other half lives,' I thought; but, feeling the comment would probably not be in order, I kept quiet and respectfully held open the rear door of the car. Rapid farewells followed, and the two officers, by now very embarrassed, climbed in. Not a word was exchanged during the whole of the journey back, and on arrival at the camp they crept through the rear entrance of the mess, leaving me to park the staff car and return to bed.

The next day the transport officer sent for me. After putting a few questions, he told me I was to forget the whole incident; if asked, I was to say that I had not been out of camp that evening – this was easy to arrange, as no official transport docket had been issued for the journey. Later that day I was hauled before the company commander and again questioned, but I stuck rigidly to my story. I began to feel, though, that he already knew the truth of the matter, for when he dismissed me, he said: 'Thank you, corporal. Would you please return this gas mask and steel helmet to Lieutenant Riley? He appears to have left them on the back seat of the staff car.'

Luckily for me there was a twinkle in his eye as he said it, and he grinned broadly as I saluted and left. Subsequently both officers thanked me for my silence, and from then on I could do no wrong in their eyes – and I have a feeling that the orderly sergeant did well out of it also.

Our regimental sergeant major at that time was a man called Morton who, for reasons which he kept to himself, had never been known to smile. Rejoicing in the nickname of Laughing Boy, he was a strict disciplinarian, and his insistence that everything be done by the book made him far from popular. It therefore came as a no great surprise when late one night a signalman from one of the line sections went berserk with a loaded rifle and went charging around the camp yelling for his blood. There was total uproar: NCOs dashed from tent to tent shining their torches inside and scaring the hell out of the sleepy occupants, while officers, hurriedly roused from their beds, gathered in small knots uncertain what to do next. The sergeant major, whom some kindly soul had warned of the danger, had locked himself in his quarters where he stayed until the guard commander managed to corner and disarm the would-be assassin in the sergeant's mess and locked him up in the guard room. Mr Morton disappeared some days later, conveniently posted to another unit. As for the lad, he was court martialled and then discharged from the army, no doubt thankful that he was never called upon to pull the trigger.

This potentially serious incident was, however, soon over-shadowed by a real tragedy which, as I was personally involved, made a deep impression on me. I had volunteered to take part in a scratch football match, and a mate and I had set off to collect our kit from the sports tent, which was pitched some way away from headquarters in a small field. It was an overcast day with low clouds scudding across the sky, and as we walked I thought I heard the noise of a plane engine, although as yet no machine was visible. Quite suddenly a Halifax bomber appeared through the clouds, plunging earthwards. It kept on coming and hit the ground with a rending, tearing sound, not two hundred yards from us, sending bits flying into the air to drop on the fields around. Black smoke started to rise from the wreckage and we, momentarily stunned and unable to comprehend what we had just witnessed, found our senses again and dashed forward. But there was nothing we could do; the crew, thrown clear by the impact, lay spreadeagled, only too obviously dead. The pilot was still strapped to what remained of the cockpit; he was drooping over the side, his face ashen and his mouth open and shutting as though with his last breath he was trying to say something. I got to him and started tugging and pulling at the hot metal, trying to locate the safety harness which held him, but to no avail. Fortunately, several other men had arrived on the scene by this time, and the sergeant who was with them immediately took charge, order-ing me to get back. I obeyed, and having got over the initial shock of what I had been involved in, was unashamedly sick.

They worked frantically to free the trapped pilot, but soon realized there was little point; the safety harness around his middle had cut through him like a cheese wire and he was literally in two halves – in a few minutes he too was dead. Looking at those young lads lying dead in that Yorkshire field, the futility of it all suddenly struck me. A short while ago they had been alive, but now their war was over, casualties of a senseless exercise, their dependants never to know the horrific details of their last moments.

I watched as the bodies were gently raised and carried clear of the scene, to be laid down then and covered with blankets. Slowly I made my way back to camp; death, which had only been a word to me before, was real and present now, and I was numb with shock.

We sat around the mess table that evening in silence. Gone was the good-natured banter which usually marked these occasions; it was going to be a long time before we would be able to put to the back of our minds the deaths of those young airmen. However, as is the way of things, life eventually returned to normal and soon all traces of the incident were removed by the RAF salvage teams who came to clear up.

By now we had settled in to our life under canvas – that is, with the exception of our friend Sunter, or James the son of John as we called him. James was a regular soldier, known to everyone in the unit as company odd job man and scrounger, and in these capacities he was unexcelled. Small in stature, he had a lean and hungry look and was inclined to be a bit of a loner; however, he was a good mate and I supposed you could have called him a likeable rogue. Officially his job in life was headquarters runner, and the position gave him vast scope for his nefarious activities. Unobtainable items appeared miraculously on request and officers in search of those little extras which made life more tolerable, benefited from his accomplishments, turning a blind eye to the times when James would disappear from the camp for a few days, ostensibly to visit his home in Middlesbrough – most of us doubted if it had ever existed – to make sure that it had not suffered from the attentions of the Luftwaffe.

Now, James was very fond of his pint and could often be seen staggering the few miles between the camp and the village of

Gilling West, hands in pockets and swaying from side to side along the narrow country roads. One night, having enjoyed a convivial few hours at the pub, he was overtaken by the commanding officer in his staff car. Sensing that some form of recognition was called for, James stepped to the side of the road where, coming rigidly to attention and swaying like a leaf in the wind, he flung up a very precise salute. The centre of his balance thus disturbed, he fell backwards into the ditch which at the time was full of muddy water. The CO was highly amused and ordered his driver to stop the car and render what assistance he could. James, eventually rescued from the ditch and dripping with water, immediately assumed his best 'at attention' stance, and flung up another salute. This proved no more successful than the first, the effort causing him to fall backwards into the ditch for a second time. At which point the CO, deciding that events were best left to sort themselves out, drove off, leaving James, who by then had relapsed into silence, lying peacefully in his watery bed to sober up.

This little escapade was shortly followed by the mysterious disappearance of the four hens which the sergeants' mess had installed in a specially prepared pen to be fattened up for their Christmas meal. The area around was declared strictly out of bounds and no one below the rank of sergeant was every allowed to get near them, thus ensuring that the birds would arrive safely on the festive board. Bets were placed and James, seeing the opportunity to make some easy money, ran a book giving the odds of five to one against. On Christmas Eve, to everyone's amazement, they were still there, clucking away merrily, and completely unaware of their impending fate. Came the morning and in the half-light the pen stood empty. In the sergeants' mess pandemonium reigned. We were all paraded and questioned, and there followed dire threats as to what would happen if the culprit was not found. However, as no one seemed to be able to thrown any light on the matter, we were eventually dismissed. Now, whether James was involved or not I cannot say, although we all had a shrewd idea as to what had happened. Nothing was very proved, but it was rumoured that the officers dined rather well that day – while our friend suddenly disappeared on seven days' leave, smiling all the way to Darlington station.

About this time there was a call for volunteers for the

paratroops, and in a fit of enthusiasm I put my name forward. In retrospect it wasn't the best of decisions but, as they say, it seemed like a good idea at the time. Reporting to Leeds for a medical examination, I found myself standing stark naked in a dingy little room, to await the arrival of the examining officer. Much to my surprise, this turned out to be a young lady doctor, who prodded me all over without the slightest sign of embarrassment: by the detached way she carried out the examination, it was obvious she had seen it all before. Bending, standing, coughing and breathing in and out, I was subjected to the most rigorous tests, the final one being to stand on a chair and jump on and off. This continued for quite a time. However, at the end of it all, she told me that I had one weak ankle – a defect not calculated to help when having to land burdened with kit and equipment on some field or hard roadway.

So that was that, and I returned to my unit. But I was still determined to have a change of some sort or other, and at length, after turning the problem over in my mind, I asked to be regraded as a despatch rider. My request was promptly granted, and within a week I was posted to Catterick and assigned to No. 38 DR Training Squad, ruled over by a canny Scot named Cameron and his assistant, Lance Corporal Turnbull. I enjoyed the nine weeks of training, finding my pre-war motor cycling experience very handy. Sergeant Cameron was a hard master but an extremely good instructor, and under his guidance I soon learned how to handle the heavy BSA machines in all sorts of conditions. Our motto was 'One man one bike' – and this applied even when we found ourselves bogged down on the moors with wheels stuck in good Yorkshire mud.

There were incidents, of course, some funny and some not so funny – such as the day when, out on a training run, one of our squad nearly rode straight through the front door of a roadside cottage. Lined up in single file, bikes on their stands, we had been enjoying a ten minute break for a smoke, at the end of which the order was given to remount and 'Wind 'em up'. Now, it was common practice to lay our gauntlet gloves on the tank, these being the last items to be put on before moving off. One of the lads, responding to the order, engine duly revved, bike in gear and clutch held in, suddenly remembered his gloves. Letting go of the clutch he reached for them, whereupon he and his machine took off, heading straight across the cottage garden towards a dear old lady who was standing watching the proceedings from her front door. Confronted by a charging motor cycle with its rider desperately trying to regain control, she dived for cover, literally falling into the house and slamming the door as she did so. I don't think I have ever seen a lady of her age move so quickly. Meanwhile, rider and machine finished their brief career in an embarrassing heap in the middle of her flower garden. The rest of us enjoyed this hugely, but Sergeant Cameron was not so pleased and he only seemed to revive when, having rescued our unfortunate companion from the shrubbery, we moved off.

When I had completed the course, I was detailed to assist in training, soon finding out that this too had its pitfalls. One day I wanted to demonstrate to a squad of would-be Don Rs, the correct way to tackle a sticky patch of mud outside a farmyard. Arranging them in a semi-circle so that they could get a good view of my expert tackling of the situation, I mounted up and charged the mud, only to realize too late that the farmer had laid a pair of galvanized water pipes across the area: needless to say I hit them with my front wheel. Away went the bike in one direction, whilst I continued in ungainly flight, finally coming to rest face down in the mud. Picking myself up, I said: 'Now, that's the way NOT to do it'; however, my captive audience, determined to make the most of it, cheered loudly. A farm worker standing nearby joined in, shaking his head sadly; no doubt he was wondering what I intended to do for an encore.

It was now the early spring of 1942 and another move was in the offing. This time, quite unexpectedly, I was posted to an anti-aircraft battery in London where, after the peace and quiet of the countryside, I found it hard to adjust to nights without sleep and the almost continual wail of the sirens and drone of the enemy bombers. In the night sky the searchlights probed restlessly, lighting up the silver-grey barrage balloons which swung at their mooring cables, and catching infrequently the fugitive silhouette of a plane. Then the descending bombs would whine and strike their targets with an awful crunch. The sound caused me to dive for cover on many occasions, at the same time sending shivers up and down my spine. There was always a feeling of great relief when the all-clear sounded and we could relax. In the night sky a menacing red glow showed where the bombers had done their work and my thoughts would go out to the defenceless civilians who, come morning, would either be dead or return to find homes and ways of life gone for ever.

In the cold light of the new day men, women, and children wheeled their few possessions in prams and makeshift hand-carts through the littered streets. Slowly they came, their faces showing the strain of the previous night. They returned to homes which, if they were lucky, were untouched, but, more often than not to find them roofless and with shattered windows from which ragged curtains blew unhampered in the morning breeze. Picking their way through the rubble they searched for treasured possessions, their indomitable sense of humour and courage giving them the strength to face the new day. In the Dockland area most of Shandy Street had been razed to the ground. Lying on roof tops where they had been blown by bomb blast I saw the bodies of men, women and children; the survivors, numb and dry eyed, watching as the rescue teams gently lowered the corpses to the ground, and searched the ruins in the vain hope of finding anyone alive. On the sidewalk the pathetic remains, sheeted over to preserve some sort of dignity even in death, reminded one of the price that was being paid. I asked myself again and again then where God could be that he allowed this to happen. Had it been in vain that these same people had spent hours in His house, praying for peace on earth and goodwill towards all men? Had He deserted them in their hour of need? The silent ones would not now be interested in the answer even if one could be found.

Night after night similar scenes were enacted, and their aftermath, until it almost became an accepted way of life for the thousands of Londoners who were forced to remain. Their spirit was remarkable, but I wondered how much more of this they would be able to take. My own experience of it was not destined to last long, for the battery to which I had been attached was disbanded, and I was posted back to Catterick. In those more tranquil surrounding, the suffering which had been so vivid in London, blurred as memories do, but was never to be completely forgotten.

Back in barracks, I returned to a routine existence, filling the days awaiting posting with guard and picket duties and other boring details, visiting Sandy's Home in the came centre and paying occasional visits to nearby Darlington. At the camp theatre I listened to the music of Glen Miller and his band and sampled the tea on offer at innumerable church and NAAFI canteens, but whenever I could I visited Richmond where I spent many happy hours. Set high above a valley its cobbled streets, which for so long had brooded in silence, now echoed to the sound of army boots. The castle, watching over the severe stone houses which nestled beneath its walls, had no doubt seen many wars in its day and had long since learned to cope with the upheaval and disruption of its peaceful Yorkshire way of life. It provided a sanctuary where for a short while I could get away from barracks and sitting alone on its crumbling walls I spent hours drinking in the tranquillity of the scene below where, down in the valley with its river running through, high flying rooks complained noisily and timid water fowl went about their business, their world unaffected by war. Often I thought of Kathy, wondering when I should see her again, not realizing that in later years Richmond would play an important part in both our lives. But all that was to be in the future.

Leave periods came as a welcome relief and within a few weeks I found myself on Darlington station awaiting the arrival of the train and the long journey to Hereford. Seated in the carriage I wandered mentally back in time trying to get some sort of perspective and order into the events of the last few years. Things seemed to have happened so quickly, giving me very little time to adjust. Gone was the easy ordered way of civilian life; at present I was so regimented and ordered that I had almost ceased to be an individual. It was as if I was gradually becoming a part of a huge and not always well-oiled machine, which was sweeping me and my life irresistibly along with it. I thought of Yvette and that warm summer evening long ago, when she and I had shared those few intimate moments: I wondered where she was and how her war had gone. I thought of Hereford and the river flowing close under the walls of its ancient cathedral; but, as always, Dumbleton and the wooded heights of the Cotswolds were uppermost in my mind. A long buried quotation returned to the surface: 'To travel hopefully is a better thing than to arrive.' Up to then its full significance had escaped me, but now I realized just what it meant: the looking forward to leave spiced the days before departure, but on arrival I would only find that the little world I had left behind had changed, and would never be the same again.

Walking the streets of Hereford I sought out old friends and well-remembered places. Visiting the now empty camping site at the Butts Wall, I stood for a while to wonder where all the young lads had gone who had shared those carefree days. Some were no doubt serving in foreign lands, in the steamy jungles of the Far East, on the plains of India, on the high seas and in the air above. Others, less fortunate, lay buried in lonely graves in places which to them in years gone by had only been insignificant names on the coloured maps of the world which had hung in their school classrooms – but that was the way of war: death chose its partners at random and had no favourites.

My parents in their work at the local munitions factory, always seemed to be on different shifts and consequently I saw very little of them together. As for my brother, he was still serving with the Army Pay Corps and had got himself married, but our leaves rarely coincided. Things, however, did have their lighter side: Mother, in her patriotic enthusiasm, had given my collection of some two thousand matchbox tops, which had taken me years to collect, to the waste paper campaign, and the ten gallons of petrol which I had buried in cans at the top of the garden against emergencies, had gone to the milkman.

Tragedy had already reached out to the occupants of our little avenue. Across the way at No. 21, the curtains were drawn and the house was silent, their only son having been killed on his first operational flight over Germany. The event had cast a shadow over the whole area; neighbours, when asking after my health, tended to speak in whispers, and to enquire: 'How long have you got?' – a question which could be taken in many ways.

On the third day of my leave I decided to visit Dumbleton to see Mumford, and after a tiring and devious journey I reached Evesham only to find that the last six miles would have to be travelled on foot. Fortunately, after a few miles an army truck on its way to Winchcombe stopped and gave me a lift to the bottom of Nutmeadow.

The afternoon was warm and sultry and the fields to either side of the road were heavy with crops. In the distance a dog was barking, the sound seeming lost and insignificant in the blue haze which shimmered over the woods backing the village. Born on the still air the church clock announced the passing hour, its mellow tones bidding the inhabitants of the cottages which nestled around it to stir the pot and rattle the tea cups, the weather beaten tower which housed it, gazing impassively down the deserted street.

Lifting the latch of the gate to the cottage, I made my way round to the back. Poor old gate, it seemed so much smaller than it did when, as a boy, I had swung to and fro on its protesting hinges. Its white paintwork was now peeling and discoloured, but there, on the top rail, were the deep notches I had carved with boyish enthusiasm, marking as they did, the passing of time. The cottage door, unlatched and half open, swung inwards at my touch and, crossing the threshold, I stood for a while gazing at the familiar surroundings. The marble clock on the sideboard still ticked away the minutes, the same old iron kettle on the hob all ready for boiling and, under the window which looked out on the village street, the leather couch on which as a child I had been forced to sleep an hour away in the afternoons, still waited invitingly. On the mantelpiece above the fireplace the motley collection of china ornaments stood in brave array and, in pride of place as ever, Grandad and Mumford looked down from the silver photograph frame safe in their sepia world. Nothing seemed to have changed and fleetingly I was transported back to my boyhood, when I had sat dreaming in front of that fire while the flames flickered and danced their way up the dark chimney.

Then Mumford came in. She cried a little as I held her, so small and grey she hardly came up to my shoulder. However, after much fussing and discreet wiping of her eyes on her pinafore, she made the tea and we whiled away the hours until bedtime talking of the past and of the lads of the village who were now serving with the forces.

Beyond the soft lamplight in which we sat, the world had fallen apart, and Monty the cat, waiting patiently at the closed door, gazed up at the latch, waiting for it to be lifted so that he could go about his nocturnal business. At last, taking the lighted candle I made my way to the old familiar bedroom where, lying half asleep, I watched the shadows cast by the flickering flame waver and dance across the papered walls.

Behind the wire grilled doors of the old bookcase *King Solomon's Mines* and *The Sorrows of Satan* still stood secure in their musty covers, while in the dark unused chimney, bats fluttered, squeaking in their conversation before venturing out into the night. Reaching out I snuffed the candle and lay in the darkness, savouring the acrid smell as the wick cooled, until at last I fell asleep in surroundings which had been dear to me since childhood.

The next day, free to wander, I walked the village, pausing now and then to talk to old friends. Bill Wood the carrier, now beginning to stoop with age, shook my hand and wished me well. Charlie Staight the butcher, still larger than life, stood bedecked in striped apron and straw boater outside his shop; up at the dairy George Nurden and his son Charlie pumped my hand, enquiring what I was doing to win the war – a question which for the life of me I couldn't think how to answer.

On my way back from the dairy I stopped to lift the lid from the well to see if my old friend the frog was waiting to play the game we had indulged in so many years ago. But, alas! he was away on other business. Over the years, patiently sitting on that protruding brick, he had lost contact with our morning ritual. In the woodyard the old steam engine was still earning its keep. I lingered there for a while to watch the bright steel circular saw rip through the great tree trunks, the smell of fresh sawdust bringing back many happy memories. Then on to the churchyard where, sitting on the wall by the gate leading into the plantation, my mind roved back to the time when, as a grubby little youngster in short trousers, jersey, flat cap and hob-nailed boots, and with stockings down around my ankles, I had played my games of make-believe. So much seemed to have happened since then; the world had been turned upside down, scattering boyhood friends to far distant places. I began to feel lost and alone, causing me to search even more frantically for incidents from the past. It was as though I was trying to convince myself that all these things happened only yesterday, and that I should wake up to find that it had all been a dream.

And so I sat in the warm sunshine. On the face of the grey squat tower, the minute hand of the clock jerked away the passing minutes and in the wild grasses that bordered the neglected graves, bees droned lazily in the scented air. Suddenly I glimpsed a figure making its way towards me through the shady plantation. As yet unaware of my presence, she walked slowly under the old yew trees, dress swinging with her gait and large brimmed straw hat held tightly in one hand. Pausing she lightly brushed away the wisps of her dark hair from her face, and then came on again. Hardly daring to breathe I slipped down from the wall where I had been sitting and turned to face her. Suddenly she saw me; with outstretched arms she ran the last few steps between us, then for the first time in years I held her. There was so much I wanted to say but the words wouldn't come. However, there seemed no need of them as I gazed in admiration at the beauty that stood before me. She had blossomed into early womanhood, her open face and dark eyes still radiating the innocence she had possessed as a child, an enchanting creature to whom I lost my heart all over again.

Walking the old familiar footpaths we talked, always avoiding the inevitable question which I knew she was eager for me to ask, and so the hours passed and soon it was time for her to return home. Standing at the gateway to the farm, I had an uncomfortable awareness of business as yet unfinished. In the distance first rumblings of thunder gave warning of a storm gathering away to the west over the Malvern Hills and I knew it was time for me to leave. Kathy, as if reading my thoughts, raised her face to mine lips slightly parted, eyes dark and misty, and invited the one meaningful kiss of the day. Taking her in my arms I held her close, stroking the long dark tresses of her hair and struggling to say the few words which would have made all the difference, but none came. Reluctantly I let her go, the last I saw of her was when she turned and smiled before disappearing into the gloom of the farmyard. Slowly I walked away. Pausing at the turn of the lane I took one last look back, but she had gone and so for the time being was lost to me.

☆　☆　☆

Back in barracks, in the small room set aside for NCOs, I lay listening to the sounds of the men stirring in the hut beyond as they searched for socks, boots, and clothing discarded the night before and which lay scattered between bed spaces in untidy heaps. Others, outside, bleary-eyed and unshaven, were making their way towards the wash house, towels draped scarf-like around their necks, braces dangling from trouser tops and unlaced boots clomping up and down with every step. There would be little or no conversation between them, for, until the first sharp intake of smoke from the inevitable cigarette had been enjoyed, and the first mug of hot sweet tea had been drunk, the day, for them, had not yet begun. In the crowded wash room they jostled for space, plying their razors more by feel than sight as heads bobbed this way and that. Then, with mess tins clanging, they made their way around the perimeter of the parade ground for breakfast.

Soon after my return, my posting came through and I was not sorry to leave the routine of barrack life behind. I was sent north to join a divisional signal unit stationed in Walton, a small village some six miles from Morpeth in Northumberland. Here the army had taken over the large manor house together with several other smaller houses nearby which were to be used as stores and company offices. The village, standing as it did close to the border with Scotland, had no doubt seen many troubled times but now, in a war much larger and more devastating, it had somehow managed to remain rurally isolated, that is until we descended upon it. However the inhabitants seemed to take it all in their stride, making us welcome and involving us in many of their local activities. The vicar, an earnest young man, took on the job of padre and entertainment organizer, and it was he who was responsible for the arranging of several concerts in the village hall, one of which I shall never forget.

I was called upon to supervise the building of a stage. It was a makeshift, constructed of planks and trestles, and I must confess that on completion, I had grave doubts as to how much punishment it would take; however, keeping my fingers crossed and hoping for the best, I left things to fate. On the night of the concert the hall was packed with troops and villagers, officers and their guests occupying the front row of seats. The first act went down rather flat, a quartet of elderly ladies giving renditions of chamber music which, towards the end of their recital, provoked much shuffling of feet and murmured comments from the back rows. However, the disturbance was contained and the quartet retired to the side screens, the lady with the cello, judging by the look on her face, being very relieved to get the instrument from between her knees where it appeared to have been giving her a great deal of discomfort.

A female contralto came on next, and ended her zestful contribution with *Land of Hope and Glory* in which we all joined, accompanying her singing with foot stamping and clapping of hands. Taking this as a mark of appreciation, she immediately proceeded with an encore much to the consternation of the young man at the piano who, looking as though he had had enough, constantly wiped the sweat from his forehead with a handkerchief which he kept at the ready in his breast pocket. With the audience now thoroughly warmed up our well meaning young vicar stepped on to the stage to do his conjuring tricks. He meant well, but the lads, now beginning to get bored, were in no mood to appreciate the appearance of several coloured flags of all nations which he produced from his clerical attire. The various card tricks he undertook invariably went wrong at the critical moment but then came the high spot of his act. Producing a rather scruffy rabbit from a top hat he held it up saying 'And what shall I do with this then'. For a moment there was silence. Then several of the lads in the back row stood up to give him the answer, only to be hastily pulled down into their seats to the accompaniment of loud cheers. The vicar, taking several bows to acknowledge the applause, then turned and walked straight into one of the side screens which collapsed noisily.

The commanding officer by this time was beginning to fidget in his seat, no doubt dreading what would come next. In view of what had happened, he had need to be concerned. Out on to the makeshift stage came a troop of young maidens, not one of them under ten stones, who proceeded to give their interpretation of the Tiller Girls. My worst nightmares were about to be realized. The planks forming the stage were now being tested to destruction and bounced and wobbled on the trestles. Every time the girl at the end of the line performed her high kicks, the one she was on dipped, causing the other end to rise up. The inevitable result could not long be delayed: one of the supports, unable to bear the strain any longer, collapsed, and three girls disappeared up to their middles.

There was absolute pandemonium in the hall. At the back the lads cheered and clapped wildly, having no doubt in their

149

minds that this was the best act of the evening, while those in the front row dashed forward to give what assistance they could. Fortunately, no one was hurt physically, though there were probably a few dented egos. The commanding officer took it all rather well, I am glad to say, being able to see the funny side of it. So ended an entertainment which I feel sure the village would not forget for a long time.

Adjoining the driveway to the manor stood a row of terraced stone houses in one of which lived Annie, a dear old lady who would insist on inviting two or three of us to tea on Sundays. These visits were always rounded off with hymn singing which she accompanied on an old treddle harmonium – an instrument whose pure tones were somewhat handicapped by one partially collapsed bellow. But Annie was a well meaning soul and it gave her great delight when we loosened our collars and sang lustily until the teacups on the table fairly rattled. Many of our pairs of socks which required darning found their way to her, and if one of them had a larger than usual hole in the heel, she knitted a square of the appropriate size and sewed it over the offending part. I like to think that our visits brought a little gaiety into her life, and that somewhere in heaven there is a place for a little old lady with a wheezing harmonium and a flair for darning socks – for if ever there was a deserving case, she was it.

The manor house, largely used for billets, was said to be haunted by a phantom fiddler, the ghost of a previous owner of the house who, according to legend, was buried somewhere in the grounds. One Saturday night myself, the company sergeant major and the quartermaster, returning from an evening out in Newcastle, decided to stage a revival of the haunting. waking up one of the lads who was known to be fairly competent at playing the fiddle and who by chance happened to have his instrument with him, we doused him with flour taken from the cookhouse and sent him into the large hall where the lads were sleeping to do his stuff. The result was unbelievable – in the half light his ghostly appearance caused a near riot, half clad bodies fleeing in all directions, bumping into and falling over each other in their panic to escape. Some of them even got as far as the village street where, clad only in their long johns, they sought sanctuary in the guard room. The next morning the three of us where hauled before the CO and given a good dressing down, but we couldn't help notice the twinkle in the old man's eye as he delivered it. And so the ghost was laid to rest, hopefully for ever.

The days passed and our training and regimental duties continued. Our hopes began to rise: perhaps we had been forgotten, and would be spending the rest of the war in this pleasant little village? But it was not to be as, out of the blue, we were informed that our section was being posted back to Catterick to reform. Rumours were rife and a great deal of speculation was entered into; back in depot, however, we were kept far too busy to worry. All inoculations were brought up to date, visits were paid to the dental unit to have teeth checked, there were endless kit inspections and, lastly, any medical undesirables were weeded out, though thankfully there were few of these.

Eventually we were reorganized into a unit consisting of one line section, one wireless, and one despatch rider. A young officer was posted to us, a second lieutenant fresh from training, and we took to him right from the start, realizing that he would no doubt need our support. As a mark of our affection we nicknamed him Taddy; as it happened, he and I were to remain firm friends for many years after the war.

Our role as a DR Section was not at this time clearly defined, neither was our destination, the only information given being that motor cycles would be made available 'on the other side', so we spent the days brushing up our map reading, attending lectures and getting our stores and equipment organized. As we were now excused all duties, I found time to catch up with my correspondence, writing letters home, to Mumford and one to Kathy. Replies were not to be expected, as our forwarding address had not yet been made known to us: no doubt this would be given later when we were all well on our way to wherever we were bound for. Our letters were being censored now and I found it difficult to put on paper the things I so much wanted to say to Kathy. The result was probably more formal than I intended. It was not that any declaration of my true feelings would have been erased by the censor, but somehow writing under those conditions destroyed the mood for me.

One afternoon the trucks arrived. We were bundled in and taken to Darlington station where, once aboard the train, we

151

settled down for the journey, discussing amongst ourselves, as always, to which port in the UK we were heading. As it turned out, no one came near the target as, to our great surprise, we finally landed up at Huddersfield, from where we were transported to Kirkburton and installed in an old malt house standing in the main street.

On the second day after our arrival we were issued with tropical kit: this consisted of lightweight shirts and underwear, shorts, long khaki stockings and, last but not least, pith helmets. I can still remember the look on Taddy's face when he came to inspect us in our finery – it reminded me of the day in Harrogate when we had been issued with our first army uniforms. There were long shorts on short people, short shorts on long people; pith helmets too small on big heads and large ones too large on small heads. After a bit of swapping and adjusting and a few minor alterations, we didn't look too bad; but we were relieved when next day our pith helmets were taken from us and returned to the stores.

Our next move took us to a deserted anti-aircraft site high on the moors above the town. Here, much to our delight, we were issued with motor cycles, thus enabling us to spend the remaining days of our stay training in the surrounding countryside. In our off-duty periods we lazed about sunbathing and taking life easy, spending most of our free evenings in Huddersfield where, whenever the opportunity presented itself, we danced away the hours at the local Co-operative Hall.

During this period of comparative inactivity I managed to wangle a seventy-two hour leave pass and returned to Hereford. Naturally my parents were pleased to see me, as by then they had visualized me on the high seas bound for foreign parts; however they realized only too well that this was only a reprieve and that before long I should be on my way. It was an uncomfortable leave in a way, too short, and with my parents trying hard to steer the conversation away from any reference to what might be in store for me. It was like having to be on one's best behaviour all the time and I finally got away with a sense of relief.

It was late evening as I set off to walk the two miles to the station. At the end of the avenue I paused and looked back, just in time to see the lights in their bedroom extinguished. How long it would be before I saw them again was anyone's guess;

and it was with this thought in mind that I made my way through the darkened streets. The only person I met on the journey was a solitary policeman who stopped me and asked to see my leave pass. We chatted for a few minutes, then, after wishing me well, he disappeared into the night. In a way I was sorry to see him go. However, in a short while I reached the station where I was fortunate enough to share a compartment with a young sailor who was returning to Scotland to join his ship. With boots removed and kit stowed away on the rack above, I stretched out full length on the seat and slept for most of the journey, arriving at Huddersfield in the early hours of the morning. Here again the problem of transport awaited me and I was baffled to think how I was going to get back to our isolated camp on the moors. Luckily I managed to hire a taxi and arrived with only ten minutes to spare before my leave pass expired.

The days passed quickly but soon our peaceful lives were shattered, movement orders came, and before long we found ourselves once again on the station platform at Huddersfield. It was late evening, and darkness was falling when we eventually climbed aboard the troop train where, once settled and kit stored, we watched, with a certain amount of apprehension, the porters locking all the carriage doors, presumably to prevent any of us attempting to abscond during the night. Soon we were off and I, bundled into the luggage space between two carriages, snatched what sleep I could on a pile of kit bags, being occasionally wakened by some suffering fellow traveller who, unable to bear the strain any longer, climbed over me to visit the toilet.

The train rattled on, passing through dimly lit stations whose platforms, cold and deserted, showed not a vestige of life. It was clear that we were going north and a great deal of speculation was entered into as to our final destination, Liverpool and Glasgow being the favourites. Not until the following morning, however, was our port of embarkation revealed when, tired and hungry, we arrived at Greenock where we detrained and assembled on the quayside from where we were transported to a troop ship moored in the river.

# 5

*In which I cross the sea, get my first*
*taste of active service and lose a very*
*dear friend*

Straining at its anchor chains, the tall steel hull loomed above
me and looking up at the row upon row of portholes I could see
where the salt spray of many voyages had left long rust marks.
No time to paint and make her pretty now, I thought, for soon
she would be engaged on more urgent business. Pulling alongside we clambered up the narrow catwalk to an open steel door
which gave access to the lower decks where once again we were
checked for number, name, and unit, before being conducted
down steel gangways to the deck that was to be our temporary
home. Sitting on my kitbag, taking stock of things, I couldn't
help noticing that the only way out was by means of a wide
stairway at the top of which was a large hatch cover which
would undoubtedly be secured at night or on other unthink-
able occasions. However, there was no time to dwell on all the
possible eventualities. Left to our own devices we soon got
ourselves organized, grabbing floor space or alternatively
hammock space, the art of getting in and out of the latter being
demonstrated by members of the ship's crew.

For three days we lay at anchor, whiling away the time
playing cards on blankets spread out on the deck and exploring
as much of the ship as lay within bounds. In between times we
carried out boat drill and PT sessions, had our inoculation
records checked and attended lectures on the mess deck. Twice
a day the ferry passed under our bows and we rushed to the
rails to whistle at the girl passengers as they journeyed backwards and forwards to work, a pastime which provided a
tentative link with home.

It was on a dull evening in late October that our convoy

finally got under way, the first indication of our departure being the rattle of chains as the anchor was weighed and the steady throb of the ship's engines as we slowly nosed our way down river. For me it was the beginning of a great adventure and I felt a strange sense of elation as I stood and watched the now familiar shore line fade into the mist. Men crowded to the rails to gaze at the dark outline of the Scottish hills as they mingled with the gathering darkness. With hands in pockets and collars turned up they walked the deck conversing in low tones. Suddenly a rich tenor voice raised itself above the subdued conversation and the words of *Annie Laurie* drifted through the gloom, captivating each of us with its lilting air. One by one we took up the song until the whole deck became one great choir. How apt the words seemed at that moment;

> 'For the sake of Annie Laurie,
> I would lay me down and die.'

Probably I was not the only one who wondered how many of the men singing on that misty evening would be called upon to do just that in the coming months.

Morning found us off the coast of Northern Ireland where we got our first taste of the Atlantic swell. All that day we steamed close in, the gun crews taking the opportunity to test their equipment and ready themselves for any confrontation in the open sea beyond. Escorting corvettes and destroyers in their grey-green Atlantic camouflage patrolled the outer perimeters of the convoy like sheep dogs shepherding their flocks, and we found their presence comforting.

Day Two, and we woke to the pitch and roll of the open sea. Many of the troops had been seasick during the night, and as there was no escape to the latrines, and portholes and hatches had been made secure at dusk the previous evening, the stench was unbearable. The poor unfortunates in the hammocks, unable to move, had vomited on those sleeping on mattresses below. Within minutes of waking, I too had succumbed. I was staggering towards the steel stairway when, by lucky chance, the hatches were opened and I was able to make it to the latrines. There I stayed for the best part of four hours, unable and unwilling to move, and wishing with all my heart that a German U boat would come along and put an end to my agony.

Those four hours were the worst I can remember. Slowly I got my sea legs and was at last able to get up on deck where, finding a convenient coil of rope, I collapsed into a sitting position and buried my head in my hands. It seemed like ages afterwards that I was jerked out of my trance of self-pity by one of the Dutch crew members. He had sized up the situation and, taking from his pocket a wad of black chewing tobacco, he sliced off a lump which he forced between my teeth. I was so far gone by then that I couldn't have cared less, and accepted it with the same grace that I imagine a condemned man accepts his last breakfast before facing the gallows. It tasted awful, but strangely enough it seemed to do the trick as within half an hour the sickness left me. Breathing a silent prayer to that unknown sailor, I made my way back to D Deck and my still suffering companions where much to their envy they saw me able to enjoy the white bread and fresh butter that came with the meal. Once fed I returned to the open deck and, after a brisk walk and a few lungfuls of sea air, I began to feel more like a human being again – although I very much doubt if I looked like one.

That first time at sea was a great experience; it was truly awesome to stand on deck surrounded by nothing except the heaving Atlantic in its immensity. The convoy seemed to stretch for miles, but frequent signals flashed between the ships kept us in touch with our escort, and often resulted in a change of course. At their posts the gun crews, protected from the elements in duffle coats, gloves and balaclavas worn under their steel helmets, stood ready for action. And so, for better or worse, we steered further and further out to sea, followed at a discreet distance by one lone empty ship whose job it was in case of accidents to pick up any survivors – a comforting thought indeed.

Early one evening, just as dusk was falling, I was in the bows of the ship watching as it ploughed its way through the turbulent waters, my thoughts as always being on Dumbleton now so far away; suddenly, I felt a hand on my shoulder. Turning quickly, I saw to my amazement and delight, the grinning face of Badger Robinson. For a moment words failed me but, once having got over the shock we shook hands, hugged one another and danced around like a couple of schoolboys, much to the amusement of several members of the

Dutch crew working nearby. As is always the case in such situations, both of us started firing questions at each other and were incoherent for a time; but eventually I learned that he was accommodated two decks above me and that he was serving with the Royal Army Service Corps as a driver. Seeking cover under one of the lifeboats we spent the next hour or so swapping experiences, smoking endless Woodbines and reminiscing about the old days. He told me that on his last leave he had married a girl from Alderton a village just over the hill from Dumbleton, and from the photograph he showed me she looked a very attractive young lady. It occurred to me then that perhaps I should have carried a photograph of Kathy; however, Badger soon brought me back to reality, asking if I had heard from her and how things were between us. He seemed surprised at the diffident answers I gave, and finished up by giving me a good old roasting for dragging my feet in the matter, he having assumed that there must have been some understanding established between us by now. His news of Dumbleton was more up to date than mine, and I gathered that Kathy was still working on her father's farm, and was, as far as he knew, still unattached. This piece of news was a great relief to me, for had she taken up with someone else I don't think I could have borne it – though, properly speaking, I had no right to adopt such an attitude.

When he had gone, I stood for a while in the darkness remembering Dumbleton, around which our whole conversation had turned. I thought of its quiet street, deserted at this hour and only illuminated by chance beams of lamplight escaping from between half-drawn curtains; come the morning, it would wake unaware of the drama being enacted here on the lonely Atlantic. I thought of Kathy, picturing her asleep in the farmhouse, her dark hair spread across her pillow and the steady rise and fall of her breathing. Suddenly the distance between us lost its magnitude and I felt closer to her. Then the freshening wind hurled the salt spray in my face and the dream broke; chilled, I made my way back to D Deck where I settled down to face the long night ahead.

In the early morning of the sixth day we steamed through the Straits of Gibraltar and as many of us as could, crowded the decks to catch the first sight of the famous rock as it loomed out of the mists. Our convoy, now augmented by other ships which had apparently joined us during the night, stretched as far as the eye could see, while our escorts had been changed to units of the Mediterranean fleet in their grey and sand camouflage. Overhead, American planes kept watch, and diverted us with their weaving and low level flights. Looking closer at some of the newcomers, we could see that many of them were flying the Stars and Stipes, making it fairly obvious that whatever landing we were eventually to be involved in would be a joint effort. As yet we had no idea just where and when this would be, although the more knowledgeable amongst us were confident that North Africa was to be our destination.

Primed with anticipation and speculation we spent the waiting hours attending lectures, checking kit and equipment and, when we could, lazing on deck, and it was on one such afternoon that we experienced our baptism of fire. Lulled by the steady throb of the engines I lay watching the gossamer clouds drift slowly across the blue sky. All around groups of men chatted and played cards, while others, writing pads on knees, sat in the more secluded corners to pen their letters home. On the promenade deck above, the officers strolled around in ones and twos, pausing occasionally to lean on the ship's rails and stare into the distance. At their stations the gun crews searched the sky with binoculars, the muzzles of their guns pointing upwards in readiness; suddenly the peace of the afternoon was rudely disturbed as over the ship's tannoy system came orders for all hatches to be battened and all personnel, except those on duty, to take cover below. Klaxons sounded, decks were cleared, and we awaited our first air raid at sea.

The escorting fighters came at us out of the sun, with engines screaming; some of them passed so low over us that we could see the markings on their wing tips. The guns were already in action, hammering and juddering as they swung to follow the flight path of the attackers; while all around plumes of white water showed where bombs had fallen short or wide.

Then the fighter planes turned and came back, raking the decks with machine gun fire. With every nerve in my body stretched as taut as a violin string, I crouched in the shelter of a lifeboat wondering how in God's name I was going to reach the gun mounted on the forward deck, to which I had been detailed to act as standby. Judging the moment carefully, I raced across to join them, feeling a kind of fearful elation. It was all so unreal, an incident seemingly mushrooming from nowhere. However, I had no time to analyse the situation further, as I busied myself with my duties.

In the sky above, puffs of grey smoke showed where the gunners had ranged the bombers' progress. From the escorting corvettes and destroyers round after round was being pumped into the air, each salvo causing them to heel over until their decks were almost awash. Still the planes turned and came back again, the machine gun bullets ricocheting from steel coverings and throwing up splinters of wood from the decks: the air was thick with smoke and the smell of spent cordite. Away on our starboard side an American fighter with smoke pouring out behind it, hit the sea, bouncing across the surface like a rubber ball. I thought of the game we used to play called Ducks and Drakes when, with acquired skill, we used to skim flat stones across the surface of the pool at home. Then, at the end of its momentum the plane stood for a brief moment on its nose, before sliding below the surface, leaving no trace of aircraft or occupants.

I carried on mechanically at my station, the sweat now pouring from me, soaking my shirt and running down into my eyes till it almost blinded me; my throat was dry and scorched from the acrid fumes. Nearby, one of the gun crew staggered drunkenly, his hands covering his face to stop the flow of blood where a bullet had grazed his head; quickly the medics pulled him to shelter and attended to him.

Again the planes came. A young sailor attempting to reach safety was hit as he ran, the impact of the bullets stopping him dead in his tracks. He staggered a few steps, then collapsed and lay still. Almost without thinking I crawled over to him, but it was too late: he was beyond help. So I left him there, till the stretcher bearers should come round and place him beside other still forms.

By now the convoy had scattered, each ship being left to fight its own battle. In the confusion, orders continued to be rapped out by unseen commanders, and followed implicitly, while underfoot the empty shell cases rolled hither and thither with the tilt of the deck, before being rescued and stacked out of the way.

Then, just as suddenly as it had commenced, the raid ended,

almost as if someone had switched the whole thing off. The breeze blew and the clouds of smoke parted to reveal the chaos of those eventful few minutes. Away on our port side, a supply ship had been hit and was on fire, tongues of orange flame mixed with furious black smoke rising skywards like a funeral pyre. Around it small boats searched for survivors in the oil-covered water, and strong arms pulled the occasional man to safety. On our deck the cooling guns, now silent, still pointed upwards, their crews wiping the sweat from their faces and drinking the welcome mugs of hot tea, which had begun to arrive.

Sitting apart from the rest, I tried to piece together the horrors of those last few minutes, but somehow my confused mind couldn't make sense of it; its having happened so suddenly and unexpectedly made it seem like a bad dream. It was only when I looked around at the pock-marked cabin sides and battered decks that I began to take it in. My fingers were shaking as I delved for a cigarette in the pockets of my sweat-soaked shirt. Lighting up I sat back to enjoy the comforting taste of a ship's Woodbine, but I had hardly taken a few drags when an officer came along and detailed me to help in the clearing up; this was just as well as it took my mind off things.

With guns checked and fresh ammunition brought up in case our friends decided to pay us another visit, we relaxed. Casualties were taken below to the sick bay and slowly order was restored. Our convoy, now regrouped, steamed steadily towards the now gathering gloom and I was mightily glad when, tired and dirty, I was ordered below to rejoin my comrades on D Deck.

The next day being Sunday, we assembled for a church service on the forward deck where the padre, white surplice and hair blowing in the stiff breeze, lead us in prayer. We stood awkwardly shifting from one foot to the other while he entreated the Almighty to bless our efforts and ensure us victory. I remember thinking that it just didn't make sense; surely at that very moment the German priests would be making the same request: I didn't envy the task of him upstairs who would be faced with the job of sorting it all out.

In the fading light we sang the closing hymn, *The day thou gavest Lord is ended*, a hymn that brought back memories of quiet summer evenings in the church at Dumbleton where as a child

I had sat with Mumford and sung the same words, little realizing that one day I should be singing them again under very different circumstances and with a great deal more feeling.

☆ ☆ ☆

November 7th and last minute preparations, kit and arms were checked and endless instructions given on what and what not to do on landing. All through the long night we stood to, smoking endless cigarettes and swapping confidences with unknown faces under steel helmets. Photographs of wives and girl friends were passed around offering a brief glimpse of a world now seemingly far behind us. Officers and NCOs picked their way through checking men and equipment, stumbling over outstretched legs in the darkness. And so we waited for the new day and whatever it would bring.

At first light we heard the rattle of anchor chains and as the sun rose above the grey horizon we could make out the dark outlines of other ships floating motionless on the calm sea. Corvettes and destroyers weaved in and out, their signal lamps piercing the gloom with pinpoints of light as they flashed last minute instructions to the convoy captains. Back from the dark outline of the shore searchlights swept the sky to the left and right of the port of Algiers. The French troops there, caught up in a web of political intrigue, were debating whether to join us or to fight. Then, just before dawn, one by one the searchlights threw their beams upright in the sky – a signal that they would offer no resistance.

Away in the distance the dull boom of heavy naval guns indicated where the ships at sea had found it necessary to neutralize small pockets of resistance, the muzzle flashes of their guns being plainly visible in the semi darkness.

Dawn broke to reveal the flat sandy beaches of Surcouf, some fourteen miles east of Algiers. Now that the waiting was over the ship hummed with activity. Landing craft were lowered and scrambling nets flung over the side, by means of which the heavily laden troops descended to the boats below. Laughing and cursing they groped their way downwards, packs on back and rifles slung across shoulders, glad at last to be involved in some sort of action. Backwards and forwards between ship and shore the landing craft plied, depositing their human cargoes. Guns and heavy equipment were quickly manhandled clear of the beach by both British and American troops and tanks ploughed their way through the last few yards of low water to make their lumbering way inland. Beach masters shouted their instructions through loud hailers, marshalling small knots of men who had become detached from their units, endeavouring to keep the beaches clear for the follow up detachments who were now beginning to disembark. At last our turn came and I found myself scrambling down the nets to the waiting craft below. Secretly I had been dreading the moment the ship, heaving with the swell, swung the net backwards and forwards, while the pitching boat towards which I was making my way looked terribly small. Looking up at the steel hull above me, now slimy and slippery with sea spray, a feeling of nausea came over me. However, due no doubt to the excitement of the moment, the feeling soon passed and I made it to the boat safely where, clinging to the gunwales, I closed my eyes, said a silent prayer, kept my head down, and waited eagerly for the security of the now approaching beach.

Once ashore I stood on the hard sand wondering why the ground beneath my feet was not still moving. Ahead columns of men were making their way inland and we joined them in their upward march, soon getting clear of the activity below. After a further half hour or so of struggling on, a halt was called and thankfully we sank down for a short rest.

Slowly we got ourselves organized and nightfall found us comfortably billeted in a collection of holiday huts, a relic of more peaceful days which stood on a high promontory above the beach. The Americans, to whom we were attached, treated us at first with a certain amount of indifference, not being quite sure what to do with a bunch of limeys, who, devoid of transport, were regarded as something of a liability. But we helped where we could, moving stores and heaving vehicles out of the sand where they had become stuck. Characteristically, some of the British lads had already got a brew going and whenever we could we joined their unofficial councils of war, handing round our cigarettes and drinking Compo tea from enamel mugs which not long before had held shaving water.

For the next few days we lived a comparatively peaceful life,

162

scrounging rations from the nearby American units and gradually accustoming ourselves to our new surroundings and it was during this calm interval that my 'barbering' skills were exercised on every member of our small group. By sheer chance I had, before leaving England, come into possession of a pair of hair clippers which, having several teeth missing, had no doubt been discarded by their previous owner. With these I set to work, with the result that three or four lines of hairs were left sticking up like a hedge down the middle of every scalp. Taddy, unwilling to see his section paraded like Red Indians, ordered that the ridges be eliminated. My victims submitted and emerged with scalps duly shorn, looking for all the world like young hedgehogs. However, our haircuts proved to be most practical later when, beset with summer heat and flying sand, which penetrated eyes, ears, and clothing, we found it easier to keep clean and avoid the irritating sand rash from which many others suffered.

After two days we forsook our friendly beach huts and moved to Algiers airport where, to our surprise and delight, our motor cycles awaited us: now at last we felt we could carry out the job we had travelled so far to do. Attached to the Americans we operated between the various units, guiding convoys and escorting staff cars and their occupants between the various headquarters.

The American way of soldiering was to us a revelation. Officers frequently addressed their subordinates by their Christian names, and salutes between them resembled a wave of the hand, so unlike the rigid acknowledgement we gave them. Nevertheless, the abiding impression was of people who were kind in the extreme, being only too anxious to share their rations and the many extra goodies which appeared from tunic pockets on the slightest provocation. In their leisure hours they played cards and threw dice – both accomplishments being carried out with a great deal of noise – chewed vast amounts of gum, and strolled around with incredible nonchalance. I was reminded of extras in a Hollywood movie 'waiting to go on'; but they were a great bunch of lads, and I couldn't help but admire their attitude to life.

In Algiers, the reception accorded us by the French colonists and native population was predictably warm: they lined the streets waving and cheering, slapping us on the back, giving the inevitable V sign and generally treating us like conquering heroes. The Arabs, initially, were much cooler; if in time they mellowed, it was because they had cottoned on to the fact that rich pickings were to be had from the strangers in their midst and they would be wise to make the best of their opportunity. I felt sorry for them in a way; the French appeared to be exploiting them, and had fixed their standard of living at a very low scale. Their children were appealing in their poverty, scrambling for the chocolate and cigarettes thrown to them and generally behaving as children do all over the world, although it didn't do to leave anything portable lying around, as they were as nimble-fingered as their elders.

Algiers was a beautiful city with broad tree-lined streets and shining white buildings. Its magnificent post office looked more like a cathedral than a place of commerce; once inside, you felt that somewhere hidden from view there ought to be an altar with candles fluttering. Exploring the streets, I peered into the doorways of the more well-to-do houses where, in quiet courtyards, fountains played into limpid pools surrounded by palm trees and exotic flowers. How glaring was the contrast they made with those in the native quarter set high in the hills above – an area we rarely visited unless accompanied by an escort.

The harbour itself had escaped serious damage, the main casualties being two destroyers, the *Martin* and the *Broke*, the latter having been lost forcing the boom across the entrance. Idling by the docks, I watched the gangs of native labourers carry unbelievable loads from ship to quayside, each group being controlled by a foreman who would deliver a hefty kick to the backside of any flagging worker. They were an argumentative bunch and seemed to spend a great deal of time gesticulating and shouting at each other. At each instance of this their military overseers would charge to the spot and attempt to restore order, so they too were kept busily employed. On one occasion during unloading, a large crate slipped its securing ropes and crashed down on to the dockside, bursting open and scattering its contents around. At once all work came to an abrupt halt and dozens of Arabs, appearing from nowhere, dived in, gathering up what they could before the watching guards moved to intervene; in no time the whole consignment had disappeared from view. Then, as if nothing had happened, they resumed work. It reminded me of Ali Baba and his Forty Thieves; and I felt sure that this is where they must have received their training.

The city, rising above in tiers cut into the hillside, was a grand sight: the people, on closer view, left one astonished and amazed. The diverse forms of transport available were a tribute to their ingenuity. There were old single deck buses fuelled by a mixture of cheap native wine and other ingredients best left unmentioned, which chugged up and down leaving clouds of intoxicating smoke behind them; and cars and vans which, having no other means of propulsion, had been fitted with shafts and were being pulled along by sad-looking horses and mules. The buses, filled to capacity, took on extra human cargoes on the roof, where passengers were to be seen hugging chickens in wicker baskets, bundles of firewood, and other possessions as they clung on for dear life. The military traffic endeavouring to make its way through this melée only added to the confusion. At crossroads the American Military Police, affectionately known as 'snowdrops' because of the white helmets they wore, frantically tried to keep things moving, but no one could claim that their efforts were very effective. The native drivers seemed unable to comprehend their signals or commands, or perhaps they chose not to – whatever the truth, they went their own way regardless, the result of it all being traffic jams the like of which I had never seen before.

For the first few weeks we suffered from Montezuma's Revenge, a form of diarrhoea which, besides being very debilitating, resulted in us spending long periods in enforced isolation at the latrines which had been erected on a small hillock a short distance from our camp site. The frequency of our visits was such that we decided to form the seating accommodation into a circle. With an upturned box placed in the middle we sat for hours playing cards. It didn't do a lot for our egos, but it certainly saved many a weary trip backwards and forwards and afforded endless amusement for the natives, watching and wondering from a distance.

But the time soon came to move on. The main body had already commenced its long journey east towards Tunis and its ultimate rendezvous with the Eighth Army; we were to catch them up. Those were busy days for us as we accompanied convoys and guided straying transport back on course. On and on we pushed, passing through many small settlements set close

165

to the roadside, with the high ridges of the Maritime Atlas Mountains to our right, and the single track railway which ran from Algiers to Tunis. At night we slept where we could – inside trucks or beneath them – and ate our meals at the temporary cookhouses set up along the way. Water was rationed for both drinking and washing, as we were strictly forbidden to use the local supply. At first this created quite a problem, as none of us were able to keep as clean as we would have wished. However, we did very well for eggs, of which there seemed to be an inexhaustible supply, judging by the basketfuls that the native Arabs brought to us whenever we stopped.

It was during one of these temporary halts that I managed to catch up with Badger again. He had changed, he looked older than when we had last met on board ship; but for all that he still retained his sense of humour. I suppose it was inevitable under the circumstances – our youth was fast fading and we were now doing a man's job: overnight we had grown up. He had received several letters from home which he gave me to read, and I gathered that one or two of the older villagers had passed away, but otherwise life seemed to be going on much the same as usual. The Hall had been taken over and now housed Land Army girls, and some troops had been billeted in the surrounding areas. The most exciting news, though, was that his wife was expecting their first child; he was over the moon about this, so we could do no more than toast the expected arrival with mugs of tea.

Soon it was time to part and, shaking hands, we said the inevitable words, 'Take care of yourself.' He moved off, then turned and waved; the last I saw of him was when he climbed in the cab of his truck and drove away. Deep inside I had the feeling that I should never see him again, but I shrugged it off; probably talking about Dumbleton and the old days had made me a bit morbid, I thought.

The advance continued, as yet untroubled by any enemy air activity. In spite of this, I had only one night's decent sleep during those first days, and that was in a deserted villa, the former home of some well-to-do French colonist, I suppose, who must have fled to one of the larger towns for protection. It was strange to wander through the rooms. In a way it reminded me of the *Marie Celeste*: so much was left, it was almost as if the owners, suddenly deciding to go, had packed a few belonging and walked out of the front door. Upstairs we found a bedroom containing a large four poster bed complete with sheets and pillows and, unable to resist the temptation, we piled into it fully clothed, boots and all. The next morning we were rudely awakened by an irate British sergeant who, after giving us a good ticking off, admitted that he wished he had had a camera to record for posterity the sight of two unshaven, bleary-eyed despatch riders lying in magnificent splendour, with two pairs of muddy boots sticking out at the end of the bed.

Although we were now continually on the move, the journey was far from monotonous, as the countryside was ever changing and there was much to see. Whenever we stopped, groups of Arabs would show up, always with children in tow, to beg for cigarettes and sweets and any other items they could cadge – or, if all else failed, steal. For they were natural born thieves, and we did hear of one instance where a crew sleeping in a wireless truck had had their boots and socks taken in the night without the owners even being woken – quite an achievement considering that the lads were wearing them at the time. Children gathered by the roadside raised their pathetic rags to expose naked bodies beneath, chanting 'Shufty Cush' – which, roughly translated, means, 'Look what I've got.' We were also invited, in broken English, to sample the delights of elder sisters, with: 'Lovely sister, Johnny; jig a jig egg and chips,' the latter apparently weighing with them as powerfully as more fleshly pleasures. It was amazing how quickly they adapted themselves to marketing the only commodity they had to offer, and I can only assume that they had at some time been told that foreigners existed on a diet of egg and chips and young females.

And so we came to Constantine, a city set high in the mountains and approached via the Route de Steif, by means of a long arched bridge spanning a natural cleft in the rocks. The first sight of it, clustered around the heights of a deep horse-shoe shaped gorge, was breathtaking, and the more so when compared with the often squalid roadside settlements we had passed through. There was an air of prosperity about the place, the buildings clearly showing Moorish and French influence.

The convoy split at this point, part travelling on towards

167

Phillipeville, while the remainder prepared for a short stay in Constantine: fortunately, our section was included in the latter. Headquarters were set up in the Maison de L'Agriculture in the main square, and we were allocated temporary accommodation in the Ecole Voltaire, a large school not far away, in whose deserted classrooms we spread ourselves. However, before we could get settled in, our Don R Section was moved to a small garage in the Rue Pinget. We took over the workshops here, leaving the French owner and his wife and family still occupying the flat above. The arrangement seemed to work well, and we soon struck up a friendship due in no small way to the fact that they had two daughters with them, Alex and Charlotte. The girls spent a great deal of their time in our company perfecting their English, whilst we in turn endeavoured to master French. Alex was an attractive sixteen-year-old, while her younger sister was plainer and more of a tomboy. Their father, a reservist, had been called to the colours and was adjutant at the local French barracks. He used a little moped to travel the distance between home and his place of duty, and I well remember the trick we played on him one night, when we removed its engine: luckily he had a sense of humour, so no harm was done. His wife, Madame Crepin, was a plump cheerful woman who took us all under her wing, and even once, with the best of intentions, offered to make tea for us. Not realizing the niceties of that very important ritual, she poured a whole tin of tea into the pot, brought it down into the garage and, smiling benevolently, seemed to be waiting for our expressions of approval. Of course the resultant brew was quite undrinkable, and it was with great difficulty that we managed to take a few sips of the stuff, expressing our appreciation with broad grins and chants of 'Good! Good!'

Although they continued their own lives quite apart from us, we were occasionally invited to take a meal with them in their flat, these visits providing a welcome relief to our rough existence at that time. As we sat in the candle light round a table covered with a crisp white cloth, bottles of wine glinting, the war seemed a long way away. Alex acted as interpreter and we were able to learn a great deal about Constantine and the surrounding countryside. In return we told them of our lives in England and the homes and families we had left behind. Well primed with wine and nostalgia, we would then return to our

168

billet below, feeling more than a little homesick but nonetheless grateful for their kindness and hospitality.

Whenever she could, Alex came and sat with us. Looking at her, I kept being reminded of Kathy: she had the same dark shoulder length hair, the same youthful vitality, and had things been different there is no doubt that I could have fallen for her. However, Madame kept a close watch on things and made sure that no war-time romance developed. As it turned out, Alex and I were to keep in touch after the war, but that lay far in the future and a lot of water would pass under many bridges before then.

Between duties I found time to explore Constantine and on one of these excursions, quite by chance, I landed up in the souk or Arab market place which, although I did not know it then, was strictly out of bounds. I found it a fascinating place, crowded as it was with small workshops where various trades and skills were being carried on, and where groups of swarthy men from the hills sat cross-legged on the ground engaged in noisy barter. At first they viewed me with suspicion, but fortunately I was befriended by an old shoemaker who had at one time been a merchant seaman and spoke reasonable English. Sitting with him in the open window of his workshop, I spent many pleasant hours talking of England and hearing him speak of the ports that he had visited during his travels. He explained to me the customs and ways of his people and introduced me to many of them. Thereafter, whenever we met in the market place, they would acknowledge me with a slight bow of the head, and I knew that I could visit the old man in safety. Many of our lads, however, were not so fortunate; lured into the native quarters by the promise of drink and female company, and not realizing the strict codes by which these people lived, they got themselves into all sorts of trouble. Their usual fate was to be found by the patrols that went in search of them, lying drunk and incapable in some hovel, with most of their clothing missing. A few even paid for their folly with their lives, their bodies being discovered in the morning, dumped outside in the narrow streets with their throats cut. It was a dirty business, but in spite of the many casualties they never seemed to learn.

Of all the sights to be seen in Constantine, the suspension bridge spanning the Gorge du Rhumel was the most impressive. Named Le Pont Sidi M'Cid, the drop from its centre span to the floor of the gorge must have been all of eight hundred feet. In the late evening I often stood watching the eagles soaring below, while the setting sun sent velvety shadows creeping across the expanse of the great coastal plain, till finally they lost themselves in the high mountains behind.

Our war so far had been comparatively uneventful. As the days advanced, convoys of troops, British, American, and Free French, together with companies of native auxiliaries, passed through on their way eastwards, and all too soon orders came for us to join them. Reluctantly we said goodbye to Constantine and took our leave of Madame Crepin and her charming family. Addresses were exchanged and promises made to write when the war was over. My last picture of them as a family is of them standing outside the garage waving farewell. What became of them ultimately, I never knew. It is true I received a few letters from Alex, but these suddenly ceased just about the time that revolution was sweeping through Algeria in the postwar years. I applied to the French Embassy in London for help, but the only information they could give me was that Alex had been teaching in a small hill town, when all trace of her and her family had been lost. I often wonder what happened to them, and hope that by some miracle they survived. The sudden breaking off of our correspondence was very strange; I'm sure that had she been able to do so, Alex would have got in touch.

The coastal road to Tunis offered a never ending panorama, running as it did through deep scrub-covered gorges and over high wooded hills with their great spurs and crests of rock. Magnificent in its immensity and splendour, it protected us from enemy air strikes, only the occasional sniping from the hills by Arabs, seemingly using us for target practice, disturbed the serenity.

On reaching Bone, we were relieved of our convoy duties and spent a short while under canvas on the outskirts of the town. Here we had our first experience of organized army washing and delousing in the field, a great improvement on our usual methods of coping with our laundry in streams along the way. Stripped off, we bathed in a large communal canvas pool while our clothes passed through an intricate system which finally delivered them clean and deloused at the other end. In the afternoons we bathed in the sea, naked as the day we were born, endured continued kit and firearms inspections and overhauled our motor cycles, which by then were showing signs of wear and tear.

To our great delight, mail finally caught up with us and as always there was a mad scramble to open letters and parcels. Home-made cakes and other little luxuries which somehow had managed to survive the journey were shared and enjoyed, but the best of all were the letters, which were read endlessly, the more spicy bits being related to anyone who cared to listen. I received one from Mother in which she gave all the local news. It seemed both she and father were still working at the local munition works, although direct reference to this had been erased by the censor. My brother, now somewhere in the Middle East, had been commissioned in the field and they had heard from him recently. She mentioned some of my letters having reached them, so at least they knew that at the time of writing I was fit and well.

My greatest joy, however, were the rare letters from Kathy which I read over and over again. What I was searching for in them, however, was not to be found. Desperately I needed some sign from her that my enforced absence had strengthened the slender bond between us. It was not there in her words; however, I was grateful that she should write at all.

At Bone a curious incident occurred which made me realize just how small the world really is. Near to us there was a large mess tent which not only served the troops in the immediate neighbourhood, but also any visiting staff car drivers who happened to be passing through. Sitting at a table one day I caught part of a conversation taking place a few feet away. One of the speakers had a broad Wiltshire accent which I would have recognized anywhere, knowing that part well, I leaned forward and enquired what part of the county he came from. He was an elderly soldier who wore a row of First World War medal ribbons on his tunic. He told me he was from Devizes, so I moved to a vacant seat beside him and struck up a conversation. In the course of this I learned that his home was in Longcroft Avenue close to the grocery shop now owned by my uncle who apparently he knew well.

Suddenly he asked me what my father's Christian name was and on being told that it was Jack, he paused for a moment, then said: 'I'm going to tell you something, lad, which I feel you will find hard to believe. I knew both your parents before the First World War when I was an apprentice in a clothing shop in the Little Brittox in Devizes where your father worked. Your mother was employed in a haberdashery store across the street, and I used to take notes between them when they were courting.'

For a moment this link with my parents seemed incredible: that I should chance to meet him of all people in that vast country! But there it was, and for a long time we sat chatting about Devizes and my days there at school. In my next letter home I recounted my meeting with their dear old friend, hoping that it would revive many happy memories of their courting days. I never ran across him again, but I seem to remember that he wrote to my parents after the war.

From the signs of activity around, it was plain that we should soon be on the move again, but in the meantime we carried on with our normal duties, delivering despatches to outlying units, sometimes on our own and occasionally in pairs, where a greater risk seemed to be involved. During one of these runs a couple of incidents occurred which at the time I found very amusing. It had been a long hot day and, feeling the need for a break, I had pulled up at the side of the road and was stretched out on the grass verge smoking a cigarette. Just as I was getting settled, I saw in the distance an old Arab approaching. He was wearing a black dinner jacket and a battered bowler hat, while a rolled umbrella swung on his arm: had it not been for his baggy white trousers, he could well have been some City gent strolling down Bond Street at home.

He took his time on the road till, reaching a point some fifty yards from me, he suddenly stopped and stepped into the shade of a nearby tree. He then proceeded to divest himself of his clothing which, once removed, he placed carefully in a neat pile on the ground. By now fascinated by his performance, I half expected him to break into a sand dance – but no, the occasion was more basic than that. Crouching down he attended to the call of nature and, this done, he retraced his steps, resumed his strange attire and with the umbrella once more safely tucked under his arm, came on towards me.

As he drew level, I got to my feet and offered him a cigarette, having some idea of engaging him in conversation. He took it,

172

examined it carefully, lit it from the match which I held out to him, puffed away for a few seconds with obvious enjoyment at the luxury of an English cigarette, then, bowing his head, he continued on his way without a single word having passed between us! Such an encounter could have only happened in the wilds of North Africa; for the life of me I couldn't imagine someone going through that performance along some dusty road back in England.

My second amusing encounter came a little later on when, out of sheer curiosity, I stopped alongside an Arab family busily preparing a meal at the roadside. They greeted me with friendly gestures, and indicated that I was welcome to sit and join them. So, dismounting and propping my motor cycle on its stand, I walked over to where they were, admittedly feeling rather out of place but hesitating to offend. On a smoky wood fire they had placed an old oil drum which had been cut in half lengthwise, and bubbling away inside it was a sort of stew which had lumps of meat and other unrecognizable items floating about on the surface – a rare delicacy judging by the expectant expressions of the family crouching beside it. As I was the guest, they gave me to understand that I was to start the proceedings by having first choice of the contents of the pot. Dipping my fingers into the container, I fished around for something solid to hold on to; what it was I finally ate I shall never know – probably just as well, as I learned after that goat's meat and sheep's eyeballs were considered great delicacies. However, protocol having been observed the rest of the family joined in a grand free for all, which they accompanied with numerous belches of appreciation. When the meal was over, I passed my cigarettes round which seemed to please them greatly, as even the children took one and we all sat puffing away contentedly. After this, feeling that I could now leave without causing offence, I shook hands all round, mounted up and rode away. Thinking back on the incident I couldn't help feeling that the code by which these people live could well teach the western world a few things about hospitality. To give something when you have plenty of it is easy, but those poor people had shared what little they had with a complete stranger.

From Bone we moved on towards Souk Ahras, having been attached to a convoy which was slowly making its way across the Medjerda Mountains and down the valley of the Medjerda River. All around the large concentration of troops, tanks and artillery indicated a push towards Tunis and when, in late November, we found ourselves in Bedja, and within striking distance of the enemy, things began to hot up. In this forward sector, units tended to move rapidly, continually changing their locations so that the task of finding them to deliver despatches was made much more difficult: maps were provided, but more often than not we were feeling our way about by sheer instinct. Vehicles temporarily lost in the confusion had to be located and shepherded back to rejoin their respective convoys, the Americans being the worst offenders. They charged about firing at anything that vaguely looked like enemy transport – although this was not much in evidence as the Germans had now firmly entrenched themselves blocking the road to the coast. There was a none too polite saying going around to the effect that: 'When the German aircraft come over, the British duck; when the British come over the Germans duck; but when the Americans appear everybody ducks.' I thought this sentiment very unfair as the Americans certainly pulled their weight, and there were many occasions when we were mightily glad to have their fighters in the sky above us. However, just to be on the safe side, I always ducked.

It is strange how fate takes a hand in things from time to time; I could never have imagined the circumstances in which I was to meet up with Badger again. Returning to Bedja one day, I came upon a convoy which had halted along the road to Medjez-el-Bab. Chatting to the driver, I learned that there was one who came from Gloucestershire, and with this information I made my way along the line of trucks, hoping to enjoy a few minutes' conversation with a fellow Gloucesterite. Suddenly and without warning enemy aircraft decided to pay us a visit. They came out of nowhere, flying at almost ground level, and raked the convoy from end to end. What a few minutes before had been a peaceful halt turned into a chaotic scramble as men dived for cover under vehicles and in the scrub which bordered the roadway.

I too flung myself down into a nearby ditch where, with steel helmet pulled well over my head I lay hugging the ground and licking away the salty beads of sweat that had begun to drip from my forehead. Above and around spent bullets ricocheted

174

from the hard surface of the road to bury themselves in the soft earth of the bank behind me; from further down the column I could hear the frantic calls for stretcher bearers. Then they came again.

A few yards in front of me, a driver crawled out from underneath a truck where he had been sheltering and started to run to the cover of the ditch where I was lying. He never made it – a hail of bullets catching him in the open, he was spun half round. With head thrown back and hands clutching at his chest he staggered a few yards before collapsing on the road where, after a few convulsive twitches, he lay still.

I half rose to go to his aid, but I soon saw that he was past that now. Lying in the shelter of the ditch I watched as the blood seeped from under his body, staining the dirt around as it congealed into a dull red paste. So this was what it was all about, I thought, life's journey, ending in this God-forsaken spot. At least it had been quick, no suffering, no prolonged agony – little consolation to him whose war was now over. In those moments of my helplessness, my thoughts went back to Armistice Day services of long ago when, as a choir boy, I had stood under the shadow of the war memorial in St Nicholas churchyard singing:

'O God, our help in ages past,
Our hope for years to come.

remembering all too well the lines:

'Time, like an ever-rolling stream,
Bears all its sons away.'

How apt those words seemed at that moment, for surely the stream must now be in full flood.

Just as suddenly as it had begun the raid ended, and an eerie calm settled over the scene. Smoke from burning vehicles drifted across the road, and men began emerging from their places of safety, scanning the sky where the enemy planes were already lost to view. The work of assessment and rescue was quickly under way; the wounded were attended to and the few burnt out trucks were towed and manhandled to the side of the road where they were eventually left. Further down the

175

column an ammunition truck was on fire, its exploding cargo sending tracers of orange light into the lowering black smoke.

I retrieved the motor cycle I had so unceremoniously dumped when the raid started, and cautiously picked my way down the road. The fallen, now arranged in silent rows with blanket-covered faces, awaited identification, the searchers going quietly and efficiently about their business. Officers and NCOs passed me, issuing instructions and directing those vehicles which could be moved further down the road to be regrouped. I, having no part in this activity, slowly advanced, until I was confronted by a three ton truck which lay on its side partially blocking the road. It was clear what had happened: the driver, having lost control, the vehicle had careered up the bank and overturned, the poor fellow lay half in and half out of the cab.

I dismounted and hurried across to where he lay and, with the help of a passing officer, dragged him clear. We laid him on the verge at the roadside where, on my knees beside him, I opened his tunic and felt for any sign of life. But there was none; his eyes, open in death, stared sightlessly; gently I pulled the lids down.

All the time I had a chilling feeling that there was something familiar about that blood-covered face. But it was only a feeling, and it was not until the officer read out the name from the identification discs hung around the man's neck that the full horror of it struck home. '347862 Robertson': the words seemed to come to me from a distance until at last a name came. Oh God, not him! Not dear old scruffy Badger with whom I had shared my childhood and climbed trees in the plantation all those years ago in Dumbleton! But it was. Uncontrolled, the tears rolled down my cheeks and, burying my head in the still body, I cried like a child. How long I knelt there I cannot remember, but at last the officer, who had been standing beside me, took me by the shoulders and gently lifted me to my feet. He asked me if I knew the dead soldier, but there was no need for me to answer. Then realizing that there was little else he could do, he gripped my shoulder, turned and walked away, leaving me with my sorrow.

Poor old Badger, he had been there all those years ago when we had buried that tiny chaffinch in the mossy bank. It too had blood trickling from its beak, but there would be no mossy bank for him. He now lies, hopefully at peace, in the military cemetery at Medjez-el-Bab alongside his British and German comrades – just another casualty of war. Eventually one of his officers would write the usual letter of condolence and forward his few possessions. Future generations will read his name along with others, but they will never know from whence he came or the story of that tiny chaffinch. He rests now with other young men who died in rain-sodden fields and waterless deserts, and who had crossed wide oceans; boys who, knowing the secret of killing rabbits had been taught new and quicker ways of killing their fellow men – all too soon to learn that the dead, of whatever race, colour or creed, were all alike, for in death all men are equal.

Soon they came and, wrapping a blanket around him, bore him to where the other motionless figures lay. My thoughts went out to his wife and to the child he would never see, at least not this side of eternity. And to his parents who, even now, might be sitting in their tiny cottage at the top of School Lane in Dumbleton, reading and re-reading his last letters home, unaware of their loss. All too soon would come the knock on the door, the telegram, and the slowly dawning realization that he was lost to them for ever. I hope they buried his wife's photograph with him; at least he deserved that.

In silence I made my way through that scene of desolation. What a bloody waste it all was! How many more young lives would be sacrificed before the world realized the futility of it all? No wonder Christ on the cross had cried out: 'My God, my God, why hast Thou forsaken me?'

And so I rode back to Bedja. I shall never forget Badger and the sorrow of our last meeting. There would be others, no doubt, but none like that. From then on I seemed to age mentally. The strain had begun to tell; what up to now had been an exciting adventure had now taken on a more sinister aspect; the war games we had played during our training had become stark reality; and it was time to grow up.

8 December and down came the rain, turning everything into a sea of mud. There is something universal about mud; whether it be in the fields of England or there in the uplands of North Africa, it sticks to boots and clothing just the same and makes life just as unbearable. By now all transport was virtually immobilized as the grand push for Tunis which had

started so well slowed to a halt. After ten days of ceaseless fighting in the low hills east of the Medjerda River, along the Terbourba Road and in the high ground above the Sidi Nair valley, the Allied armies had been forced back, and dug in. Many times we attempted runs to outlying units, but our task became hopeless and, defeated by the rain and mud, we were obliged to resign ourselves to our uncomfortable situation. The shelling from enemy mortars was very heavy. The British 25 pounders, American 105s and French 75s replied with everything they had got, pounding the German armour which was attempting to thrust its way through from Djedida and Massicault. The Americans, their tanks bogged down and unable to manoeuvre, lost heavily, but in spite of everything that could be thrown at them they held their ground. Eventually, the impetus of the enemy advance was sapped by the same appalling conditions, and they decided to call it a day. And so, for the time being, the race for Tunis was halted.

Sitting under an overhanging rock wrapped in a groundsheet I celebrated my birthday, or perhaps it would be truer to say, I remembered it. An American soldier who happened to be passing, stopped and joined me in my temporary shelter, and for a while we sat chatting and trying to light damp cigarettes with equally damp boxes of matches. Abandoning the attempt we gave ourselves up to watching other unfortunates sloshing through the mud. There was little else we could do, as the rain lashing down penetrated even the best of shelters, and clothing was worn for the most part until it dried, only to become wet again: a most miserable time and best forgotten. Christmas came and went, the only signs of the day's significance being the extra rations and mail which by some miracle had found its way to us. And so, whiling away the time brewing tea and keeping as dry as we could, we wished each other a Merry Christmas without giving much feeling to the words.

The history of the final stages of the campaign has been far better recorded by others. January and February passed and the Axis armies, now beaten and in retreat, were beginning to surrender in their thousands. During the last hours of their resistance I found myself on the outskirts of Tunis, where an uneasy calm had settled over the area. German armour and transport, abandoned in flight, littered the roadways. In a nearby house, a half track had been caught by our artillery and blown through the front wall, bringing the roof crashing down on it.

Strangely enough, a moment of humour stands out for me amid the devastation. Rounding the corner of a street I came upon a small Arab boy waving a Union Jack and wearing an Arsenal football jersey which reached almost down to his knees. Grinning all over his face he gave me the V sign; and just at that moment I wished I had had a camera to record the incident. However, I suspect that somewhere he must have had a German flag all ready, just in case.

In an adjoining road one of our tanks careered through a row of small houses bringing them crashing down. Clouds of gritty dust rose in the air and a bewildered and terrified group of Arabs, caught up in the turmoil and unable to escape, crouched down behind a low wall, their few possessions scattered about them.

We were billeted in a small village some five miles to the west of Tunis, our detachment having taken over a villa which stood back from the road. The weather had now changed for the better, and we were glad to see the back of the rain which had plagued us for so long. The sun came out and dried up the roads, enabling us at last to visit many of the units in the surrounding countryside to check on our small signal detachments. And it was on one of these trips that Taddy and I became involved in the incident of the mule.

It was a pitch dark night and the roads, although fairly passable, still had to be negotiated with caution. Our feeble masked headlights were of very little use and we literally had to feel our way towards the seaside town of La Calle, Taddy riding some fifty yards ahead whilst I, in the rear, kept a wary eye on the flickering glow of his tail light. Suddenly there was an almighty crash, sparks flew from the metalled surface of the road, then all went quiet. Pulling my machine on to its stand, I raced forward to find his motor cycle lying on its side, its engine still running but no sign of its rider. Hastily shutting off the engine I stood in the darkness calling out his name. At that moment I heard sounds of movement from the ditch at the roadside and there to my astonishment I found him crawling on hands and knees looking for his glasses: these had fallen off and without them he would have great difficulty in navigating.

After a prolonged search we finally located them and Taddy, extracting himself from the ditch to which by now he seemed to have become quite attached, regained his composure and helped drag his crashed machine to the side of the road.

Searching more by feel and touch than anything else, we tried to ascertain the extent of the damage. Suddenly I heard a movement ahead and creeping forward I found a mule making frantic efforts to get to its feet. Examining the poor animal as best I could by the faint beam from the headlight of my machine, I found that both of its front legs appeared to have been broken. Pitifully it struggled to rise but without success and I knew that there was only one thing to do. Reaching for my service revolver I checked the chambers and was just about to put an end to the mule's misery when Taddy stopped me. I explained that it was the most humane thing to do in the circumstances but he would have none of it and so, he being the officer, he finally won the day. With a great deal of heaving and lifting we at last managed to get the stricken animal to the side of the road and there we left it. I doubt whether it survived for long, however, as a few miles further on a French convoy passed us coming from the direction of the incident; most certainly the mule's untimely end came under the wheels of the leading heavy vehicle.

Fortunately, the damage to Taddy's machine had been superficial, and after straightening out a bent footrest and repairing the clutch and brake levers, we continued on our way towards Bizerta. Here we came upon another obstacle in the shape of a deep ravine, the bridge over which had been demolished by the retreating Germans. Our engineers had carried out a temporary repair by laying supports and planks across the damaged section, but it was obvious that this had been done more with four-wheeled vehicles in mind, as down the centre there was an ominous gap through which the dry river bed some twenty feet below, could clearly be seen.

I knew that the longer I thought about it, the less likely I should be to attempt the crossing; so, revving up, I started off, keeping my eyes fixed firmly on the far bank and not daring to look either to right or left. All went well until I reached the centre section; then I felt the planks under me begin to joggle violently, and the sweat pouring from my forehead was blinding my eyes. But there was no help for it, having got so far there

180

was only one way to go. So, gritting my teeth, I rode slowly on, and was greatly relieved when I finally made the far end where, turning around, I waited for Taddy to join me. After several false starts he finally won through, although I must admit that there were moments when I feared he wouldn't make it. About half way he seemed to lose concentration and his machine wobbled alarmingly; however, to his credit he kept going and at last drew up alongside me. Grinning all over his face, he admitted that that was the one ride he hoped he would never have to do again – a sentiment with which I heartily agreed.

Pressing on we soon reached the outskirts of Bizerta, or at least what was left of it: Allied bombers had almost razed it to the ground and the harbour, littered with sunken ships, stank with the smell of dust and death. Our destination was the American tactical headquarters on the far shore and, searching around, we found the only way across was by means of a hastily improvised ferry. On this craft we duly installed ourselves, complete with motor cycles, and slowly set off. There was an American major on the ferry with us, and during the journey I managed to flog him my heavy storm coat. Taddy viewed the transaction with a certain amount of incredulity, but on being assured that the coat was not lost but only borrowed, he relaxed, waiting to see what I had in mind.

Reaching the far side we disembarked and I followed the major to one of the huts. He went in, hanging the coat as he did so, on a peg just inside the doorway. I waited until he had disappeared into an inner office, then walked boldly in and retrieved it. I was making my way back when two American officers passed me and I felt sure that they were going to ask me what the hell I was up to; however, slinging them up a very precise salute, I continued on my way unchallenged. Rejoining Taddy, I stuffed the coat into one of the back panniers, then we mounted up and rode off at speed, thus completing a very successful deal.

We arrived back at our billet to find, to our joy, that the mail had caught up with us. I had received two letters, one from home and the other from Dumbleton. Mother, in hers, sounded very war-weary, and reading between the lines, I sensed that the strain of shift work was beginning to tell. The censor in his wisdom had erased several references to air raids but, not having been too heavy with his pencil, I was able to gather that there had been a few scares in her part of the country.

However, it was the contents of Mumford's letter that were far more shattering. Wisely or unwisely, she had saved what was for me the most important news until the end, and it was with a sinking heart that I read that Kathy was to be married. At first the words didn't register, and when they did I didn't want to believe it. Kathy to be married! It didn't seem possible; all my dreams were rudely shattered. It was a cruel blow delivered at the wrong time and in the wrong place. I felt a sense of anger that she should have left me to find out through Mumford's letter.

How far and for how long I walked that day I cannot remember, but it must have been obvious to Taddy that something was wrong for, taking me to one side, he asked if there was anything I would like to talk over with him. On impulse I drew out the letter and gave it to him to read. Good old Taddy, he handled the situation with great tact and, having shared my misery, I began to feel better. After all, there was very little I could do about it as, due to the long delay in our mail deliveries, she was probably already married. Too late I realized what a fool I had been. It had been a mistake on my part to assume that I had any claim on her; in all fairness she had never encouraged me in that belief. Mercifully, as the days and weeks passed the hurt became less and less, leaving in its place a dull ache of unhappiness.

Life for our section had become hectic, and long runs with despatches meant nights and days in the saddle, leaving little time for remorse. Prisoners came in droves to be accommodated in hastily prepared compounds. The Italians with their 'Me no fascist Johnny' (and then they would spit) almost convinced me that Mussolini must be the most unpopular bloke in Italy; on the other hand the Germans, proud and arrogant, seemed to dislike their allies more than we did. In spite of this, I couldn't help admiring them, for whatever they might or might not have been, one thing was certain, they were good soldiers and very proud of their race and country.

Many of the Italians were eventually released to serve in the camps; one of them, a middle-aged corporal named Giovanni, was allocated to our section. Soft in speech and ways, he was an excellent mechanic and we found him very useful to have around. Often when off duty he would sit with a dreamy far-away look in his eyes. He liked to speak of his life before the war, and eagerly presented for our inspection photographs of his wife and family of whom he was immensely proud. He had a beautiful tenor voice and in the evenings, sitting around in the billets, he sang songs of Naples and the blue waters of the Mediterranean, the feeling he put into them plainly showing on his face. Listening to him, I couldn't help but hope that one day he would be safely restored to the bosom of the family he so dearly loved. For myself, I felt sure of one thing: if I ever managed to get to heaven, the first thing I should wish to hear would be his golden voice rising above all others; then, as friends and enemies no longer we could sit in peace.

# 6

*Sees the end of my army career
and my return to civilian life
where I take up a new challenge*

The campaign had ended and life settled down to a familiar routine. Units were being split up in preparation for the impending invasion of Italy, and our journeys became longer and longer as, uninterrupted, we worked the links between Tunis and Algiers. Taddy and I did our rounds to outlying detachments and very little occurred to disturb the tranquillity of our existence.

One day, requiring the services of a dentist to see to a filling which had come out, I set off alone to locate a mobile dentist unit which was some forty miles away in the direction of Mateur. It was midday when I finally found it, a tented encampment tucked away in the foothills. I searched around for a while till I came across what I assumed to be the surgery, where a most unco-operative corporal sat busily finishing his meal, at the same time managing to smoke a fat cigar. Grudgingly, he took details of my name, rank and unit, entering the details on a rather tea-stained army form; then I was ushered into an inner sanctum and left seated in a rather battered dental chair alongside which stood an old treddle drilling machine. Looking around I cannot say the set-up gave me any confidence, and I had just resolved to make my escape when the tent flap was pulled aside and a Canadian officer entered, reeking of whisky and far from steady on his legs. Coming over to me, he examined the offending tooth and, without saying a word, commenced operations. I will not dwell on the agonies that followed; suffice it to say the smell of his breath as he leaned over me acted as an anaesthetic, while his variable pressure on the treddle, caused the drill to be at full speed one minute and at full stop the next. However, the treatment was finally completed and I staggered out into the fresh air, leaving the officer slumped in the chair, no doubt to reach for the whisky bottle as soon as my back was turned. Strange to relate the filling lasted for years, far outstaying the others I had done later with more modern equipment; perhaps if he had been sober he would not have made such a good job of it.

On my return I found a letter from Kathy waiting for me, and it was with mixed feelings that I took it up, for I must confess that my first impulse on recognizing the handwriting was to destroy it unopened. It was a sweet letter, direct and to the point, and I could well imagine the heartache it must have caused her to write it. For the first time I realized that her feelings for me went far deeper than I had hoped. Now I could see plainly how I had mismanaged the whole affair, for she intimated to me that, had I been more forward in my courtship of her, matters might have been very different. She told me about her husband; I gathered that they had met while he was stationed near Cheltenham and that they had married at the registry office there. Even so, I sensed that things were not quite right with her. I knew Kathy, and hers was not the letter of a radiant bride in the first flush of marriage; something was wrong. However, on reflection I thought that perhaps I was reading more into it than was necessary.

She concluded with the wish that perhaps we should all meet again when the war was over, but that in the meantime I was to take good care of myself. So for the moment that was that, and in due course I replied, offering my congratulations and saying that I looked forward to meeting them both. The words and sentiments came hard, for if I had written from my heart it would have been a very different letter.

It was now high summer with us and the heat was at first unbearable, but we soon adjusted to it. Taddy, having business in Tunis, took me along and, as we were to be there for a few days, we contacted the local billeting officer. He arranged for Taddy to stay in a local hotel which had miraculously escaped damage, and which had been taken over by the military, while I was given the choice of either the transit camp or civilian billets. Without hesitation I chose the latter and, with Taddy in attendance to act as interpreter, we made our way to what eventually turned out to be a large block of flats some two miles outside the city. A young French woman answered the door with whom Taddy entered into negotiations, with me standing by, unable to understand. The arrangements were soon completed and he left, promising to return the next day with my rations and any extras he could lay his hands on. When he had gone, Madame busied herself preparing a meal of sorts from her meagre stock; and it was a pleasant change for me to be able to enjoy a taste of home cooking for a while.

After we had eaten, we sat talking for I was relieved to find that she could speak English – not perfectly, but sufficiently well to enable us to carry on a reasonable conversation. Her name was Odette and her husband, a member of the Free French forces, was a prisoner-of-war in Italy. It appeared that she had been educated at a convent in France; after her marriage, she and her husband had emigrated to North Africa to start a new life together, but then the war had come and he had left to join up.

She was very easy to talk to and, as the evening wore on any reserve or awkwardness I may have felt initially disappeared; and before long I found myself telling her about Kathy and my life in England. The conversation drew us closer together; I suppose it was finding a sympathetic listener in her that made me confide in her as I did, and no doubt it was the same for her. However this may be, it was soon time for us to retire and, bidding each other good night, we made our way to our separate rooms.

The night was hot and humid and for a long time I lay tossing and turning, unable to sleep. All was quiet, only the steady ticking of a clock on the landing breaking the silence. It was then, in the darkness, that she came to me. Without a word she lay down beside me, her soft breathing being the only indication of her presence. Reaching out she gave herself to me without restraint, and all through the long hours of that unforgettable night we lay in each other's arms, two lonely people caught up in a war which at the moment seemed very far away. Dawn broke and the sun had just begun to chase away the night shadows when she left in the same silent way she had come. I felt no guilt for what had happened, only a deep feeling of peace and a sense of belonging to someone who, if only for that brief moment, had cared and shared my

186

loneliness.

For three days and nights we held on to each other, dreading the moment of parting – which came all too soon. Standing in the doorway, she did not want to let me go. In other circumstances I would have promised to keep in touch; however I realized that it was far better that we go our separate ways and treasure the memory of the few stolen hours we had shared. And so, without even looking back, I descended the stairs to the courtyard below where Taddy was waiting.

Before returning to our unit we decided to take a short detour to visit Carthage; it seemed a pity to miss it as we were so near. Before long we found ourselves standing on the heights above the bay where, resting for a while we sat to take in the beauty of the scene below. As far as the eye could see the blue waters of the Mediterranean rested gently in the summer heat, topped here and there with white breakers where it lapped the shore. Nestling in the curve of the bay lay the ancient city with its tumbled columns and scattered stone work. Like a magnet it drew us as slowly we made our way down winding paths through the olive groves until at last we reached the shore. All was still, the hot sun, beating down, sent heat shimmers dancing across the dry earth. As I stood there, captivated by its atmosphere, I tried to visualize what it must have looked like in its heyday. In my imagination I could almost see and hear the bustling crowds, the street traders going about their business and the groups of chatting soldiers of another age, wandering by examining the goods displayed on the many stalls that lined the streets. Hannibal would have known this harbour and, as a young man he would have trodden the same paths, stopping no doubt to watch the comings and goings of merchant ships, which had sailed to and from the far corners of the then known world and their dark skinned crews busy with loading and unloading. But it was silent now, its age of glory long since gone; now only the breeze playing amongst the ruined stonework disturbed the silence that wrapped itself around the ancient columns lining the weed strewn sidewalks. The Romans too would have known it; leaving their mark they too had disappeared into the mists of history and I couldn't help but wonder if, with the passing of time, we should leave such treasures to be enjoyed by future generations. Somehow I doubted it as at the moment we were far too busy destroying the future, such being the stupidity of man, his course destined to be shaped by his failings until the end of time.

Regretfully we made our way back into the present. The days passed quickly and in November, much to my surprise, I was recommended to attend a selection board with a view to taking a commission. This was Taddy's doing and I must admit that, at first, I didn't take too kindly to the idea, preferring to stay with the lads I had been with for so long. However, I decided at least to give it a try; and so, after saying my farewells, I left to report to the board, which was located in a small village to the east of Tunis.

I spent three interesting and exacting days there. The examining officers, notebooks in hand, put us through our paces and our every move was duly recorded and scrutinized. A harder test, though, was the final interview with the commanding officer, who questioned me at some length as to my suitability to hold a King's Commission. I cannot remember how I managed to persuade him that my mathematics were up to the standard required, but he seemed convinced and, contrary to common belief, failed to ask if my father rode to hounds or was a member of any fashionable club in London. I left the interview room being far from sure that I had done enough to impress him, but I consoled myself with the thought that the worst that could happen would be to be returned to my unit if I failed. At long last the results were pinned up on the notice boards. There were two columns, one headed 'Suitable for onward transmission to the UK for Officer Training' and the other 'To be returned to unit'. Eagerly I scanned the former and there, on the very last line, was my name and number. So that was that, and I prepared myself for the long journey back to England.

The trip back to Algiers by rail was unquestionably quite an adventure in itself. Accommodated in box cars originally designed to hold horses, we sat back to enjoy the ride. The native crew never seemed pushed for time; occasionally they would stop the train to gather firewood to stoke the boiler, the engine itself needing to be coaxed up every incline and frantically held in check down every decline, seemingly having made up its mind to commit suicide at the bottom.

One waggon was kept free to serve as a cookhouse and on the way we managed to set fire to it. I should explain that we were equipped with our Bengazi stove, an empty oil drum part filled with sand soaked in petrol into which wood was added. In order to get it going, we held it outside the waggon so that the breeze would fan it into a blaze; and one morning, having done this, we stood it on the floor of the waggon, forgetting that the bottom half was by then nearly red hot. Before long the boards were well alight and the flames spread quickly.

The train shuddered to a halt, and out jumped the crew to run up and down shouting and gesticulating. Then, deciding that the whole thing was about to blow up, they withdrew from the scene and hid in the bushes. Fortunately the truck was at the end of the train, so that we were able to unhitch it and manhandle it off the track, where we left it to burn itself out. Then we rounded up the crew and went on again.

The first stop of any duration was at El-Khrob. Temporary halts along the way had, however, been not infrequent, usually depending on the whims of the engine driver and fireman, as, once they had decided to stop the train, no amount of coaxing, or worse, would induce them to move until they were ready. If an argument broke out between them, as it often did, they would leap down and carry on the dispute at the side of the track, where more often than not they would come to blows. Attending to natural functions took at least half an hour on each occasion. All this was very frustrating for the officer in charge, who would pace up and down muttering threats – though he had no intention of carrying these out, for I firmly believe that if he had upset them, they would have disappeared into the blue and left us to it.

Arriving at El-Khrob hot and dusty, we were relieved to learn that we should be there for some hours. This gave us a chance to stretch our legs and catch up on our laundry, which by then was in need of attention. After a while, however, the lads became bored and started looking around for some diversion: they soon found one.

The line, which had been a single track for most of our journey, now branched out into three or four sidings, at each of which stood a train loaded with locals: these had evidently been held waiting our arrival before taking off in the direction from which we had just come. The waggons were packed to capacity, families complete with pigs, goats and chickens having found places inside or on the tops of the waggons where they sat impassively. A number of the menfolk, however, had got down and squatted in small groups on the ground where, smoking their terrible Algerian cigarettes, they were engaged in a spot of bartering.

For a while all was peaceful until some of the lads, sneaking up between the waggons, released the livestock, resulting in an hour or so of what can only be described as absolute pandemonium. Chickens, ducks, pigs and goats charged about in the semi-darkness hotly pursued by their swarthy owners, whose shouts and clouting of anything or anybody that came within reach, only added to the confusion. Their wives sat quietly by, watching the efforts of their lords and masters whilst we, from the safety of our waggons, yelled words of encouragement and took care to stay well clear. All this went on far into the night and when the last of the livestock had been rounded up, they spent the rest of the time until daybreak sorting out what belonged to who.

Early next morning we moved off, the natives watching us go in sullen silence; fortunately they failed to hear the cackle of a few hens which had somehow found their way into our cook waggon.

Our next stop was at Hamman Meskoutine where we were able to enjoy a whole day bathing in the hot springs. Lazing about in the sunshine we played cards and generally relaxed, and it was during this halt that a small and seemingly insignificant incident occurred which, for some reason, left a lasting impression.

He came towards us, proud and erect, an ageing Arab holding the hand of a little girl who was limping. When they were within a few yards of me they stopped and the old man bowed and muttered something in his native tongue. Not fully understanding, I gathered from his gestures that he wished me to examine a wound on the leg of the little girl. It was a nasty gash, just below the knee and really needed stitches. However, in the absence of anything better I washed it in the spring water and applied my field dressing. The child was a brave little soul; during the whole operation she remained silent, not even flinching when I cleaned the wound. Her dark eyes looked into my face, innocent and wondering. I was a foreigner whose ways were unknown to her, but childlike she trusted me. I must say, I was deeply moved. Acting on impulse I put my arms around her and gave her a gentle hug; she offered no resistance and before I realized it, she planted a kiss on my cheek. All this while the old Arab, who I took to be her grandfather, had stood silently by, but when the little girl at last rejoined him, he reached down and took a cooper bracelet from her arm which he handed to me. Then, bowing slightly, he turned and soon the two of them were swallowed up in the scrub beyond. That was a scene I shall never forget. I still have the bracelet upon which I place great value and often, when sitting alone, I take it down from the hook above the fireplace where it hangs, to remember that small child of the desert.

Our journey continued and, with many unscheduled stops, the train brought us at last to Algiers, where we were billeted under canvas on the race course, to await shipment back to the UK. I found myself sharing a small two-man Pup tent with a Canadian sergeant who, by way of introduction, produced from his kit bag two bottles of rye whisky. With these and a few bottles of the local wine we settled down to relieve the boredom, the result being two inebriated days of which I have little or no recollection other than the hangover. On the third day, feeling terrible, I reported sick and I clearly remember the medical officer telling me that a few more drinking bouts like the one I had just had would no doubt finish me off just as quickly as an enemy bullet, and perhaps not as painlessly. His fatherly lecture on the evils of drink had its effect, and from that day to this I have been strictly teetotal. As for my drinking companion, I never did get to know what happened to him: one morning he just disappeared, kit bag and all.

Although looking forward to returning to England, I knew I was going to miss North Africa and all the friends I had made there. It was of them, of Badger, and of all the others who would not be making the return journey, that I thought as we slowly left the shelter of Algiers harbour. It seemed like only yesterday that we had started out on that great adventure. Now, staring back at the white buildings which clung to the hills along the receding shoreline, some lines from the long-forgotten poem came to mind:

> 'For I have a rendezvous with Death,
> At some disputed barricade.'

Moving on, we made our way out into the waters of the

Mediterranean to join the homeward-bound convoy, and soon the coast of North Africa disappeared into the blue haze.

The first few days passed uneventfully. Then I suddenly succumbed to an attack of influenza and was confined to the sick bay, where clean sheets and comfortable bed proved ample recompense for a high temperate and snivelling cold.

I was just beginning to feel better when, late one evening, we had our first U Boat alarm. The 'stand to' signal came blasting over the ship's tannoy and I hastened to obey, donning my greatcoat over my pyjamas, slipping the Mae West lifejacket over my head and, last but not least, stuffing the contents of my recent chocolate and cigarette issue into my pockets, figuring that if the worst came to the worst, I should be able to enjoy a few creature comforts while 'adrift in an open boat'. The 'stand to' order was soon followed by 'boat stations', so up we all trooped to our allotted positions on deck.

God, it was cold up there! All around the sea was black and uninviting, and the wind, shrieking through the rigging, penetrated our clothing and blew the salt spray on to our faces. Too late I realized that I had forgotten to put on my socks and boots. Hopping from one cold foot to the other, I drew my greatcoat tighter around me and waited. Away in the distance our escorting destroyers were dropping depth charges and, although we couldn't see them, we could feel the vibrations on the ship's sides as the charges went off.

After about an hour, fortunately, things quietened down and the order came to 'stand down'. Feeling like death warmed up, I staggered back to my sick bay where I snuggled down in my warm bed and pulled the sheets over my head.

Two further days of idle luxury followed, until eventually much to my regret, I was discharged from the Sick Bay and sent back to duty. Curiously, I had as yet not suffered from the seasickness which had plagued me on my outward voyage, even though the conditions were much rougher.

Time passed and we slowly edged our way through the grey waters of the Atlantic. Then, sitting at breakfast one morning, the news, which was relayed over the ship's speakers, suddenly gave way to Workers Playtime and we knew that at last we were in friendly waters. With feelings of nostalgia we listened to familiar programmes being broadcast from the canteens of factories. It seemed a long time since we had heard Vera Lynn

and *The White Cliffs of Dover*, and Tommy Handley and his
'Can I do you now, sir?' Crowding the decks we searched for
the first sight of land, speculating on what our final destination
would be. The northerners amongst us were hoping for Glasgow or Liverpool, while those from the south naturally wanted
it to be Southampton. Early one morning the question was
resolved for us, when we awoke to find that the ship had hove
to and was waiting alongside a concrete anti-aircraft platform
built on stilts into the sea bed; and there on the horizon we
could see the twin towers of the Liver Building which dominated the skyline of Liverpool. As the tide turned, we cautiously moved forward into the maze of docks, accompanied by
blasts from the sirens of tugs and other ships lying at their
moorings; until we finally reached our berth where we found a
band waiting to welcome us.

Crowding the rail we gave vent to our feelings of relief at
being safely back in England, shouting greetings to the
watchers below and throwing packets of cigarettes to the
dockers clustered on the dock side! Soon, however, we were
ordered below to collect our kit and prepare for disembarkation and, at about four in the afternoon, the gang planks were
lowered. Bronzed and cocky, we made our way down them to
the railway terminus where a train was waiting to whisk us off
to St Helens, where, in a large park, we were accommodated in
wooden huts and left to our own devices.

The next morning almost at first light we dashed out to
enjoy running barefoot in the frost-covered grass, just why we
did this is hard to explain, but I remember how strange it was
to feel the soft turf beneath my feet after spending so much time
on the hard sunbaked scrubland of North Africa now so far
away. After a few days we moved again, this time to Catterick
where we were medically checked, re-kitted and given fourteen
days' disembarkation leave.

I spent mine in Hereford, not wanting to visit Dumbleton
and risk meeting Kathy. That was something I was not yet
ready for, as the wounds had not completely healed – if indeed
they ever would.

Father greeted me at the door with the immortal words:
'Where did you spring from?' and, bearing in mind that
neither of my parents had had the slightest inkling that I was
back in England, I was rather taken aback; but that was just

193

his way. Mother, on the other hand, who was out in the kitchen at the time, burst into tears when she saw me, and it was some time before she could be consoled. We sat talking late into the night, they asking many questions about my stay overseas. Some things I answered truthfully, while others I either avoided or glossed over. In a way I was still numbed by the experience; indeed, years were to pass before I was able to catalogue events into some sort of order. I made no mention of Kathy, or the death of Badger, feeling that these memories were for the moment too personal and private to be shared with anyone.

And so I spent my leave walking the countryside and visiting one or two old friends. Luckily, my parents respected my bouts of silence, probably guessing something of what I had been through. I remember my mother telling me years later, that she had noticed a look in my eyes – a far-away look that hadn't been there before. And she was right, for my experiences had left their mark.

With leave over I returned to Catterick, only to be posted down to Wrotham for a month's infantry training, my stay in Kent proving to be quite eventful. Under the watchful eye of the officers and NCOs of the Durham Light Infantry, we carried out endless exercises – crawled under barbed wire in 'Happy Valley', while being peppered with live ammunition; scaled the heights above the Pilgrims Way loaded down with Bren guns and full equipment; and generally got chased from backside to breakfast time.

On one occasion our battle training included charging with bayonets fixed, down a long incline through the woods at the bottom of which lay the rifle range, where we were supposed to drop down and fire five rounds at the targets. What they had neglected to tell us was that the pathways by which we were making our descent were strung with trip wires – and, of course, being me, I soon found one. Charging downwards, yelling like a banshee, I suddenly tangled with one of their wires which was strung across the path at ankle height. Still clutching my rifle, I lunged forward, the bayonet stuck into the ground and I was vaulted into the air, finally coming to rest in the middle of a large thorn bush – from which, encouraged by the shouts of the sergeant instructor, I endeavoured to extricate myself with as much dignity as I could muster.

Other activities included the firing of the Canadian Piat anti-tank gun. This devilish piece of equipment, when loosed off from some hastily dug slit trench, which more often than not was half filled with mud and rainwater, had a mind of its own and could only be held in by bracing one's feet and back against the sides of the trench. Assault courses figured largely in our programme and in addition we took driving tests on light and heavy vehicles – most of these things, to add to our tortures, being done at the double – but there were more welcome breaks in our training. These we spent either at nearby Gravesend or in the little village of Meopham where we gathered at the local pub – in my case to try and get merry on glasses of lemonade and orange juice.

The days of the Normandy landings were now fast approaching, and we could feel the excitement and tension in the air. At Gravesend we watched the great Mulberry Harbour sections being towed down river preparatory to their final trip across the Channel. Overhead, aircraft droned all day long on their way to soften up the beaches. But I, for the moment at least, witnessed the build-up as an observer rather than a participant, and was not sorry that it should be so.

With our training completed, we returned to Catterick and the officers' OCTU. It was to be a twelve months' course and I soon settled in to take advantage of the superior living conditions provided – a great contrast to those I had endured at Wrotham. We now wore collars and ties, with white flashes on our epaulettes and round our forage caps, and were expected to conduct ourselves like officers and gentlemen, our instructors addressing us by our surnames prefixed by 'Mister'. In the classroom I soon found my meagre knowledge of mathematics a distinct disadvantage, but I managed to scrape through, due mainly to the help of a fellow cadet named Lawson, an ex-school teacher from the north of England. Without his help I should probably have foundered; though, as it turned out, all such things were soon to be irrelevant to me.

One miserable wet day, when returning by motor cycle to headquarters during an exercise, I became involved in an accident. The rain had been falling steadily for some hours and, tired and hungry, and perhaps not as alert as I should have been, I suddenly encountered a three ton truck coming round a bend on the wrong side. There was no avoiding it and we collided head on. I knew nothing more after that until I came to in Catterick Military Hospital. There they told me that I had been lucky to escape serious injury, owing my life to the fact that the machine and I had parted company on impact, causing me to be thrown on to the bonnet of the truck and over on to the road.

I was thoroughly shaken up and, with damage to my left shoulder and side, I lay in hospital for some weeks. On my recovery, I was surprised to learn that I was to appear before a medical board. Subsequently, I was examined and they, in their wisdom, decided that I would be of more use to my country back in Civvy Street doing my old job with the Post Office Engineering Department. And so it was that one cold November morning, I handed in my army kit and was issued with a suit of civilians clothes, a hat and an overcoat. Home I went, eventually to find myself back on Hereford station where, years ago it seemed, I had started on my long journey. Standing on the platform clutching the brown paper parcel containing my few possessions I thought of all the heartaches and moments of foreboding that I had experienced on that very spot. Of my return from Dumbleton when tearfully, as a young boy, I had watched the train depart for Evesham, taking Mumford with it, and that memorable morning when, with battered suitcase, I had started on that long journey to Harrogate. I remembered the many times when, returning from leave, I had stood on that deserted platform, a lone uncertain figure illuminated by the subdued light of war time, but now all that was behind me so, gripping my paper parcel, I made my way out into the street ready to take up my new life.

On reaching home the first thing I did, after the reception committee had finished with me, was to discard the clothing which a grateful government had provided. Luckily several of my pre-war suits which had been carefully stored during my absence, still fitted. It was strange how a simple thing like a change of clothes altered my outlook. I could now walk the streets without fear of being checked, pass an officer without saluting, and not be constantly having to count the days before I must return to the army.

However, in spite of my new found freedom I had to admit that I was already beginning to miss the comradeship and ordered way of life of the last few years. I had returned expecting to find my world more or less the same as when I had left it but the illusion was soon destroyed. Great changes had taken place, young men with whom I had shared my adolescence had grown up and were now older and wiser; those few, who, like myself, were already home were restless, finding it hard to settle back into their old routine. Drifting, they searched for something to hang on to, a difficult period which, before long, thousands would have to come to terms with.

Victory in Europe day came and the crowds that gathered in High Town to celebrate, sang and danced late into the night, the relief showing plainly on their faces. They had come through a war and now it was time to start living again. From church and cathedral towers the bells, released from their long silence, rang out across the city. Streets were festooned with flags and, above front doors banners of welcome hung for sons and husbands who, after having fought their way half across the world were coming home. I paraded with them, kissing girls I had never seen before, linking arms with complete strangers to sing *Roll out the Barrel* with an enthusiasm I didn't really feel. However, time enough to face reality; the day was for rejoicing, and whatever lay ahead could wait.

Before settling into my old routine, or before I laid any plans to change it, I knew there was one visit I had to make. I had to go to Dumbleton again, at risk of re-opening old wounds now beginning to heal; and if I went there my duty would be to visit Badger's parents and wife, though that experience might be hard to face. However after giving the matter a great deal of thought I decided to go.

Mumford was overjoyed to see me, and although she looked older and more frail, was as fit as ever. It was good to be back and for the first time in months I began to relax. As we talked I told her about Badger and my intended visit to his parents and wife, realizing as I did so that I was seeking justification for what I meant to do. However I need not have worried as she agreed whole-heartedly, saying that it would be kinder to tell them all I knew about his death.

The following morning I made my way down the village street to their cottage, secretly dreading the moment when, face to face with them I should have to relive those tragic events. Lifting the latch of the garden gate I made my way to the front door and knocked. Mrs Robinson answered and, after

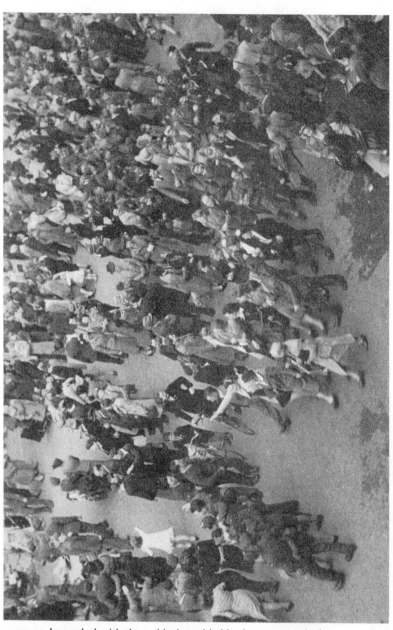

I paraded with them, kissing girls I had never seen before, linking arms with complete strangers to sing *Roll out the barrel.*

shaking me by the hand and bidding me welcome, conducted me into the parlour where I was greeted by her husband who rose from his chair in front of the fire where he had been sitting. Badger's wife Helen, who was living with them, was out in the kitchen attending to her young son; and so the scene was set.

For a while we talked of things in general but I sensed that it would not be long before they would ask the many questions to which they wanted my answers, so, after Helen had joined us bringing the young lad with her, I decided that the time was now right to do what had to be done. They listened in silence as I went back over the events of that fateful day; Mr Robinson sat quietly in his chair gazing into the fire and occasionally tapping out his pipe on the side of the grate. His wife, hands folded on her lap, eyes lowered, fidgeted with the folds of her apron, while Helen, holding her young lad close to her, stared impassively at the ceiling, stifling back the tears that I knew would soon come.

At last it was over. There was no more I could say and for a while we sat in silence. Then, without saying a word, Helen rose and taking the young lad with her, went out into the kitchen from where I could hear her sobbing. Mrs Robinson, now close to tears, went over to her husband and, kneeling before him, buried her head in his lap.

Feeling like an intruder in their grief, I let myself out of the cottage; it was no place for outsiders. Then, standing alone in the street I wondered if I had done the right thing; however, knowing Badger as I did I was sure that he would not have wished me to do otherwise, so, with this comforting thought I returned to Mumford where, alone in the parlour I sat for a long time deep in thought. The past hour had brought back many memories and I couldn't help wondering if things would have turned out any different if I had been able to put the clock back. Somehow I doubted it.

That night, sitting with Mumford in the lamplight, I recounted such parts of my experiences as I thought fit to tell, talking of a life which already seemed so far away. Change there had been in plenty, but for the moment I was back where I had started, in the peace and quiet of the country. No doubt the same thrush would be singing from his perch in the fir trees outside the village stores, and the same family of blue tits would still nest in the old hawthorn at the bottom of the garden. To them it was no great matter, the events which had taken place outside their little world; perhaps in the continuity of these simple things I should find myself again.

The next morning I wandered up to the cricket ground and stood for a while leaning against the fence where, as from a distance, I fancied I could hear the sound of happy voices on Flower Show Day, but it was only the wind playing through the branches. They were long gone, those carefree days, but I had the strangest feeling that I was not alone – that the past with its presences was all around me. Badger, Titch, Lofty and Ernie Lane, I could almost see them again chasing and climbing trees in the nearby plantation. Then something touched my cheek and, half-turning, I expected someone to be there, but it was only the wind.

On a sudden impulse I decided to visit Kathy's parents up at Manor Farm. They were surprised and pleased to see me and we talked at great length, though very little about Kathy. However, her sister Margaret, who joined us later, soon brought the conversation around to that important subject and, reading between the lines, I gathered that all was not well. She did not seemed inclined to go into details and I thought it better not to pursue the matter. Feeling ill at ease and fearing to outstay my welcome, I made my excuses and left, promising to visit them again when next in Dumbleton.

The following morning I returned to Hereford and to my work in the Post Office. By this time I had more or less decided to let things take their course, feeling that whatever was meant to happen would happen. I had by now managed to get fixed up with a small car, and taking advantage of a few days' holiday, I made a tour round the lovely countryside of the upper Wye Valley. Stopping in the old-world Town of Hay, perched on the banks of the river, I was wandering along the High Street when I chanced upon a vacant shop premises. Now, at that moment I had no definite plans as to my future, but somehow the magic of the town got to me and, standing in front of the shop, an idea was born. Noting the name of the agent, I made my way to their offices and soon found myself seated before an elderly gentleman who gave me details of the property. It had apparently been standing empty for some time, and consequently was in need of restoration and repair. However, I was not deterred and, being eager to look it over, I borrowed the keys.

The two large ground floor rooms, heavily beamed, with a fireplace in each seemed admirably suited to my purpose, and I saw how easily they could be converted into the picture gallery which by now I had decided upon. I had always been interested in art and in my mind's eye I could already see the rooms hung with oils and water colours.

Now at last I had a sense of direction. It would be a gamble, but one that I was prepared to take. The house had an air of having been lived in for generations and the atmosphere was a happy one. The more closely I examined the possibility, the more excited I became. The upstairs rooms I had already earmarked for living accommodation – on the first floor, a kitchen and large lounge, and two smaller bedrooms above: this would be more than adequate for my needs. A small garden at the rear could, I thought, with the right planning, provide a delightful area in which to enjoy my leisure hours.

Without wasting a moment, or waiting for my enthusiasm to cool, I returned to the estate agent and made them an offer which they promised to pass on to their client. For now there was little more I could do, so it was back to Hereford to battle with the question of finance and break the news to my parents. They had their doubts, of course, but when they realized that my mind was made up they gave in with good grace.

I totted up all the figures and, allowing for alterations and repairs, I found that the project was just within my means: fortunately I had saved a little and the small bequest which had been made to me by my grandfather in Devizes, had been invested for some years. Imagine my pleasure then, when in a short space of time I received notification that my offer had been accepted. There were still the legal formalities to tie up, but at last everything was settled; I gave in my notice to the Post Office Engineering Department and prepared to seek my fortune in the world of art.

Having now secured the premises in Hay, the next thing to arrange was the alterations and repairs, and here I was lucky, being recommended to a firm of local builders who turned my ideas into reality. The foreman in charge, Bill Wentworth, was a grand old man who had lived all his life in the town and who took great pride in the restoration of its old buildings. Under his loving care and guidance the place was soon transformed, and I was almost sorry when the work was finished; however I had made a friend in Bill, and he was to visit me many times in the future.

Meanwhile I had been touring the local auctions in search of furniture and fittings, and was agreeably surprised at both the cost and availability of the items. I chose old furniture, feeling that this would be in keeping; and here again Bill proved to be of great help, restoring some of my purchases to their former glory, a task which he carried out in his spare time and at week ends.

The days passed quickly and soon the gallery was ready for stocking. Once more I roved the neighbouring counties, visiting house sales, auctions, and other galleries in search of suitable pictures. Petrol rationing was still in force, but I managed to obtain extra supplies, coupons being readily available if one knew the right places to go. The stock I bought first was selected more by personal taste than by any expert knowledge, but I soon learned and, after making a few mistakes, became quite expert in recognizing the better quality items. The dealers with whom I came into contact were invariably helpful and full of advice, and so I had soon collected together sufficient stock for my immediate needs.

It was essential at this stage that I learn the art of picture framing, and here again I was lucky as an old school friend of mine, who also ran a gallery in Hereford, offered to take me in for a few weeks to teach me. I stayed with my parents during the period that I attended his workshop, and soon became fairly proficient. Then, armed with my new-found knowledge and with keenness undiminished, I decided that it was time to strike out and get cracking.

I will not dwell on the ups and downs of my first year, suffice it to say that the business finally got into its stride and began to show a profit; dealers came to know me and my knowledge of the art world improved by leaps and bounds.

All this while the domestic side of things had had to take second place, my standard of living being, to say the least, basic, though well fitted to my bachelor way of life. But as I prospered, I began to be conscious that I was not wholly fulfilled. I needed someone to share my triumphs and disappointments; but most of all I needed love and companionship. I was getting older and didn't want to go through the rest of

202

my life alone. When I was younger it was different, but now that I was approaching middle age I began to have doubts.

Strange how I kept recurring in my mind to this problem. Of course, I knew that there was only one person who could properly have filled that vacant space – Kathy, whom I never had nor ever would forget, but all that was wishful thinking. Perhaps in reaching for the moon I should gather a few stars on the way? We shall see.

I made many friends in Hay and was a frequent visitor to their homes, yet I always felt like the odd man out. During our conversations, sometimes they would ask why I had never married, a question to which I always managed to avoid giving a direct answer – if indeed there was one. However, life has a habit of arranging things in one way or another and, being at a certain place at a certain time sometimes gives fate a shove in the right direction.

It was on a warm spring morning that they first visited the gallery. There were two of them, an elderly lady and a much younger one who I assumed to be her daughter. However, listening to their conversation as they wandered around looking at the paintings, I was surprised to learn that they were aunt and niece. I was immediately struck by the bubbling personality of the younger one, who seemed to have a considerable appreciation of art. After a while I approached them and asked if there was anything I could do to assist, and soon we were chatting away like old friends. On impulse I invited them to join me for coffee in the flat above, an invitation, I must admit, that I rarely extended to customers; however, there was something about the niece that gave me the feeling that I wanted to get to know her better.

As we sat drinking our coffee, they introduced themselves: her name was Elizabeth, and I gathered that she was living with the auntie in Builth Wells, a town not far away. They were both very easy to get on with and I soon found myself inviting them to call again when next they were in the district, which they promised to do. Then they left and though the meeting had seemed to have more than ordinary significance to me, I did not think that I should see them again.

But I was wrong, for the following week they called again, and from then on our friendship blossomed. I found myself looking forward to their visits, particularly Elizabeth's, with whom I had struck up a genuine friendship.

Then one day she came alone, explaining that her aunt had business elsewhere; and rightly or wrongly I must confess that I assumed that she had made the journey through interest in me, and not in the gallery. She invariably came alone after that, and the more I got to know her the more attracted I became, until at last the day arrived when, feeling that I now knew her well enough, I asked her out for a meal.

I remember that evening so clearly: it was when I began to learn something of her past. It appeared that during the war she had married a young Canadian pilot officer named Peter, but, like many others, had been widowed after only a year of marriage. Since then she had moved in with her Aunty Mary, unwilling and unable to face life without her late husband. However, the years had rolled on, and she now felt able to talk about her sorrow.

I could see the tears beginning to well in her eyes. Reaching across the table, I took one of her hands in mine, half expecting her to shy away – but she didn't. It had been intended as a gesture of friendship on my part, but I had a feeling that soon our relationship would go much deeper.

From them on, things progressed quickly. Our conversations, as we sat together in the flat of an evening, ranged over all we had done before we met. To my surprise, I found myself telling her about Kathy, which might have seemed ill-advised. However, the fact that I still harboured affection for another woman did not destroy our relationship; Elizabeth, too, made it equally plain that in her heart her late husband would always come first. It was good that we started in this way, hiding nothing and being open about our past lives. To say that I was falling in love with her would be wrong – or she with me, for that matter – it was just that we were two lonely people adrift in the world, and looking for companionship.

And so things took their course and we were drawn closer and closer. Then one evening, greatly daring, I ventured to speak of marriage. Her long silence made me dread that I had been too hasty or had chosen the wrong moment, but eventually she replied. She said that I must be clear in my mind that any such arrangement would have to be entered into on the understanding that, at present, there was no question of love or any deeper feelings. If I was proposing companionship and was prepared to accept what she had said, then the answer was Yes. That night she stayed with me and I held her through the long hours. There was no love-making; each time I touched her she trembled and stiffened her body against mine. I knew then that the time was not ripe and that I should have to be patient.

We were married in the small registry office in Hay, attended by her Aunt Mary and a few close friends. Back at the gallery we held a small reception, in the course of which Mary and I had a long talk. Some of the things she told me I already knew, but I assured her that Elizabeth would be in good hands and that we had both discussed our relationship fully. After a short honeymoon spent touring North Wales we returned to Hay to take up our lives in the little flat above the shop.

From the start Elizabeth had an immediate effect on my domestic life. Vases of flowers appeared on tables and window sills, and no longer was the tiny kitchen a necessary evil in my life. From it came the clatter of saucepans, the contents of which sent tantalizing aromas of good things down into the gallery. However, most important of all she was there to share my problems, providing a shoulder to cry on when things went wrong. She proved a delightful companion, enlivening as she did the long winter evenings, when we sat in front of the fire discussing the day's activities.

Sometimes our talk delved back into the past, a past which for her I gathered had not been easy, her parents' marriage having ended in divorce. Eventually however, her mother had re-married and they had gone to live in London. Elizabeth hadn't taken too kindly to her stepfather, who had made it very plain that he resented her presence, intimating that it was time she left home and made her own way in the world. Soon after, as it happened, tragedy took a hand. One night during an air raid the house received a direct hit and both her parents were killed. Fortunately Elizabeth was away at the time visiting her Aunty in Builth Wells, and she told me that it was about then that she met and married her late husband. In the uncertain conditions of war time their lives had been fraught with anxiety and change, but in spite of this they had managed to share many happy times. Peter's death had robbed her of that and she herself had died a little.

I could see how the experience pained her still, and sitting there by the fire I resolved to do all within my power to make up for those unhappy years. And so we lived and prospered, visiting our many friends and exploring the lovely countryside around, unaware of another tragedy that was to be enacted in the not too distant future.

The letter arrived on an overcast January morning. Elizabeth was busy in the kitchen and I was getting ready to open the gallery. Snow had been threatening for some days and the wind that moaned around the old chimney stacks gave notice of this. Outside the frost had turned the spiders' webs hanging precariously from the window frames into jewelled lace, and our tiny robin, with hunger making him more venturesome, had taken to coming right up to the back door to beg for food.

As I read the words, my eyes blurred and I could read no more. Mumford, after a short illness, had passed away and was to be buried in three days' time. With the best of intentions they had kept the news from me until the last minute, realizing how upset I should be.

I sat down and stared into space. My last and only link with childhood days had been severed for ever. I couldn't cry, the tears refused to come; only a dull ache was there, and I had a feeling that I had betrayed her by not being with her in her last hours. Elizabeth came in and reaching over took the letter from me. There was so little that she could do or say. Quietly she slipped away leaving me alone.

How long I sat there I cannot recall. Memories came flooding back until, unable to bear it any longer, I broke down and cried like a child. Elizabeth came back into the room and, putting her arms around me, laid her head on my shoulder. Little did she realize what a great comfort it was to have her there.

The day of the funeral was cold and dull and the roads all but deserted as I drove. Elizabeth had wanted to come with me, but after discussing it we decided that it would be better if I went alone. At Hereford I called in to pick up my father who, during the journey tried to steer the conversation away from the present and talked of happier times. However I don't think I was even listening.

The village was stilled as if in mourning. A few solitary black rooks flew silently, riding the biting wind which was sweeping down from the North. Reluctantly I lifted the latch on the back door of the cottage and entered. There was a smell of death in the room, causing me to shiver slightly as I stepped across the threshold.

Mother came forward to greet me, words of comfort falling from her lips, but in truth I didn't even hear what she was saying. For a while we sat, drinking innumerable cups of tea and talking in hushed tones until at last came the moment to face what I knew must be done. With a heavy heart I made my way alone into the bedroom where, in the half light of the January morning, Mumford lay in her coffin. It was the same room in which as a child I had lain in bed, watching the sunlight chasing the shadows across the walls, while the sounds of summer drifted in from the open window. Death had turned back the years for Mumford. She looked younger as she lay there; the rosy cheeks still showed through the pallor of her skin, and her snow white hair, now carefully brushed and arranged, lent her dignity even in death. Soon they would come and screw down the coffin lid and she would be lost to me for ever, taking with her the happiest days of my life to be buried in the cold dark earth, leaving only memories.

The short walk to the churchyard seemed interminable. Standing beside the open grave I watched as the coffin was lowered. Flakes of snow drifted this way and that harassed by a biting wind that chased the dead leaves amongst the grave stones. At a distance the few villagers who had come to pay their last respects stamped their feet on the frozen turf and pulled the collars of their coats tighter about their faces to escape the bitter wind. The vicar, eager no doubt to return to the shelter of his church, said the brief formal words, then left us alone in our grief. There was no sense in lingering so, after taking a handful of earth and gently throwing it on the coffin below, I turned and left, taking my mother's arm as I did so.

The cottage, although now full of mourners, to me was empty; the soul had gone from it. I looked around that familiar room, seeing no kettle steaming on the hob, just a cold empty grate. Above the fireplace Mumford and Grandad gazed down from their silver frame, united as they now were in death. The restless cat, unable to understand, paced up and down. From living room to bedroom he wandered, looking for the hand that had fed and loved him through many years. Poor animal, his loss must have been in its way as great as ours, but how would one explain to him the inevitability of death?

I stayed on for a few days, helping to put Mumford's affairs in order and to dispose of her few possessions. The only personal item I took was her small gold wrist watch, feeling that at least I should have one memento of her which I could keep. Later my mother very thoughtfully sent on to me the photograph of Mumford and Grandad in its silver frame, also the copies of *King Solomon's Mines* and *The Sorrows of Satan*. They still hold the same magic and I often take them down from the bookcase to thumb through their well worn pages.

Time passed and Elizabeth and I entered middle age with dignity. The business prospered and we filled our days happily. However, as is invariably the way of things, dark clouds were gathering on our horizon and I was soon to grieve for the second time.

# 7

*In which the wheel
turns full circle*

They do say that our destinies are planned for us and, looking back, I believe this to be true. Fate is not always kind in the gifts she hands out; if we could we would evade them, but we cannot choose.

There was an auction at a large country house near Gloucester which I had meant to attend; however, at the last moment something cropped up which prevented me and Elizabeth volunteered to go alone. It was a beautiful spring morning and the countryside was beginning to awaken from its long winter's sleep. When the time came for her to leave, I hesitated to let her go alone, but she was familiar with the road and insisted that she would be all right. She was looking forward to the run out, she said; she would make a day of it and added that she would ring me later.

So away she went, and I busied myself in the gallery. About mid-afternoon our local bobby came in, as he sometimes did, for a chat and a cup of coffee. But this time it was with no cheery greeting that he met me and, seeing his expression a cold fear gripped me, it was almost as if I already knew that he was the bearer of bad news. He was a kindly man and broke it to me gently. Sparing me for the moment the details he told me that Elizabeth had been involved in an accident and had been taken to hospital in Gloucester. Listening to him, numb with shock, I hardly heard what he was saying, his voice seemed to be coming from a distance, almost as though it wasn't me he was talking to. At last pulling myself together, I managed to ask how she was and was she in any danger but tactfully he avoided answering. Taking me upstairs he seated me in a chair and soon had a cup of tea going, then, leaving me for a while, he returned downstairs and locked the shop door, drawing the curtains as he did so. There was something awfully final about his actions and in my heart I think I already knew the worst. On his return upstairs he told me what had happened. An empty coach negotiating a steep hill between Gloucester and Ross-on-Wye had suddenly gone out of control. Elizabeth coming from the opposite direction had stood no chance, the coach had overturned after running up a high bank, pinning her car beneath it. The driver was already dead and Elizabeth, although badly injured, was still alive.

Before we left I got in touch with Elizabeth's aunt, arranging to meet her at the hospital; I also rang my parents telling them that it would be better if they stayed put and promising to ring them when I had more details. After a silent and seemingly endless journey we finally reached the hospital where, on arrival, we were conducted to a private ward. Before entering I was met by a doctor who explained that Elizabeth was in a coma and would probably never regain consciousness: with that realization I opened the door to her room.

She lay very still, her eyes closed, her chest faintly moving with her breathing. Her face was not marked, she could have been deeply asleep as I had sometimes seen her. I took her hand and hoped, but in vain, for a flicker of response.

All that night I stayed by her bedside, holding her hand and reliving the years we had shared. I thought of the day when she had first come into my life, the way she walked and the way she smiled. Gently I leaned forward and kissed her pale cheek, but my lips felt no warmth there and I knew that the end was near. Just before dawn she seemed to rally and at that moment I had a feeling that we were not alone. I turned quickly, expecting to see a nurse or doctor, but there was no one.

I pressed the bell and the nurse entered. Quietly she made her examination, but there was no need for words; eventually she left, closing the door behind her.

When the end came, Elizabeth's grip suddenly tightened. Opening her eyes she turned her head towards me, her lips moving as if she was struggling to say something. I bent to hear, but she was not making sense. Then, as if with one last effort, she raised her head from the pillow and called the name 'Peter' – then it was all over. In those first few moments I prayed that at long last she was now reunited with her wartime

210

husband whom she had never ceased to love, and as I sat there holding her hand it somehow gave me consolation. After a while the nurse returned. Gently she released my grip on Elizabeth's hand and pulled the bed covers up to cover the now lifeless body. The struggle was over. Reluctantly I rose and made my way towards the door where, before closing it behind me, I turned to take one last look at the woman who, if only for a brief moment, had brought me so much happiness.

The journey back to Hay, accompanied by Aunt Mary, who had also waited through the long night, seemed endless and I was glad when we reached its familiar streets. Opening the door of the gallery I stepped inside and, in the unreal world in which I was still living, half expected to hear Elizabeth's cheerful welcome from the flat above, but no sound came. In that empty place the silence was so acute that I could have almost reached out and touched it.

We laid her to rest in a quiet corner of the churchyard overlooking the river and the wooded valley beyond where, in happier times we had often walked together. Time passed and the flowers on the grave withered and died, eventually to be thrown on a heap under an old fir tree nearby. Soon the mound was covered with young grass to become one more grave in that silent acre. There is a stone at her head now and the plot is freshly tended; each year on the anniversary of her death a bunch of red roses brings a touch of colour to the sombre scene, reminding her, that wherever she is, she is not forgotten.

In time the wounds would heal. I threw myself into the business, determined to wrestle with my loss that way but it was hard going. Sometimes when the loneliness became almost unbearable, I would walk up to the churchyard and talk with her as if she was still with me. Gradually however I took up my life again, helped in no small measure by my parents who, having now retired, kept an eye on me, visiting frequently. I was grateful for their help as they had become, in a way, the only links left with my past life. My brother, with whom I had never been close, had stayed in the army after the end of the war and I only heard from him infrequently, in letters sent from the various stations where he was serving.

One afternoon two people came into the gallery and stood for a while just inside the entrance. Taking them to be prospective customers I approached, asking if I could be of help, but before I could complete the sentence recognition dawned on me. At first I couldn't believe my eyes, but there, standing as large as life, was Taddy who I had last seen during the war in North Africa. To say that I was pleased to see him was putting it mildly. We shook hands with delight, and he introduced me to his wife who, I learned later, he had met while serving abroad. She was a charming French lady and I took to her at once.

Up in the flat we talked of old times. It was so good to see him again; in a way he brought a touch of reality back into my life, reminding me of the days of our comradeship long ago. It was by sheer chance, he said, that he happened to be in Hay – and luckier still when they saw my name above the shop. He hadn't changed a lot, the years had been kind to him and so we talked well into the evening until at last it was time for them to go. Climbing into their car they promised to call again; but it was to be a while before we met again.

It was about this time when, undecided as to what my future should be, and with some idea of selling the gallery and moving away, that I received a letter from Kathy's mother: it reached me via my parents in Hereford. Naturally I was surprised, for all contact between our families had more or less ceased in recent years, though with no ill will on either part; it sometimes happened when old friends drift apart.

She did not say plainly what her purpose was in getting in touch with me, though reading between the lines, there were things that she wanted to discuss. Having no reason to deny her, I replied and suggested that perhaps they might wish me to visit them in Dumbleton.

And so it came about, and I found myself back in the village where, before calling on them, I took a walk around to try and recapture some of the magic of the place. But it was strange, I felt like an outsider, as if the past was buried indeed. Mumford's cottage had passed into other hands and been altered: the new work stood stark against the village street. I did not knock, it would have been useless. Far better to remember it as the house that I had known.

Retracing my steps, I made my way up to the churchyard to visit her grave. I was shocked when I saw it. It was so sad and neglected, the headstone leaning and moss-covered, the words almost blotted out. With a pang, I vowed then that never again would it be allowed to get into such a state. However, as there was very little I could do about it at the moment, I returned to my car and drove up to Manor Farm, wondering what awaited me there.

They were obviously pleased to see me and., after greeting me warmly, we retired to the comfortable lounge to enjoy a cup of coffee. For a while the conversation seemed fraught with difficulties, and silences which I found hard to bridge. Gradually, though, after Kathy's name was mentioned, the tension seemed to ease, and soon they were telling me the story which I knew was the reason for my presence there.

It appeared that, prior to her marriage, Kathy had confided to her mother her true feelings for me, leading both parents to hope that we should eventually get together. Then, out of the blue, they had received the news that she intended to marry a more or less complete stranger. It was wartime when such things tend to happen; Kathy's mind was made up and there was little they could say or do. The husband was a Yorkshire man, a builder having his own business in Richmond. He seemed a decent chap, and Kathy assured them that she was happy, so of course they were glad for her sake, and would not have dreamed of putting obstacles in her way.

When the war ended, the couple had settled in Richmond and they saw very little of them, the distance to travel being so great. In her letters to them, Kathy did confess to being homesick, but they had accepted this as being perfectly natural under the circumstance. However what did come as a shock was the news that she was unable to have children, and that there had been some talk of adoption. Now, whether this had any bearing on the eventual break-up of the marriage they never established, but gradually the husband's attitude had changed, and he took to drinking heavily. During the frequent rows that followed, he used physical violence; on one occasion, they were shocked to discover that she had actually been admitted to hospital with a broken arm, he in his drunken state laying about him blindly.

Immediately they received the news, they decided to visit Richmond and arrived without giving any notice of their intentions. It had been a tearful reunion and they had found that Kathy was just about at the end of her tether and very frightened. Her husband had ordered them out of the house and uttered such threats against them that it was clear the situation was impossible. Secretly they arranged for Kathy to pack her few belongings and be ready to move at a moment's notice. Then they left the house and put up at a local hotel to wait their opportunity: it was not long in coming. One evening while the husband was away on one of his drinking bouts, they collected her and all three returned to Manor Farm.

As might be expected, the matter did not end there. The husband, soon figuring out where Kathy had gone, had phoned them and subjected them to considerable abuse, warning them what would happen if she did not come back immediately. When this failed to have the intended effect, he turned up himself one morning and burst in, demanding to see his wife. Fortunately she was out, having gone on an errand to Evesham. He stormed and ranted until at last, fearing for their own safety, they had called in two of the farmhands who happened to be working out in the yard. After a short scuffle, they managed to get him outside and back into his car, telling him in no uncertain terms to make himself scarce. He had gone, and they had not seen him since.

Realizing that her marriage was now over, Kathy had filed for a divorce on the grounds of cruelty. This had finally been granted and, wounded in spirit, she had gone to live with her sister Margaret in the small village of Upper Seaton just outside Cheltenham, where she still was.

So their story ended and for a while we sat, absorbed each in our own thoughts. My own were in turmoil. I was distressed for Kathy, and I blamed myself for it. I was stirred by the knowledge that she was free and that I was still in love with her; and disturbed by cross currents of memories of long ago.

To the two people sitting opposite me, I offered what words of comfort I could, however after a while and feeling that there was little else I could do or say, I took my leave of them promising to visit again very soon.

During the next few weeks the problem of whether I should contact Kathy again caused me many sleepless nights. Stopping off at Hereford to talk things over with my parents, I tried to gauge their opinion but, rightly or wrongly, they refused to commit themselves, saying that the decision must be mine and the sooner I came to one the better.

At last my mind was made up and, sitting down one evening, I wrote to Kathy's sister Margaret, a letter that was to change my whole life, although at the time of writing I didn't realize it. Slipping it into the post box I sent it on its way, and within a week received a reply.

At first its contents seemed to hold out very little hope. Kathy, it seemed, had read my letter and was reluctant to meet me, intimating that with the passing years and all that had happened, she felt it better that we left things as they were. This was no more than I had expected, but I must admit that I was disappointed; however, there was one ray of hope. Margaret had obviously talked things over with her sister, and she advised me to be patient. Kathy was surprised, disturbed; at the moment she did not know what to do or think.

I decided on a bold action. I would visit their cottage unannounced, for it was not only Kathy I had to persuade now, but myself: was I, after all, only in love with a memory? Would a meeting disappoint me as well as her, seeing the toll that the long years had taken?

I put the suggestion to Margaret, and in due course she replied: yes, let the visit go ahead.

At last the day came to make the journey. I felt like a youth on his first date, finding myself glancing in the rear mirror to make sure that my tie was straight, ignoring the streaks of grey hair which were now beginning to show. Three times I drove past their cottage before summoning up enough courage to stop; then, realizing that there was no going back, I pushed open the garden gate and made my way up to the front door. At the very last moment I panicked, being of half a mind to turn and race back to the car and drive off. However before I could do so the door was opened by Margaret who, after greeting me warmly, ushered me into the small front parlour where a log fire was burning, and there left me.

It was a pleasant room with its old oak beams, and gleams of firelight reflecting on the rounded edges of a copper warming pan standing in the hearth. A grandfather clock ticked away the minutes, its brass pendulum swinging backwards and forwards behind its glass fronted case, and on the mantle shelf above the fireplace, two white Staffordshire dogs viewed me malevolently, their bright yellow eyes watching my every move.

215

Suddenly from beyond the closed door I heard footsteps. Rising to my feet I waited. Slowly the door opened and there, standing with one hand on the latch as if uncertain to enter, was Kathy.

As she walked towards me the light from the window fell on her and I saw that she had changed. Her dark shoulder length hair was now cut short and like mine, tinged with grey. There seemed to be no vitality in her movements and her face, although to me as beautiful as ever, showed the strain of the passing years. But for all that one thing remained unaltered; those dark brown eyes that I knew so well.

We shook hands formally, both obviously embarrassed by the situation and I remember mumbling something about it being nice to see her again. All the pretty speeches I had rehearsed on the way down were forgotten, I was at a loss what to say and she, perched on the edge of her chair opposite appeared equally ill at ease. We talked of Dumbleton and her family, sentences with long pauses in between, each waiting for the other to speak, then mercifully Margaret came in bearing tea and scones and for a while the tension was relieved. Later she suggested that we might care to take a walk in the garden and so we wiled away the afternoon talking of flowers and their seasons and any other subjects which steered us away from the real reason for my visit, until at last it was time to go.

Kathy walked with me back to the car and we said our goodbyes at the gate. Tentatively I asked if it would be possible for me to call again and, much to my relief, she agreed. So, promising to ring and arrange a date, I left. Thus it was with a lighter heart that I drove back to Hay, feeling that at least I had broken the ice.

A week later when I rang, it was Kathy who answered and, although it may have been my imagination, I thought I detected a new warmth in her voice. We chatted for a few minutes and fixed up to meet the following Sunday.

Sunday came and we spent it touring around the countryside, finishing up at a wayside inn where, much to my delight, she agreed to stay and share a meal with me. Seated at the table, conversation between us became easier, and I found myself telling her all about the gallery and Elizabeth, recounting a few of my wartime experiences to keep the conversation going. It was then for the first time in a long while that I saw her smile. Reaching for the menu both at the same time, our hands touched and briefly held contact, I felt her tremble, but she gave no other sign.

In the next few months we were often in each other's company and the wall of reserve which she had built up began to collapse. She talked more freely of her past life, though I was careful not to probe, knowing that any wrong move on my part would set things back. I took her to Hay to see the gallery and she seemed greatly impressed and quite at home there, even making suggestions for improvements which I gladly agreed to.

There was, however, one question to which I needed to know the answer so, it was with some misgiving that I took her up to visit Elizabeth's grave. As we stood there I couldn't help wondering what thoughts were going through her mind; but I need not have worried. Walking back, she reached out and took my hand. Nothing was said, or needed to be: I knew that the last barrier had been crossed.

Soon the day came when, having decided to throw caution to the winds, I made up my mind to ask her to marry me. Without even hinting at my intentions, I rang and suggested that she might care to visit her parents in Dumbleton, and she agreed.

It was a beautiful spring morning when we set off, one of those days which May sometimes borrows from June. Somehow I sensed that she already knew the importance of the occasion, for as we drove along she lapsed into periods of silence, almost as if she was preparing herself for it.

Her parents, too, especially her mother, seemed privy to a secret which I had not revealed to anyone. We had hardly arrived at Manor Farm than she was finding elaborate excuses for leaving us alone together, it was a well meant gesture, and I could see that Kathy appreciated the humour of it. Over the last few weeks I had noticed many changes in her: her eyes were more alive, her step lighter, her conversation less constrained; and I was sure that her parents were aware of the fact as well.

After lunch we took a walk round the village, recalling incidents from our youth and visiting old familiar places where, blissfully unaware of what lay ahead, we had played our games in those golden years of childhood. Close by her side as we walked, I reached down and took her hand in mine, gripping it tightly. She turned her face to me and smiled and it was then that I knew that at last the end of a long road was in sight.

Alone in the churchyard we stood beside the gate leading into the plantation. In the grey squat tower the clock ticked away the minutes and a pair of jackdaws protesting noisily at our intrusion, flew in and out of their nesting hole in the brickwork. Drawing her close I kissed her, the first time I had done so since that day long ago when we had parted at the farmyard gate. For a moment I felt her body stiffen, then gradually she relaxed, clinging to me as I put the question which she herself had asked all those years ago under the cherry trees.

And so, as the clock struck the hour, we made our way back to the farm to break the news to her parents. Leaving Kathy to go on ahead I stood for a while leaning on the yard gate gazing towards the warren beyond. Soft white clouds passing across the sun sent shadows racing over its wooded flanks, and all was silent, except for the soft rustle of the wind as it played amongst the branches of a nearby tree, causing it to bend this way and that as if nodding its approval.

Entering the house I was greeted by Kathy's mother who hugged me and cried at the same time, such being the way of women. Her father shook my hand and wished us well and I was glad that they were both sharing our happiness.

The next day I set off for Hay, leaving Kathy with her parents. On the way I called in at Hereford to break the news to my parents. They were delighted and evening found me back in Hay where, opening the door of the gallery, I no longer hesitated on the threshold as I had often done in the past.

The days passed quickly until at last it was time to return to Dumbleton. We were to be married at the registry office in Evesham followed by a short service in the village church. I stayed overnight at the farm and the next day we all set off by car to Evesham where, in the company of a few chosen friends and relatives, we were joined together as man and wife. Kathy looked radiant, the years seemed to have dropped away as if by magic and as I slipped the ring on her finger she looked at me and smiled – a smile that for me said everything and was reward enough for all the years of waiting.

The ceremony over, we shook hands with the kindly registrar and thanked the young member of his staff who had stood in as witness, then hand in hand we stepped out into the sunlight, confident in our ability to face the years that were left to us. A complete stranger passing stopped and wished us luck, the gesture touching us both deeply. And so with hands shaken and bride kissed, we made our way back to Dumbleton.

Much to our delight the church was full; the villagers, knowing and loving Kathy as they did had turned out in force. Looking around I saw many familiar faces. Ted Pulley, now looking older, gave me a knowing wink as I passed while Ernie Lane, in his best suit, smiled and nodded approvingly as if the whole idea had been his in the first place. It was a meeting of old friends and I was glad that they were there to share our happiness. How I wished Mumford could have been there! How she would have loved it, sitting in her favourite pew! Still I had a feeling that she was not far away.

Standing at the altar rails with Kathy by my side, I wandered back in thought over the years, hardly hearing the words which the young vicar was speaking as he stood two steps above us. There was a new face at the organ keyboard, old Gadget Richardson having long since departed to join a more heavenly choir: had he and Polly the post lady ever managed to get together after their long years of courting, I wondered? And Badger and his escapade with Miss Hayworth's cat Clarence – a pity that he would not be with us. But the old days were gone, taking many friends with them.

After the service we all made our way back to Manor Farm where a reception had been laid on. How Kathy's mother coped with it all I shall never know, the guests seemed to fill every room in the house. With flushed cheeks Margaret dashed from kitchen to dining room with endless plates of sandwiches, while in the parlour the menfolk partook liberally of the liquid refreshments provided. I was shaken by the hand and thumped on the back so many times that I began to wish it was all over; but they meant well. Kathy was in her element, mingling with the guests and captivating everyone with her laughter and her radiance: I must admit that I was extremely proud of her.

And so the day wore on and it was late evening before the last of our guests departed – some rather unsteadily I fear. Ernie Lane and Ted Pulley with their arms round each other singing lustily as they faded into the night, while the vicar, cheeks flushed with too much wine, made his way back to the vicarage.

Sitting by the fireside, Kathy and I watched the last embers cool in the grate. In the kitchen beyond the womenfolk were busy washing up and clearing away, while apart by themselves, my father and Kathy's sat talking, getting great satisfaction from the full glasses that stood on the table beside them. Quietly we slipped away and made our way up to the bedroom which had been made ready for us and where, in the darkness, we finally came together.

Our honeymoon was spent at Lyme Regis where gradually we got to know each other all over again. Each day a new side of Kathy was revealed to me, her warm sunny personality endearing her to all with whom she came into contact. At the hotel where we were staying, the guests threw discreet glances in our direction whenever we entered the room. It seemed strange to us that they should be so coy; after all, we were no young honeymoon couple in the first flush of youth. However, our happiness, regardless of our age, seemed to get to them and we took their attentions kindly.

The days passed all too quickly and soon it was time to return to Hay-on-Wye. On the way we called in at the Manor Farm and Hereford and it was late evening, just as the sun was sinking behind Hay Bluff, that we drew up outside the gallery.

It was astonishing to me with what confidence Kathy took command there, almost from the first moment seeming to stamp her personality on every room in the place: it was as if a ray of sunshine had entered and decided to stay.

We often talked about Elizabeth and each week we visited the churchyard together to tend her grave and lay fresh flowers on it. At Kathy's insistence, a photograph taken on the day Elizabeth and I were married held pride of place on the mantleshelf, together with one taken at our own wedding. There they stood, side by side with the silver framed sepia picture of Mumford and Grandad. I was grateful that Kathy should be so understanding, but that was her way, and I loved her all the more for it.

The business continued to prosper although already in my mind were thoughts of retirement. After discussing it at great length, we decided to sell up and, if possible, make our home in Dumbleton.

The answer to our problem came one day in a letter from

Kathy's mother, in which she told us that a cottage at the top end of the village, close to the church, was becoming available. Realizing that this might be just what we were looking for, we journeyed down to investigate. The white thatched cottage was indeed exactly what we had in mind, so after obtaining the keys from the estate office, we returned to wander through its empty rooms, Kathy dashing from place to place mentally arranging things as if the house were already ours.

I think we both had fallen in love with it at first sight. Its low beamed ceilings wrapped themselves around us bidding us welcome, whilst the large open fireplace in the parlour cried out for flickering log fires and crumpets toasted slowly of a Sunday afternoon. The kitchen, clean and basic, needed modernizing but I had no doubt that Kathy would soon arrange that, it being her domain; so, without more ado, we hurried back to the estate office to hand in the keys and complete the formalities. The manager was most helpful and once the preliminaries had been dealt with things moved rapidly.

There remained the problem of selling the gallery. The success we had made of it ensured that this was no great task, and through my many connections in the trade, I found a buyer who was not only looking for a small gallery business, but who was willing to take over the stock as well. So things were going swimmingly, and before long I was able to ring Kathy and announce the final handing-over date.

She came up when all was ready and we met the new owners. In a way it was a sad occasion; there had been happy times as well as some not so happy, during my years there, and now I was handing a part of my life over to strangers who would know little or nothing of the story they were inheriting.

Just before we left, I returned alone to the flat to take one last look round. The furniture having gone, the rooms were bare and empty, yet in a strange way I could still feel Elizabeth's presence there. As I passed from room to room,, the old floorboards creaked under my feet as if protesting at being disturbed and there was a silence about the place as if it was resting and making itself ready to begin a new chapter in its long life.

After taking one last look round I closed and locked the doors before rejoining Kathy in the car outside. For a while we sat, almost as if we were reluctant to leave until at last Kathy turned to me and said 'I think we ought to visit the churchyard before we leave.' Hand in hand we stood beside the grave, till Kathy, sensing that I wished to be alone, withdrew to the gate and waited. The rain which had been threatening all day now began to fall but I took no heed of it, as I stood, bare headed, looking down at the last resting place of the woman who, if only for a brief period, had brought serenity and happiness into my life.

We left Hay and all its memories and drove out over the toll bridge towards Hereford where we called in to see my parents. Late afternoon saw us at the bottom of Nut Meadow where we tarried for a while before making the last mile into Dumbleton.

The long summer's day was drawing to a close throwing velvet shadows over the hills that backed the village nestling beneath them. Now bathed in golden light, now cloaked in purple darkness, the woods to the left of the warren rested before sinking into nightly slumber. Behind us rose the darkening outline of the Cotswolds with their sleepy little villages and hamlets clinging tightly in the folds and valleys as they had done seemingly for ever. To the right, and just discernible in the failing light, the sharp outline of Bredon Hill gazed down on the broad flat plain of the Vale of Evesham; nothing seemed to have altered since boyhood days.

Back in the car we drove slowly towards the village, passing the old gate outside Fisher's barn on whose top rail I had so laboriously carved my initials with the penknife given to me on my ninth birthday, past the clump of willow trees leaning over the small pond where, for the first time, I had climbed up to gaze in wonder at the tiny bird's nest woven in the leafy branches.

Rounding the bend by the old rectory we passed the gate of the churchyard where, near to a weeping ash, Mumford lay resting beside the grandfather I never knew, and then the stone trough with its canopy of Cotswold stone standing at the top of the village street. How often had I, as a boy, sat on its stone steps to watch the velvet muzzles of the great cart horses gently and delicately take their fill of the pure spring water, but alas, the trough was filled with the rubble of time. No more did it offer its sweet water, or yet listen to the impatient chaff of tired carters eager to see their charges bedded down for the night

And then the stone trough with its canopy of Cotswold
stone, standing at the top of the village street.

and themselves back in the warmth and lamplight of their cottages. The steady tread of great hooves no longer measured time along the village street or the slow uneven rumble of iron clad wheels disturb the silence.

When we reached the cottage, we had scarcely parked the car in the driveway when Mrs Grinnel appeared at the door. She was our part time housekeeper and we counted ourselves lucky to have obtained her services. She was a cheerful, rosy-cheeked little woman who had lost her husband shortly after the war. Her children, now grown up and married, had moved away, and I had the feeling that she had adopted us as her second family. She had her queer ways, a favourite saying being, when asked to carry out some task or other the following day, 'I'll do it if I be spared,' a saying which puzzled me as I often wondered where she thought she was going in the night. However she was a capable little body and dear to us.

Once inside we found to our delight that she had organized the arrival and placing of our furniture, some of which had travelled from Hay, and some from Manor Farm where Kathy had stored a few things of her own. In the parlour a fire was burning and from the kitchen came the comforting rattle of tea cups. Later that evening Kathy and I sat alone in front of the blazing log fire, me in my favourite chair, she sitting on the hearth rug at my feet, her head resting against my knee. Deep in thought I ran my fingers through her now greying hair and half asleep she stirred at my touch. Her eyes, now so full of happiness, still had the power to stir me, and in my thoughts I remembered her as a young girl when, with her hair flowing around her shoulders, she had so often run to meet me, alive and vibrant, petulant and changing, with an infectious love of life. Unfortunately memories are not given at birth but have to be earned and stored, so that in later life we are able to stand on the crest of the hill, and looking back, draw comfort from those memories to sustain us in the descent.

The first few months were pretty hectic, leaving us with very little time on our hands. The kitchen was stripped and modernized, an operation which gave Kathy a great deal of pleasure in the supervising and making endless cups of tea for the workmen. As for me I kept well out of the way, finding jobs to do in the garden and busying myself fitting up a small workshop in one of the outhouses.

224

At last all was finished and we settled down to enjoy life, touring the countryside around and getting to know and love it. At weekends in the summer we could always be found up at the cricket ground where, in the company of old friends, we sat under the cherry trees, listening to the sound of ball on bat and talking of old times. Our garden, tended lovingly by Kathy, was soon transformed, although our adopted cat, who we named Clarence, spent most of his time digging holes in the flower beds. Fortunately, his nature was quite unlike that of his namesake who Badger had locked in the church, but it was noticeable that on his wanderings he never ventured into the churchyard.

And so time passed until one day, after giving it a great deal of thought, I decided to undertake a journey which had been on my mind for some time. I had always wanted to return to North Africa to revisit some of the places I had known during the war, particularly Medjez-el-Bab where Badger was buried. Kathy, with whom I discussed the idea, agreed that now, if ever, was the time to go, while we had the capable Mrs Grinnel to take care of things. I also spoke to Badger's wife and parents before setting off, telling them of our intentions and promising to take photographs of his grave. I further suggested that we might carry a small container of earth from their cottage garden to sprinkle over it, and to this they agreed.

The arrangements were made and away we went to London, the first step of what was to be a very nostalgic pilgrimage. The flight over was uneventful, although I must admit that I felt a little apprehensive, preferring to have both feet firmly on the ground. Kathy loved it, though, taking everything in her stride; she seemed to have no qualms. Circling Tunis Airfield I looked down on the land I had left so many years before, a land that no doubt I should find altered, but I was prepared for that. I, too, had changed. A soldier no longer, now only a middle-aged tourist, indeed I would hardly be noticed among the young thronging crowds.

We put up in a small hotel and at once began exploring the city and soaking up the atmosphere. I remember thinking that we were not far away from the flat where I had met Odette; it occurred to me – but no, perhaps this was a chapter in my life best left closed.

In a hired car we visited many of the places I had known.

Kathy was enthralled by it all, her energy and enthusiasm, never ceasing to amaze me. There was very little evidence left of the war, although in places, a few of the buildings still showed the scars of battle and in the country the occasional rusting tank or burnt-out vehicle chassis still bore testimony to the struggle which had taken place. Other than that the hills had slipped back into brooding silence, and life had returned to normal.

The military cemetery at Medjez-el-Bab had not changed greatly, except that the noise and bustle of war had receded from it: it was quiet now, its long rows of tombstones resting in the warm sunlight. In a thousand homes across the world the names carved here would be remembered and honoured, but they were so far from their homes, these young men of another age, sleeping their last sleep: it made me sad to think about it. What a debt we owed to them, I thought, as we wended our way between the marble and granite stones. Their sacrifice could never be fully repaid; the least we could do would be to honour and remember them, and not allow the same folly and mistake to be made all over again.

At last we found the one we had come so far to see. I started to read the inscription but before I finished my voice choked and I could read no more. Gently, I laid the flowers we had brought on to the warm earth, and for a while we stood bare headed in silence. Kathy, unable to hold back her tears, broke down and sobbed. Putting my arm around her, I drew her close.

In those few precious moments, pictures of the past flashed through my mind. I saw again the rows of silent ones lying beside the road covered with blankets, and the kindly officer who had been so understanding. Pulling the small jar of earth from my pocket, I sprinkled it over the grave, the soil from far away Gloucestershire mingling with the red dust of Africa, bringing the two closer together. Then, this done, I took a few photographs of the grave and its surroundings before leaving.

Others passed us, they too had made the pilgrimage and came slowly, clutching wreaths and bunches of flowers. We left them in their sorrow, and as we walked, a few lines of a poem by Ivor Gurney which I had learnt at school came to mind:

'He's gone and all our plans

226

Are useless indeed.
We'll walk no more on Cotswold
Where sheep feed,
Quietly and take no heed.

His body that was so quick
Is not as you
Knew it on the Severn River
Under the blue
Driving our small boat through.

You will not know him now,
But still he died
Nobly, so cover him over
With Violets of pride
Purple from Severn side.

Cover him, cover him soon
And with thick set
Masses of memorial flowers
Hide that red wet
Thing I must somehow forget.'

The next day we left for home and I said goodbye to North
Africa, knowing that there would always be a part of me that
would remain, for there are some things that can never be
forgotten. Soon we were back in Dumbleton, sadder and wiser
for our experience. It was a journey I would not have missed
for anything. I took the photographs we had taken to Badger's
wife and parents, staying long enough to tell them about our
journey. They listened intently and were grateful and although
I know they will never really get over their loss, I felt that in
some way I had brought them closer together.

And so the years passed. Both my parents and Kathy's have
long since gone, and we are now alone. Thinking back it was a
hard and devious road that we trod but I thank God for its
happy ending. There are new names carved on the war
memorial at the top of the village and each Armistice Day,
Kathy and I attend the service to pay our respects to those of
our friends that are remembered there. Each year that passes
the mourners grow fewer and fewer. Season will follow season

and a new generation will take over where we left off, but I
shall always be grateful for the years of happiness spent with
my beloved Kathy.

# THE FINAL CHAPTER

And so their story ends, the rest had yet to happen. Kathy and Reg lived out their lives together respected and loved by everyone. Both their parents have been laid to rest and the little churchyard at Dumbleton overflows with friends and acquaintances. I had stood beside them in that dark registry office in Evesham to see them joined together as man and wife, and shared their ultimate happiness, but now I must write the final chapter.

Reg died first to be followed three days later by Kathy, her heart broken. Perhaps it was just as well, for in life they had been as one and neither would have wanted to go on without the other. One silent grey day I stood alone in the churchyard, no bird song breaks through the cold air and the trees, gaunt and bare, look down in pity as the last of the autumn leaves, clinging to their branches, rustled in the biting wind. Taking a single red rose from my pocket where I had held it during the service, I gently threw it down on the coffins below. The tears which I couldn't hold back coursed down my cheeks and I didn't bother to wipe them away. You see, over the long years I too had been in love with Kathy.

Reluctantly I turned and made my way out of the churchyard. The grave diggers, who had been standing by, picked up their shovels and began the final act of obliteration.

Few will remember them in the years to come and strangers will pause to read the inscription on their tombstone, but of one thing I am certain: on summer evenings, when the sun drops below the wooded hills above the village, Kathy and Reg will come together at the old gate leading into the plantation where they will shed the years and recapture their long lost youth. As for myself, I am content to wait, confident in the belief that somewhere we shall all meet again – and what a meeting that will be! Badger with his laughing face and ready wit; Giovanni with his lilting songs; and Reg and Kathy reborn and young again. I hope that there will be fields and woods there, and that the sun will shine, so that once again I can roam with them and join Kathy, to wander hand in hand, watching her toss her lovely head as the wind rustles her long black hair.

And what of the village now? I find it strange to wander past the spot where their cottage once stood. Pausing a moment, I half expect to see her in the garden, tending the flowers she loved so much – but that's just illusion: all I can see are strangers, whose faces mean nothing to me. Grinnel's Orchard has been developed and harbours stark new houses whose stonework had still to be mellowed by time. Their occupants walk the street unaware of the ghosts that accompany them, and few doors stand open inviting me inside as they had done in the past. The old lane still leads down to the deserted smithy, but the apple and pear trees that bordered it have long since gone and it is edged with more new houses; no blacksmith swings his hammer there now and the old red brick forge has other uses. I hope that some of the newcomers will care, and perhaps read my story; then they may realize and treasure the trust that has been placed with them. All too soon the few of us that are left will depart, leaving no one to grieve for the passing of an era.

As for me, I am content with my memories. They may build new houses, rename old lanes and footpaths, but one thing they can never do, they cannot destroy the Dumbleton of my childhood – leastwise not as long as I am alive.